MOTO GUZZI

THE COMPLETE STORY

MOTO GUZZI

THE COMPLETE STORY

GREG PULLEN

THE CROWOOD PRESS

First published in 2013 by
The Crowood Press Ltd
Ramsbury, Marlborough
Wiltshire SN8 2HR

www.crowood.com

British Library Cataloguing-in-Publication Data
A catalogue record for this book is available from the British Library.

ISBN 978 1 84797 576 8

All photos Greg Pullen unless otherwise credited.

Photograph on page 6:
A new V7 Racer at rest outside the old race shop. MOTO GUZZI

Typeset by Shane O'Dwyer, Bristol, Avon
Printed and bound in India by Replika Press Pvt. Ltd.

DEDICATION

For JOANNA, EVE and WILL.

CONTENTS

INTRODUCTION

Like many of my generation, the first Moto Guzzi I noticed was the Le Mans and, more specifically, the Bob Carlos Clarke photograph of a girl astride a bright red version of the original Le Mans in the August 1976 issue of *Bike* magazine. An ice-blue Le Mans spotted at a race-meeting soon afterwards kicked off a lifelong love affair with Italian motorcycles, fired by their beauty, presence and speed, even if, at sixteen, I could only imagine what 130mph (210km/h) might feel like. British motorcycles were relics from a (soon to be) forgotten age, and Japanese motorcycles looked like a comic book mix of Christmas tree gaudiness. Today I still only ride and own Italian motorcycles, inevitably including those built close to the beauty of Lake Como in Moto Guzzi's Mandello del Lario factory, home to most of their motorcycles since 1921.

Today Moto Guzzi is associated exclusively with large-capacity V-twins, yet the Italian factory can trace its history back to 1919 via a range of motorcycles of unparalleled diversity. Even within the V-twin range there is great variety: from the diminutive sporting style of the Imola, to the leviathan Art Deco monument that is the new California. Despite sharing the same basic architecture, Moto Guzzi V-twins have been produced with displacements of between 350 and 1400cc, and can trace their origins back to the 1960s, when the original 700cc V-twin ushered in a new golden era for the marque. Inevitably, therefore, much of this book focuses on the V-twin motorcycles that current brand-owners, Piaggio, insist is the only conceivable layout for all future Moto Guzzis; although they do hint at the possibility of reviving the horizontal single. Piaggio point to the recent launch of the all-new 1400cc Guzzi California as proof of their commitment to both the V-twins and Moto Guzzi, although there has been more than the odd wobble along the way. Even so, by the final chapter it should be obvious that there are great hopes and plans for the future.

Written as a chronological history, early chapters introduce the ideals of Moto Guzzi founders, Carlo Guzzi and Giorgio Parodi, together with the engineering and business genius that made Moto Guzzi by far the most commercially successful Italian motorcycle factory until the 1950s. This success allowed them to create some of the most magnificent racing motorcycles ever seen, many developed in Moto Guzzi's own wind-tunnel. Owners and riders give first-hand insight into Guzzis as diverse as the incredible V8 racer and the three-wheeled truck used to mend city roads, together with the better known lightweights, big singles and, of course, the V-twins. The story ends with details of the new California and concerns in some quarters over the future of the firm's traditional base at Mandello del Lario, a stone's throw from Lake Como and the Guzzi family's one-time home.

And yet there are omissions, some because the truth is buried in myth and legend. For example, there are those who doubt that Moto Guzzi's Spanish factory actually built anything, despite being an essential gateway to the Spanish market at a time when Franco's regime would only allow Spanish-built motorcycles to be sold in Spain. Ducati formed Mototrans to build Ducatis in Spain, and not only did Mototrans build the bikes, they developed and raced them too. Yet the rumours persist that Moto Guzzi's Spanish factory was merely somewhere to uncrate motorcycles built at Mandello. But getting a straight answer often proves impossible in Italy – the only response being a wink accompanied by a finger tapping the nose.

It is also true that some omissions must be deliberate when chronicling a factory with nearly a century of history and over a hundred production models, of which more than half a million were built – even if almost half were the Guzzino–Cardellino two-strokes. So this book's focus is on the people who were pivotal to Moto Guzzi's success (or occasional lack of it). Yet even taking this approach, the sheer number of riders who raced for

LEFT: **The California Custom Nero Basalto.** MOTO GUZZI

ABOVE: **The sign above the factory is visible from much of Mandello del Lario and the first thing you see from the station platform.**

Moto Guzzi makes a complete record impossible, unless the story is reduced to a mere list. Hopefully, instead the reader will enjoy a journey that explores the genius of the engineers, financiers and riders, and shows how Moto Guzzi's finest hours often came just as failure seemed inevitable. It was particularly rewarding to find that, despite the doubters, Moto Guzzi have bold plans and seem to have not only put recent problems behind them, but are once again relishing the future. When you read the road tests, ride the motorcycles and speak to the owners and dealers, it seems they have every reason to be confident about the future and Moto Guzzi's centenary in 2021.

As this is my first book, the experience has sometimes been daunting, especially the sheer amount of time that needs to be spent at a keyboard. Thanks first must go to those who encouraged me along, especially my wife Joanna, who made sure I had the time to type and talk to people, and allowed me to disappear to Italy on my own. Le Mans and V7 Sport owner Richard Skelton also offered encouragement and advice.

The real heroes have, however, been those owners and enthusiasts who have offered guidance and insights with cheerful affection for all things Moto Guzzi. Special mention goes to Jan Leek and Ivar de Gier, both Moto Guzzi chroniclers of note in their own right, who nonetheless assisted selflessly. Ivar's guidance was especially valuable, aided by his conversations with the great names from Moto Guzzi's history, and means that the true story of the V8 racer, the loss of Omobono Tenni and the birth of the V-twin are told in full, possibly for the first time in English. Piaggio's Daniele Torresan was my direct line to the factory, and many press officers could learn

enormously from his prompt and honest response to questions, all answered in perfect English. Moto Guzzi dealers Paul Harris of Corsa Italiana and Gordon de la Mare of Moto Corsa both gave insights, as much as enthusiastic owners as businessmen, as did Nicola Arnaudo of Agostini's in Mandello del Lario: again, in perfect English. Others who helped with photoshoots and owner's opinions include Shaun Power, Brian Rogers, Glen Parkinson, Paul Baker, Richard Varley and Andrew Gray. Thanks also to Neil Leigh who spotted the brochures used as illustrations at an autojumble in Belgium and immediately bought them to donate to this project. I owe special gratitude to Snr Morbidelli for a wonderful visit to his very special museum, where I was allowed to photograph many of the Moto Guzzis on display. Finally, and essentially, thanks for photographs provided by A. Herl Inc., Spike, Phil Aynsley and Mykel Nicolaou Photography, as well as Moto Guzzi. I am also indebted to the Moto Club Veteran San Martino, organizers of the Milano–Taranto revival and archivists of the original race, for photographs both old and new. Also to Peter Lockwood for allowing me access to his old but sadly unaccredited amateur photographer's album from the early fifties. I am also grateful for the images from Andrew Gray's team at Spa in 2011.

Inevitably I will have forgotten someone or some important event, for which I apologize. But for those who helped – and especially the people who have made Moto Guzzi such a loved and important part of motorcycle history – my thanks and admiration: you have been endlessly inspirational. I hope we can meet out on the road, ideally aboard Moto Guzzis.

THE MOTO GUZZI MUSEUM

Set inside the factory gates, to walk through the museum is to travel through pretty much the complete history of Moto Guzzi, from the very beginning. The only obvious oversights are the more recent models that are being built a stone's throw away.

It may look little more than a string of first-floor offices, but the Moto Guzzi museum must be the most complete record of any motorcycle manufacturer's history. Where other manufacturers eventually wake up to their heritage and start prowling the auction rooms of the world to try and buy (or even just borrow) some of their back catalogue, much of Moto Guzzi's autobiography is written in metal at the factory. Because most of the people involved in that history lived in, or very close to, the factory, motorcycles never disappeared into private collections or nearby racing departments. Pretty much everything is here, from Carlo Guzzi's first prototype and the bike his brother rode to the

Arctic Circle, to the V-twin record-breakers and racers. If you look past the dust and poor lighting, the modest presentation and ancient windows, there is a rich seam of history right before your eyes. No wonder Moto Guzzi's current owners, Piaggio, are keen to provide a brand-new venue, still on the Mandello del Lario site, hopefully in 2016. But for now it's down to a single hour's access most weekdays at 3pm, and sadly even that window is not entirely reliable. The factory is also notoriously poor at replying to emails, even if you can get past the enquiry box on the website. Nonetheless, it is a must-see destination for any fan of motorcycle history, let alone Moto Guzzi enthusiasts. It's also worth seeing on a quiet day – the Giornata Mondiale Guzzi (World Guzzi Day) each September might allow access to parts of the factory that are usually out of bounds (most notably the wind-tunnel) but the heaving mass of Guzzisti makes a worthwhile viewing of the museum all but impossible.

The famous Moto Guzzi factory entrance.

Continued overleaf

Continued from previous page

THE MOTO GUZZI MUSEUM

As the big factory gates roll aside you're confronted with a short tunnel and a giant poster of Sean Connery in his Bond years aboard an early California. Otherwise you could be in pretty much any old factory in Southern Europe. The curator, a slim man who has been at the factory since the sixties, ushers you to an unprepossessing door on the left, where there's a bookshop and the V11 Sport racer that campaigned in the 2003 Coppa Italia (a race series for unfaired motorcycles) to spawn a limited run of road-legal replicas. Behind it is a big red banner listing Moto Guzzi's history and achievements in chronological order; and to the right, a staircase. The curator, who seems to speak no English, waves you on.

At the top of the stairs is a hall flooded with sunlight and in a glass case is the GP – Guzzi Parodi – that is the very first motorcycle Carlo Guzzi built, pretty much on this spot, in what was then a blacksmith's workshop. Power tools were a drill and lathe powered by the waters that rush down from the Alps, which rise almost 2,000m behind the factory. The GP was made in 1919, and has been here or hereabouts since then. You then walk past early production bikes and racers that competed on the Circuito del Lario, a road circuit just over the Lago di Lecco (as the south-western branch of Lake Como is known) in the 1920s. Among these historic racing machines is the C4V on which Guido Mentasti won the first European Championship at Monza in 1924.

There's Giuseppe Guzzi's own GTC Norge (Norway), which was hidden to prevent it being commandeered during the war, named after the country he rode through to prove the worth of his revolutionary rear suspension. The sense of history and achievement is palpable as sole-surviving examples of the original 3- and 4-cylinder prototypes from the early thirties speak across the decades with a wonderful patination of unrestored metalwork. Tragically there is no guidebook, or even a list of the exhibits. The oldest bikes are reasonably well labelled, but as you drift past the supercharged 3-cylinder 500 and 250 racers, it seems somebody got bored and decided that if you got this far you know what you're looking at. In what feels like Carlo's old office there's a desk with an ancient aerial photograph of the factory, revealing just how enormous the site is. Opposite is

Sean Connery welcome visitors to the factory's main gates.

V11 Sport racer fronts the list of Moto Guzzi's achievements at the entrance to the museum.

ABOVE: **The very first Moto Guzzi, the 1919 GP – Guzzi Parodi. The Parodi family quickly decided to drop the GP name in favour of Moto Guzzi, fearful that the initials could be construed as Giorgio Parodi's and damage the family's reputation if the new enterprise failed. This prototype not only survives, it is on public view in the Moto Guzzi museum, albeit as the only exhibit behind glass.**

RIGHT: **There are prototype and production engines on display, some with cutaways.**

a life-size statue of Omobono Tenni, the man some call 'the original Valentino Rossi', so devoted were his fans. He rode for Moto Guzzi, of course, becoming the first Italian to win at the TT on the 250 racer in 1937. There is, naturally, a supercharged version of that bike on display, as well as his Bicilindrica racer, as used at the TT alongside Stanley Woods.

A period-scale model shows the layout of Moto Guzzi's famous wind-tunnel, and Bill Lomas's 1955 350 world championship winner, which it shaped. Lomas also raced the equally streamlined V8, which is central to the museum's display and probably the exhibit at the top of visitors' to-see

list. A spare V8 engine sits on a plinth for enthusiasts to pore over: in fact there are lots of engines on stands, both prototypes and cutaways. Then it's time to move on from the ghost of their designer, Giulio Cesare Carcano, and on to the era of the V-twin. This starts with a hall celebrating the record-breaking specials, developed by Carcano's successor Lino Tonti, along with the prizes they scooped setting nineteen records at Monza in June and October 1969.

Continued overleaf

Continued from previous page

THE MOTO GUZZI MUSEUM

Alongside all of this are many of the production bikes that actually paid for the racers, especially as you get to the 1970 and 1980 models. Visitors can smile at the madness of the 4-cylinder 250 road-bike, the huge V-twin off-roaders (as well as the 1963 ISDT winning Lodola 235) and more – including the 'Guzzi Matic', an automatic V-twin racer based on the Convert and built by whimsical French Moto Guzzi dealer, Charles Krajka, to race at the 1976 Bol D'Or. Of course there's Dr John Wittner's 'Daytona' race bike and then you're pretty much done. The curator's tapping his watch, and you're the last person in the museum, so it's downstairs again with no time to look in the bookshop. Waved out through the reception with a smile, blinking in the sunshine and it's over.

RIGHT: **Model of the famous wind-tunnel.**

BELOW: **The exhibit everyone wants to see – the fabulous V8 racer, with spare engine to examine.**

Roll on a new museum that would allow the time that the exhibition deserves and, armed with the knowledge this book will hopefully provide, it would be possible to spend the best part of a day getting to really know the collection, along with a fine insight into Moto Guzzi's achievements.

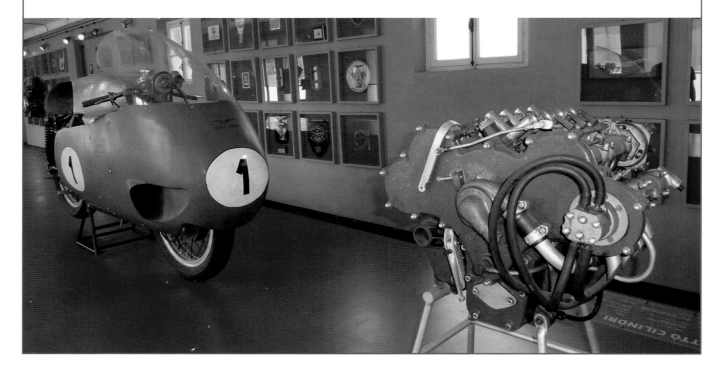

CHAPTER ONE

THE EAGLE TAKES FLIGHT

Carlo Guzzi was born into a world in which Italy had only just become a single country, rather than a collection of fractious city states, and the word 'motorcycle' had not even been coined. Yet, despite mixed fortunes as a young man, he established and nurtured a factory that would become the greatest in Italy, and the first to become famous outside his homeland. Guzzi won the inaugural 500cc European Championship in 1924, a championship that grew to become today's MotoGP. In fact there is scarcely a great race in which Moto Guzzi has not enjoyed success, from the Milano–Taranto to the TT, from Grand Prix to endurance racing. Even today, V-twins built in the same factory as the earliest Moto Guzzis, continue to win in classic endurance racing. This is the story of that motorcycle factory, the oldest, and for many the greatest, in the world. But we're getting ahead of ourselves.

Carlo's father, Palmede Guzzi, was a professor of physics at the Politecnico di Milan, founded in November 1863 a few short years after Italy's unification into a single country. Originally the Istituto Tecnico Superiore, it taught only civil and industrial engineering, until architecture was added to the curriculum in 1865. Palmede had a brilliant and innovative mind (he could arguably lay claim to inventing the light bulb) but was no stuffy academic. He had also run an engineering consultancy, and loved the outdoor life as much as philosophy, counting Friedeich Nietzcsche as a friend: Nietzcsche was the philosopher famous for the phrase, 'That which doesn't kill us makes us stronger'.

Mamma was an Englishwoman living in Genoa when she met Palmede. Elisa Guzzi-Gressini shared Palmede's love of the mountains, so, although Milan was their home, Palmede's talents and business acumen meant they could afford to buy property in Mandello Tonzanico: this was then a small fishing village at the foot of the Alps, within easy reach of Milan. The fabulous city of Milan is a fine landmark on the northern plains of Italy, in the affluent industrial heartland of Italy, but in summer can be unbearably hot, and in winter hidden in gloomy fogs drifting across the flat landscape. Mandello was just about the closest point to Milan of the Italian lake district, where the cooling waters of the lakes and streams make the heat far more bearable, and snow in the mountains makes the area a winter playground. The Guzzi family's second son, Carlo Ulisse Daniele Guzzi, was born on the 4 June 1889, joining his older

Carlo Guzzi enjoying a ski-ing holiday.
A HERL INC.

brother Giuseppe and followed by younger sisters Mary and Fanny. The family would holiday at Mandello as often as they could, perhaps skiing in the mountains or picnicking on the shoreline of the Lago di Lario, up in the northernmost region of Italy. It was here that a young Carlo became intrigued by engineering and the mysteries of the internal combustion engine. His appetite was fed by the family and a local blacksmith-come-mechanic, Giorgio Ripamonti, who was already a fan of the new technology, particularly when fitted to a motorcycle. He and Carlo would dismantle broken and failing engines, the young pupil seemingly not so much fascinated as to how a motorcycle worked, but rather how it might be improved. So it was no surprise when Carlo went on to study engineering at the Regia Scuola Industriale in Vicenza, a city between the Italian lakes and Venice, famous as the birthplace of Palladian architecture. But Carlo's studies were tragically cut short when his father died and the family had to abandon Milan for Mandello, with what had been a holiday cottage being pressed into service as the family home. Yet Carlo's future as one of Italy's greatest industrialists seemingly grew from this hardship, and he took to selling and renting out the new-fangled motor car, his engineering skills presumably helping to keep the vehicles running and his customers happy.

Success proved Carlo's independent and entrepreneurial spirit, and he was soon able to resume his studies. Once awarded his Diploma di Copo Tecnico, he started working for Singer cars in Milan. Carlo went on to join one of the greatest names from the early days of motoring, Isotta Fraschini, working on vehicles more often regarded as art on wheels than mere cars.

No two were alike, and standards were the highest in the world: popes, royalty and film stars drove Isotta Fraschinis, but not just because of their looks. Truly pioneering engineering drove the firm, which in 1912 produced the Tipo 8, regarded as the world's first mass-produced inline 8-cylinder engine. They were also early to use overhead cams in their engines, and one of the first to fit brakes to all four wheels in 1910, a good ten years before it became common practice. And they went racing to prove the stamina and speed of their cars, taking three of the top ten places in the 1907 Targa Florio, and winning that year's Coppa Florio, as well as the 1908 Targa. These magnificent Sicilian road races were seen as one of the ultimate car races of the era (and for decades afterwards), and even simply finishing the event brought credibility to a marque.

So this was Carlo Guzzi's life, working in a Milanese engineering business that valued excellence, innovation and racing success, which in turn allowed it to build and sell the finest motor cars imaginable. In a way, this was Carlo's apprenticeship, teaching him the values and standards required to succeed in the brave new world of motor vehicle production. The future must have looked bright indeed by 1911, the year of great celebrations to mark fifty years of Italian unification. This was also

Sectional early 500 single cylinder engine.

An early example of the 500 Normale.

the year Carlo married Francesca Mandello Gatti, who bore their only child, a son, Ulisse (1911–80). They would have holidayed at the old family home in Mandello, and it's nice to think of Carlo visiting his original mentor Giorgio Ripamonti to see what problems he was trying to fix on customers' motorcycles. Carlo was already talking of building his own machine, and seeing the failings in others, while working with innovators at Isotta Fraschini, would have provided a fertile source of ideas for the engines he would one day design. Carlo disapproved of things like manual hand-pumps that required a rider to provide an engine with its oil. A moment's inattention or a particularly steep gradient could seize an engine, especially if the rider was inexperienced or concentrating on another matter – racing, for example. Surely, he reasoned, the engine could drive a pump? And the exposed chain, which usually transferred the crankshaft's power to the gearbox, was dirty, dangerous and prone to breaking. An enclosed gear was an obvious solution to Carlo Guzzi but it took decades for other engine designers to see that he was right. Carlo was also unusual in not seeing a motorcycle as just an engine that could be fitted into a bicycle-style frame: he appreciated that such a layout was never going to create a motorcycle as fine as one where the engine and cycle parts were designed to work as a single machine. These are obvious ideas today, but in the short years before World War I they amounted to radical thinking.

War and New Horizons

Carlo's innovations were, however, ideas that would have to wait. With political storm clouds gathering, war engulfed Europe and, in 1915, Carlo was called up to serve his country. War was not unfamiliar to Italians back then, a series of battles and wars having been fought within living memory to unify what we now call Italy and create new borders. Initially posted to the infantry, Carlo's true talents were quickly recognized when he was posted to the flying corps as a mechanic, where he was soon transferring his instincts and training to aero-engines. Without careful setting up, the aircraft of this period were difficult to fly, but above all, aero-engines have to be absolutely reliable, especially at times of war. Carlo must have proved himself valuable to the pilots, because he soon became firm friends with two volunteer flyers, Giovanni Ravelli and Giorgio Parodi. Both came from wealthy families, Parodi being heir to the family's shipping and armaments interests. Right through his life Carlo attracted friendship and loyalty, despite a dry sense of humour and unassuming manner. He is rarely seen

smiling in photographs, and it is occasionally said he shared an English-like reserve with his mother. Or it may have been that this modest, and modestly-built, adopted son of a small fishing village was a little star-struck to find himself rising through the ranks of Isotta Fraschini and counting affluent gentlemen pilots amongst his close friends.

From our perspective it might seem odd that Carlo Guzzi obsessed about motorcycles, when his working life had revolved around some of the most glamorous cars and aircraft of the time. Yet this was a passion he shared with Ravelli and Parodi, and they would spend their free time discussing motorcycles and how they might eventually develop their own world-beater. A motorcycle was still the preserve of the rich, and even a bicycle required the wages of a hard-working northern Italian – the south was so poor that even bicycles were unheard of. Sicily might have had the glamour of the Targa and Coppa Florio (the 'Florio Shield' and 'Cup') races, but these were established so that the island's only car owner, Vincenzo Florio, could have someone to race against. And racing was, then as now, something Italians loved. Their famous bicycle race, the Giro d'Italia, was established in 1909, just after the Tour de France and only a few years after the Milano–San Remo one-day event. All the various factions in Italy, from the Fascists to the Catholics, approved of sporting activity (if not outright competition), and if you were going to see how far and fast a bicycle could go, the logical next step was to attach an engine to the frame and race that instead.

Giovanni Ravelli loved the idea of racing motorcycles and had already had some success, including race wins, before the war, with a British Triumph motorcycle. That he hailed from Brescia should come as no surprise. Brescia in many ways was the home of Italian motorsport, holding races since 1899. Vincenzo Florio awarded his first Coppa to a fellow competitor in a race here in 1905 and Brescia would go on to host the first Italian Grand Prix in 1921. Most famously, races around the city grew to become the Miglia Mille. Ravelli's part in Guzzi and Parodi's dream was to involve developing a motorcycle through racing, and his undoubted talent would bring publicity and sales to their joint venture. Sadly it was not to be, because although the three friends survived the war, a tragic flying accident claimed Giovanni Ravelli's life in the first days of peace. In commemoration, Guzzi and Parodi decided to use an eagle on the Moto Guzzi logo, taken from the emblem that still hovers over the coat of arms of the Italian air force – what was then the Servizio Aeronautico and is today the Aeronautica Militare. Over the years, the same badge of honour has been seen on many Moto Guzzis and can still be seen somewhere, even if rather stylized, on all the current models. The spread eagle today not only remembers Ravelli, but also Guzzi and Parodi, and the long nights they spent during the war discussing how to build the perfect motorcycle.

And what of Parodi? His contribution in the beginning was to persuade his father to fund the venture, and to bring a clear and fine business mind to the enterprise. Once Carlo Guzzi was back at home in Mandello designing a motorcycle, Parodi set to work to raise funds to build a prototype. He had been born into wealth in Venice in 1897, although the family's business interests were based in Genoa. If Guzzi had expected funding for their venture to be a foregone conclusion, that would have been to underestimate Parodi's father, Emanuele. A careful and cautious man, he understood that trust was everything. This meant that any new motorcycle had to be reliable and capable of racing success, if it was to be trusted and so bought in sufficient numbers to become commercially viable. But, despite his son's youth (Giorgio was just twenty-one years old, almost a decade younger than Carlo), Emanuele believed in his son enough to agree to invest up to 2,000 lira in the development of a prototype. The vagaries of inflation and exchange rates over the years makes it difficult to put a value on this sum today, but it would probably have bought a small house: it would certainly have represented a great deal of money to anyone hoping to establish a business. The original letter of 3 January 1919 is still proudly displayed in Moto Guzzi's museum, promising the investment albeit 'On the condition this sum is absolutely not exceeded, but I reserve the right to examine your progress personally'. The letter also asks if Ravelli, still then alive and a partner in the proposed venture, had ever repaid some unspecified monies and wonders if he ever will. Clearly Emanuele was a watchful father, mindful of how wealthy heirs can be led astray. Nonetheless his letter promised, 'Should I like what I see I am willing to advance much more, without further limits'. The pressure to produce a fine prototype must have weighed heavily on Carlo Guzzi's brilliant mind.

The GP – the First 'Moto Guzzi'

The prototype that Carlo built, with help from his brother, was called the GP – an abbreviation of Guzzi–Parodi. Some say that Giorgio Parodi insisted on changing the name to Moto Guzzi to avoid confusion with his own initials, and certainly this gesture of respect to Carlo would have been seen as the correct approach for a man of his background. Others have wondered if this was Emanuele Parodi's caution, to make certain that if the enterprise wasn't a success, the family name would not be tainted. Whatever the truth, any concerns were misplaced. The motorcycle initially took shape in the Guzzi household, with elder brother Giuseppe helping with the chassis. As work progressed, they moved the prototype into Giorgio Ripamonti's forge and workshop. The fully functioning GP was completed in 1920, and survives as the first exhibit seen by visitors to Moto Guzzi's museum. Despite a very low compression ratio of 3.5:1, necessitated by the low quality of fuel available, the GP achieved almost 62mph (100km/h). On the roads of 1920 Italy, that was quite fast enough, especially since Carlo Guzzi had eschewed the received wisdom of building the largest capacity motorcycle he could. The world's largest motorcycle manufacturers were American, with Indian and Harley-Davidson the market leaders and principal innovators. While Europe fought a bloody war, the Americans extended their market domination, but the big V-twins the USA was famous for betrayed the differences between America and Europe: 500cc was about as far as you could stretch a single-cylinder engine and expect the motorcycle and rider to remain in one piece. America's wide-open spaces led to long-distance record-breaking and purpose-built racing venues. These demanded horsepower and the ability to hold an engine flat out for long distances, so factories usually built V-twin, or even 4-cylinder, engines that gave power through sheer cubic capacity. But on Europe's tight and twisting roads, safe handling and low weight were at least as valuable as outright power, especially on the gravel-strewn tracks that passed for roads. Europeans also expected to see their chosen marque succeed in racing, which in 1920s Europe meant competing on public roads, which, although ostensibly closed to traffic during races, still resembled pretty much exactly the sort of environment road-riders faced.

Indian had some success with their V-twins at the two great road races of the era, the Isle of Man TT and the Milano–Taranto, but that didn't stop them building a vertical 500cc single, just like the British bikes that went so well at the TT. The other reason that Indian took a sudden shine to building smaller, lighter motorcycles was that big, expensive ones looked increasingly marginalized by the world's growing economic woes and the arrival of mass-produced cars. For the foreseeable future, a single-cylinder engine of between 350 and 500cc looked like the smart bet if you wanted to race and sell motorcycles.

Carlo's 500cc engine's most obvious difference to other singles was that its cylinder was placed horizontally in the frame, keeping weight low and making the most of cooling airflow, as well as allowing Giuseppe Guzzi to design an especially low-slung frame. Carlo's insistence on gear primary drive to the three-speed gearbox required the crankshaft to run backwards compared to other engines of the time: given that a gearbox must spin in the same direction as the rear wheel of a motorcycle, driving the gearbox by a chain from the crankshaft allows it to spin in the same direction. The GP's helical gear primary drive required the crankshaft to rotate in the opposite direction, but Carlo turned this small detail to his advantage by designing the big end so that oil was thrown up to lubricate the top wall of the cylinder. The need to provide an air-cooled engine with plenty of oil (which assists with cooling as much as the air) was something clearly understood by the designer of the GP, and even extended to placing the oil tank in the airflow above the engine, rather than behind it, like most other motorcycles of the time. This attention to cooling and lubrication was one of the principal reasons the Guzzi 'flat' singles (as they came to be known) became famous for their reliability and longevity.

The three-speed gearbox was built in unit with the crankcases, which also enclosed a metal-to-metal multiplate clutch. This was lubricated by oil mist, and clever thinking ensured oil also reached the final drive chain. Again, there is evidence of Guzzi's obsession with lubrication in the detailing to the more substantial bearings, machined so that they retained a film of oil on their faces. To keep the crankcases as compact as possible, another feature of Guzzi singles, which debuted on the GP, was a huge external flywheel. This steel 11in (280mm) disc was quickly nicknamed a 'bacon slicer' and these big flywheels remained a feature of the flat singles, right up until their demise with the Nuovo Falcone in 1976, although by then at least it had a metal cover.

Carlo's aero-engine experience shone through in the design of the GP's cylinder head, where four parallel valves were closed by exposed hairsprings and opened by an overhead camshaft spun by shaft-driven bevel gears. Also following aviation practice was the dual-circuit ignition powered by a Bosch magneto. Like the crankcases and gearbox, the cylinder head and barrel were cast in aluminium alloy, and markedly over-square for the period, with an 88mm bore and 82mm stroke giving a 498.4cc capacity. Further innovation was shown in the chassis, which was far less bicycle-like than most motorcycles of the era. The way the top tubes were connected to the rear mudguard, making it part of the frame, was again closer to aviation practice than motorcycles of the time, and the twin front down tubes, necessitated by the horizontal cylinder, added rigidity. Girder front forks held an unbraked front wheel, with the rear wheel braked by a belt running around a drum on the hub,

supported by bolted up triangulated tubing. Even running the large 26in wheels typical of the period, the low seat height allowed a relaxed, armchair-like riding position, but more importantly, allowed stability and control on the treacherous road surface of 1920s Italy. Coupled with 12bhp propelling not much more than 220lb (100kg), the GP was as fine a prototype as the Parodis could have dared to hope for.

Into Production

Emanuele Parodi might have been impressed by the GP prototype, but no business ever thrived by fishing in an empty pond. While the Guzzi brothers and Ripamonti had been toiling in the workshop, Parodi senior had been quietly researching the market. Visits to various government departments and businesses allowed him to assess the number of motorcycles in Italy, the country's manufacturing capacity and the number of motorcycles imported. Despite his natural prudence, Emanuele could see potential in the business of motorcycle manufacture, if the right product could be brought to the market at the right price. This meant developing the GP into a motorcycle that would be economical to produce and own, and reliable in use. So the 4-valve alloy head and cylinder were replaced by an unusual 2-valve arrangement in cast-iron equivalents: an inlet sidevalve was opened by a pushrod below the valve stem, and closed by a coil spring. The overhead exhaust valve almost faced the inlet and was opened by a rocker and pushrod, then closed by a hairspring – unusual at the time but a feature that would become the norm on racing motorcycles. Both inlet and exhaust pushrods were driven by a rocker on the single camshaft. The idea of combining the advantages of an overhead valve with a sidevalve was not unique: a sidevalve engine was cheap to build, compact and offered good low rpm power, even when running on poor-quality fuel; but an overhead-valve engine offered the potential for more power by offering faster gas flow into and out of the combustion chamber. This was something the world's largest motorcycle manufacturer, Harley-Davidson, offered on their V-twins in 1920 but, like everyone else who adopted the idea, they placed the inlet valve above the piston and the exhaust valve to the side. The reasoning was simple: the inlet charge gains most from the easier route into the cylinder since, unlike exhaust gases, it is not propelled by the force of combustion. But the horizontal single could not really have a carburettor in front of its cylinder head, and anyway, Carlo Guzzi was more concerned with keeping the exhaust valve in the cooling airflow, since this is the hottest part of a four-stroke engine and a part prone to failing.

Constrained by the inlet sidevalve, fed by a British Amac 1in carburettor, and despite raising the compression ratio of the four-ring (plus two oil scrapers) aluminium alloy piston to 4:1, the revised engine gave 8bhp at 3,200rpm, a fraction of the GP's output. Dimensions, notably bore, stroke and capacity, were largely unchanged from the prototype, but the lubrication system was a much simplified total-loss system supplemented by the hand-pump Carlo Guzzi had wanted to eliminate. The chassis was largely unchanged, however, apart from a sturdy steel box section taking the place of the load-bearing rear mudguard and a drum brake at the rear. The final production-ready

motorcycle was called the Moto Guzzi Normale ('Standard Moto Guzzi Motorcycle') and weighing in at a still modest 286lb (130kg) could achieve 53mph (85km/h). But perhaps the most striking thing about this new motorcycle was how different it looked to everything else on the market, as if to emphasize that Moto Guzzi would tread its own path regardless of fashion or the received wisdom. Certainly painting the motorcycle a rather drab green-brown seemed perverse, but then building a factory in a small fishing village, rather than following the herd south to Milan, was just the start of Moto Guzzi's reputation for doing things its own way.

At some point over the years, Mandello Tonzanico was renamed Mandello del Lario and the lake it overlooked stopped being called Lario, as it had been since Roman times, and became Como. But it was always the place the Guzzi family called home, so it seemed natural to build the factory there. There has been talk for decades of relocating Moto Guzzi to somewhere with better lines of communication, but back in the beginning, just as now, it seemed unthinkable that a true Moto Guzzi could be built anywhere else. Emanuele Parodi, of course, purchased the land close to Ripamonti's forge and paid for a new workshop, which remains within the current factory, some ninety years later. The handful of new recruits was all either family or local, and Mandello's remote location has always meant it supported the local community, partly explaining the enormous loyalty and love for the marque. All of this was funded by Parodi senior, which explains why, when the Società Anonima Moto Guzzi was registered on 15 March 1921, Moto Guzzi became a Limited Company with its registered office in Genoa and Emanuele Vittorio Parodi as its

ABOVE: **Another Normale, this time in the Morbidelli museum. The unusual overhead exhaust valve and inlet sidevalve arrangement is clear from this angle.**

RIGHT: **The Moto Guzzi museum's Normale.**

chairman. Parodi retained the entire shareholding, and Carlo Guzzi was to be remunerated from royalties on machines produced, rather than from a salary, dividends or profits. In fact he would never have a financial stake in the company, which must have suited him since it also freed him and his family from any risk or worries over money.

In fact the greatest common ground between Carlo Guzzi and his business partners, the Parodis, might have been a marked carefulness with money. Although the GP and Normale were different to every other motorcycle for sale, in appearance they were rather down to earth and prosaic, just like their creator. Carlo was happy to sit at his bench trying ideas and new parts on a mule engine, and was open to new ideas unless he felt them unnecessarily exotic: in other words, too costly to put into production. So neither Guzzi nor Parodi were keen to spend money on the traditional route of promoting a new motorcycle by entering a high-profile race. Instead Moto Guzzi were introduced to the world with a rather clunky statement in the motorcycle press in December 1920, promising a 'new machine produced by a vigorous limited company established to build a standard motorcycle to compete with the finest in the world'.

The First Races

Unfortunately for Carlo, a local politician managed to claim a ride on one of the two motorcycles the factory had built, and was so impressed he asked to be allowed to race it. Predictably, Carlo refused, but Aldo Finzi wasn't just a Member of Parliament, he was also quite the sports star with a known love of motorcycling. Eventually Carlo was forced to acquiesce and let his precious Normale and GP go. He must have remembered that his old friend Giovanni Ravelli would have raced these motorcycles if he hadn't been killed and, even if he'd forgotten, Giorgio Parodi would surely have reminded him. The race Finzi wanted to enter was the Raid Nord Sud ('Raid North to South' – the Italians called long-distance races 'raids'), which would become the infamous Milano–Taranto. Established in 1919, the race ran 522 miles (840km) from Milan in the affluent northern plains of Italy to poverty ridden Naples on the south-west coast via Italy's most famous cities – including Parma, Bologna, Florence and Rome. Today, with a modest car, the journey should take less than eight hours; in the 1919 inaugural race, the winner took barely four minutes short of twenty-two hours. Victorious Ettore Girardi's clever split-single two-stroke Garelli 350 was a fine motorcycle, with

two pistons sharing a single conrod and gudgeon pin that passed through a slot in the wall of the parallel cylinders. In fact this was possibly the world's finest racing motorcycle at the time, so the time taken tells how poor the roads were. There was also the hardship of racing at night, with riders setting off late in the evening and any chance of success depending on the briefest of stops for no more than fuel and a snack. Chance played a huge part in even finishing the event, and in 1919, only five of the twenty-nine starters were credited with finishing. Carlo Guzzi knew failure would damn his nascent motorcycle factory and demand resources he did not yet have when he refused to enter the raid. Yet success had rewarded Garelli with huge demand for their new 350, now proudly called the 'Raid Nord Sud' in case any potential customers had forgotten about Garelli's win. That Indian, fighting Harley-Davidson for the mantle of the world's biggest motorcycle manufacturer, entered and won the event in 1920, was simply a hard-headed business decision. Oscar Hedstrom, head of the Indian factory, declared the Isle of Man TT 'The most terrific thing I ever saw' before his big V-twins dominated the 1911 race. Indian were also developing a racing 500 single, and it was one of these that Miro Maffeis used to dominate the 1920 Raid Nord Sud, winning the event in twenty-two hours, thirty-seven minutes – almost two hours ahead of the next finisher. Indian V-twins were also back in sixth and seventh place. Clearly this was a race to make or break the name of a motorcycle manufacturer.

It took more than fate to intervene in Carlo Guzzi's decision to enter the 1921 Raid. Finzi applied irresistible pressure wherever he could until Guzzi and Parodi relented, providing a Normale with upgraded lighting for Finzi alongside a second bike for star rider Mario Cavedini. Starting late on the 17 September 1921, the Raid was held a little earlier in the Italian autumn than in previous years. Even in September, the heat of southern Italy can be unbearable in the middle of the day, beneath scorching skies and on dusty, sun-baked, rubble roads. For 1921, the route was extended to almost 540 miles (869km), a fine test for a new motorcycle. Cavedini reached Bologna, 135 miles (216km) into the race, at just after 10pm, followed a few minutes later by Finzi with a smashed headlight, broken by a fall in Modena. The newspaper reports of the time tell of spontaneous applause for the Guzzi rider who 'raced through the night aided by no more than moonlight. His Guzzi is a new Italian motorcycle which sparks keen interest and favourable comments.' Bigger motorcycles than the Guzzi 500 might have filled most of the top ten places, principally Harley-Davidson and Indian V-twins, but Cavedini's

Proof that despite being perhaps ninety years old, Normales still get ridden.

Guzzi was sixth in the 500 class (twentieth overall), with Finzi in ninth (twenty-second overall). That they finished at all on the first two Moto Guzzis built was impressive enough – just twenty-seven of the sixty starters completed the Raid. Moto Guzzi's name had been made famous across Italy, and Carlo Guzzi was beginning to understand the value of racing.

Early Success

A week later, Aldo Finzi's brother borrowed the Normale to win the 500cc class of the Targa Florio and capture Guzzi's first win. 1921 was only the second year the Targa Florio had run a motorcycle event, but the car race had been run since 1907 and was famous world-wide. The race was 200 miles (320km) of closed roads running up into the mountains in the north

of Sicily, known by enthusiasts the length of Italy as the Medio Circuito delle Madonie. Gino Finzi's victory here, on a Moto Guzzi Normale, would have been a huge boost to the factory, which, despite building fewer than twenty motorcycles in 1921, had great ambitions. For 1922, the Normale gained the fully automatic lubrication system Carlo Guzzi had wanted all along, with a pump added within the crankcases, while the arguably excessive dual-circuit ignition was relegated to the role of an optional extra. Extra cooling fins and an increase in compression to 4.7:1 pretty much completed the update, unashamedly intended to improve the chances of racing success. Power was up by half a horsepower to 8.5bhp at 3,400rpm.

Of the nine races Moto Guzzi entered in 1922, they won just two, and success in the major events remained elusive. The Raid Nord Sud yielded only an eighth place, behind Harley-Davidson, Indian, Garelli, Frera and a brace of British Norton

500s. Frera also won the Targa Florio 500cc class, and Moto Guzzi failed to show well at the new Monza circuit's Nations Grand Prix (often called the Italian GP). But the season opener was the second year of the Circuito del Lario, held just across Lake Como and in sight of the Moto Guzzi factory. Twenty-two miles (36km) of public roads climbed up to the chapel of Madonna del Ghisallo, nearly 1,800ft (550m) above the lake's shore, before racing down to the coast road. The elevation changes are severe, with one stretch of road dropping over 700ft (213m) in barely more than a mile (c.215m in 1.6km). Around 300 corners challenged riders for each of the six laps that made up the event, colloquially known as the Italian TT, impressive enough to draw crowds of up to 100,000 spectators – a race worth entering, especially when it's on the doorstep of your

Much steeper than it looks, this was the early descent to the coast road and part of the Circuito del Lario. It was not tarmacked back then. The V7 Classic was loaned to the author by Agostini's dealership in Mandello del Lario.

new factory. Moto Guzzi had actually entered Carlo's brother-in-law Valentino Gatti on a Normale for the inaugural event in 1921, but he hadn't made the start.

The 1922 Circuito del Lario was held on 1 July. The crowd would have arrived early to be sure of finding the right spot, perhaps searching out shade in preparation for the midday sun and a picnic. British marque Sunbeam took the 500cc class win, the organizers having adopted the new European norm of making this the maximum permitted capacity for racing motorcycles, but Moto Guzzis took fifth, eleventh, twelfth and fourteenth places. This awarded them the Team Trophy, a publicity opportunity Moto Guzzi made the most of, even ensuring an advertisement appeared in the leading Italian publication *Motociclismo* just days after the result was declared.

This was an era when racing typically involved lightly breathed-upon production motorcycles that most customers bought simply for leisure or transport: in other words, if a motorcycle was to sell, it needed to be reliable, easy to live with and capable of winning races. The gap between a factory's road-bikes and racers was expected to be minimal, which certainly suited Carlo Guzzi when he set about uprating the Normale for the 1923 racing season. This motorcycle was known as the C2V (Corsa 2-valole – Racing 2-valves) but was in truth little more than a Normale with a new cylinder head and a lightly modified chassis. A new frame replaced the steel box section below the seat of the Normale with simple tubing, and the wheelbase was lengthened to improve stability. Most visibly, the Normale's dowdy colour scheme was abandoned for brilliant red paintwork. Red had originally been assigned to the United States for racing in the Gordon Bennett Cup, a car race that ran until 1905. Racing colour allocations, which included green for Britain, had been adopted by all international motor sport organizers, but around 1920 the Unites States successfully petitioned to change their colours to blue and white. This left red free for Italian teams who wished to enter international races and Moto Guzzi was quick to adopt the new national standard.

The C2V's cylinder head featured near parallel overhead valves, both opened by pushrods and closed by hairsprings, rather like the exhaust valve of the Normale. The option of dual-circuit ignition remained, allowing a second spark plug, and compression was raised to 5.25:1. Later bikes also had a 25mm Dell'Orto in lieu of the Normale's Amac carburettor. These modest changes doubled the standard Normale's power to 17bhp at 4,200rpm, and racing success was immediate. Valentino Gatti won the 1923 Circuito del Lario along with a fuel economy event run by *Motociclismo* magazine, and a C2V also won the Giro Motociclistico d'Italia long-distance race.

LEFT: **1926 C2V racer in the Morbidelli museum. The overhead valves are the most obvious difference to the Normale.**

BELOW: **A clearer view of the valves, rockers and central spark plug of the C2V.**

Sadly, the Guzzi entry failed to complete the Milano–Taranto or win at Monza, despite setting a new lap-record of almost 80mph (128km/h).

Some of the C2V's features found their way onto the road-going replacement for the Normale, the Moto Guzzi Sport. The Sport featured a near-identical chassis to the C2V and could be specified with a sidecar and front brake. A modestly uprated engine, however, retained the Normale's exhaust-over-inlet valve arrangement, limiting power to 13bhp at 3,800rpm, yet allowed the Sport to reach the psychologically important 100km/h (62mph) mark. This was more than enough for the Sport to be well-received and, with the demise of the Normale, it was the only road-going Moto Guzzi customers would be able to buy until 1928.

By 1924 Moto Guzzi had built some 2,000 Normales and the new Sport was selling well, in large part due to racing success. In five short years Carlo Guzzi had gone from being a man with an idea for a fairly utilitarian motorcycle to head of design at a new motorcycle factory building machines that carried his name. Quite an achievement for a modest and reserved individual, who was never happier than when wrestling with the quiet challenges of philosophy or broken motorcycle engines. If his regular motorcycles, intended for day-to-day use, could win races, what of the motorcycles Guzzi would build with the sole intention of winning races?

ROAD-RACING ITALIAN STYLE

If you haven't any race-tracks how can you go racing? Simple – you just use public roads, and hope the public stays off them.

In the early days of the twentieth century, all wheeled racing – whether bicycle, motor car or motorcycle – had to be on the road: there was simply no other venue available. The roads would also have been unrecognizable to modern drivers: typically ancient chalk pathways used by drovers for centuries or old farm tracks, patched with rubble and cinder. Yet across the world, wealthy (because early vehicles were fabulously expensive) enthusiasts persuaded governments to close roads and allow the first motorsport events. These road closures were typically enforced by little more than posters along the route, advertising the race. Organizers relied almost solely upon the enthusiasm of locals, repaying them with a free and unprecedented spectacle. Racers simply had to pray that any disgruntled locals valued their livestock more than an opportunity to register disapproval. Fortunately, people in Italy took motorsport to their heart, decorating race routes and lining the streets to catch sight of these brave new sportsmen.

The first major motorcycle road race in Italy was the Giro Motociclistico d'Italia of 1914, a tour for production motorcycles that would be relaunched as the Motogiro in the 1950s. Even more extreme was the Raid Nord Sud of 1919, a 500-odd mile (c.800km) race from Milan to Naples that would be extended to create the Milano–Taranto. A motorcycle event was also tacked on to the previously cars-only Targa Florio in the mountains above Palermo the following year, and motorcycles would continue to compete in this Sicilian event until 1940. However, the distance of Sicily from Italy's motorcycle factories, based exclusively in the north of the country, would forever limit the draw

of the Florio. The other 'Gran Fondo' ('large fund' – referring to prize money) race was the Circuito del Lario, held in the hills across the lake from the Moto Guzzi factory between 1921 and 1939, when war intervened. The Motogiro and Milano–Taranto lasted until the Italian Government banned racing on public roads, after an accident in the 1957 Mille Miglia, when twelve fatalities resulted from Alfonso de Portago's Ferrari crashing into the crowd. Racing on public roads was unspeakably dangerous, even by the standards of those more innocent times. This was also the year the Italian factories colluded to withdraw from circuit racing to save money, although MV Agusta infamously reneged on the agreement.

The advertisements for the Milano–Taranto revival deliberately mimic the style of the original posters, which means featuring a Moto Guzzi.
MOTO CLUB VETERAN SAN MARTINO

Continued overleaf

ROAD-RACING ITALIAN STYLE

While the rest of the world seemed happy to accept motorcycle and cars racing on open roads, Britain was pretty much unique in absolutely prohibiting them. There was general public disdain for the internal combustion engine, summed up by Kenneth Grahame's 1908 book, *Wind in the Willows*, in which the wicked and feckless Toad obsesses about his motor car. Indeed, following the Motor Car Act of 1903, Britain was subjected to a blanket 20mph (32km/h) speed limit, despite many warning that Britain's embryonic motor industry was being stifled at birth. Reliability and performance could not be developed when it was illegal to go faster than 20mph (32km/h), and at the time almost half of the world's cars were built in France. The ban was also humiliating to many motoring enthusiasts, especially when, for the first major international motor racing series, the Gordon Bennett Cup held between 1900 and 1905, the British round had to be held in Ireland. As a result, the British team ran in a green livery in gratitude to the Irish, the origin of 'British' racing green. The 'British' Gordon Bennett eliminating trial was then held on the Isle of Man in 1904 as a result of the Motor Car Act (the autonomous Manx Government were happy to benefit from the British legislation), and this was effectively the birth of the TT races.

But necessity being the mother of invention, help with high-speed testing was at hand. Work commenced in late 1906 on Brooklands, the first purpose-built motor-racing circuit in the world. Built by Surrey landowner Hugh Locke-King on his Weybridge estate, the 3.25 mile (5.25km), 100ft (30m) wide track with two 30ft (9m) high bankings opened on 17 June 1907, absorbing King's entire fortune in the process. The USA were quick to follow with an inaugural race in August 1909 at the newly built Indianapolis Motor Speedway.

Yet motorsport-mad Italy had to wait until 1922 for its first race-track, a circuit in the town of Monza, close to Milan. Like Brooklands and Indianapolis, the Autodromo Nazionale Monza featured hair-raising banking, and was part of the Italian post-war rebuilding programme encouraged by Mussolini. High unemployment meant that 3,500 workers were willing to toil between May and July to complete the circuit in less than three months. The initial layout was on 1.3 square mile (3.4km²) site within the walled parkland of Monza's Villa Reale (Royal Villa). Originally 6.2 miles (10km) of serpentine twin-loop track, it was officially opened on 3 September 1922.

Italy's other famous race-track is colloquially known as Imola, although the formal title is Autodromo Internazionale Enzo e Dino Ferrari: Enzo's name was added after Ferrari's founding father died in 1988 and his son Dino had died in 1956, shortly after Imola opened. It became Ferrari's home circuit, recalled in Enzo's 1980 book, *Ferrari 80*.

From the very first moment I considered the possibility to turn

This was the main 'straight' of the Circuito del Lario, although not only was there no tarmac there was nothing to stop fallen riders sliding into Lake Como. The Moto Guzzi factory is over the water, across to the left.

that hilly area [outside the city of Imola] into a small Nurburgring due to the natural difficulties condensed into the circuit that was going to be built, thus offering a really demanding track for men and machines alike. Imola race-track's proponents felt reassured by my opinion. In May 1950 the work started. I attended the ceremony in which the first stone was laid by Lawyer Onesti under the aegis of CONI [Italian National Olympic Committee] that granted 40 million Lire: I believe this was the first contribution the Committee made to motor racing. A small Nurburgring – I was saying to myself that day looking around me – a small Nurburgring, with equal technical and spectacular resources and an ideal track length. My idea became a reality over the decades that have elapsed since then.

On 25 April 1953 Imola's inaugural event was the CONI motorcycle Grand Prix, with races won by Masetti and Lorenzetti on a Gilera and Moto Guzzi, respectively. The following year, Imola hosted the first Coppa d'Oro Shell, which became Italy's best-attended motorcycle race for over twenty years.

Many of Italy's purpose-built circuits are close to, and sometimes named after, old road circuits. Unlike Britain, where wartime airfields form the basis of most race-tracks, Italy's motorsport heritage is closely linked to racing on public roads. Even the famous Mugello, host to MotoGP, started in the nearby hills as a road circuit in 1920 and was retained for rallying until 1970. A string of accidents, many fatal and often caused by drivers illegally practising when roads weren't closed, led to the new L'Autodromo del Mugello being built in 1973. So racing on public roads defines Italian motorcycle racing to this day and, historically, racing success, especially in Grand Prix and the Gran Fondo events, meant sales. These races, together with the roads and tracks they ran on, are integral to the story of Moto Guzzi.

ABOVE: **The cover of** *Motociclismo* **would carry advertisements, this one for the 1937 Milano–Taranto: note the reference to the prize being courtesy of Mussolini.** MOTO CLUB VETERAN SAN MARTINO

RIGHT: **The 1940 Milano–Taranto saw Guido Cerato overall winner on his Moto Guzzi 500.** MOTO CLUB VETERAN SAN MARTINO

CHAPTER TWO

RACING GLORY FROM SINGLES TO THE V8

In September 1922, Garelli's remarkable 350 took a host of speed records, having already won the Grand Prix at Monza and a race in Austria – the first time an Italian motorcycle had ever prevailed abroad. The versions on sale to the public bore the moniker Competizione or Raid Nord Sud, a clear boast that

**The C4V has its 4-valve head enclosed,
but the workings are still obvious.**

these were nothing less than over-the-counter production racers. The riders who sought to race them were the Italian greats, including the incomparable Tazio Nuvolari and Achile Varzi. If Carlo Guzzi was serious about winning major races and attracting the finest riders, he would need more than a lightly breathed-upon 500 Sport. Racing was also changing, with shorter circuits gaining popularity, which favoured power over the ruggedness required for the long-distance road races. By late 1923, his C2V was struggling against improving competition, especially on short circuits, as manufacturers increasingly entered purpose-built racing motorcycles, rather than tweaked production models. It was time to dust down the blueprints of his original 4-valve, overhead cam, Guzzi–Parodi, GP design.

This led to a much upgraded engine, although still obviously related to the road-going Sport that customers were buying. Wider engine cases accommodated bevel drive to an overhead camshaft opening four valves, closed in turn by enclosed hairsprings. The inlet and exhaust valve pairings were inclined away from each other with a central spark plug, as on many modern engines. Also like modern high-performance engines was the split inlet manifold that flowed gas more efficiently to each of the inlet valves, fed by a unique Amac 28.5mm carburettor. Compression was up considerably to 6:1, necessitating a decompressor to aid starting, taking advantage of improved petrol quality and new regulations that allowed racing motorcycles to use fuel additives. The end result was 22bhp at 5,500rpm, 30 per cent up on the C2V and 2bhp more than the Garelli. Although the three-speed, hand-change, gearbox remained, the wheelbase was reduced to the Normale's 54in (1,380mm), with a rim front-brake complementing the rear drum. Weight remained at 286lb (130kg), so performance was much improved over the C2V, with the new racer capable of 87mph (140km/h), a good 6mph (10km/h) faster than the Garelli.

This latest Moto Guzzi was christened – quite literally – the C4V: Corsa 4-valole (Racing 4-valves) in a ceremony held just before the 1924 Circuito del Lario on 29 June, although this wasn't its true debut. Almost three weeks earlier, the C4V had set a 500cc class record in the Cremona speed trials by averaging 84mph (135km/h) over a flying 6.2 miles (10km), raising expectations for the Lario race. Pre-race preparations included bracing the rigid rear-end and removing the crude rim front-brake, which could be a liability on the loose shale roads. The oil tank was also relocated from just above the cylinder head on to the fuel-tank, which was to become a Moto Guzzi trademark. Carlo's brother-in-law, Valentino Gatti, was again entered to ride, along with Guido Mentasti, who had ridden a C2V to victory in the previous year's Motogiro. They were joined by brothers Pietro and Mario Ghersi, who duly delivered first and fourth places, respectively, with Mentasti finishing the race as runner-up. Moto Guzzi made the most of their riders' popularity, handing out autographed photographs of Guido Mentasti in a film star-style pose, wearing a leather jacket and white silk scarf and looking every inch the flying ace.

Success at the Circuito del Lario was followed up with a win for Mentasti at the inaugural Championship of Europe at the new Monza circuit. Monza had opened in late 1922 and its major motorcycle race was the Nations Grand Prix, often referred to as the Italian GP. For 1924, victory in the Nations would also bring the honorary title of European Champion, which in years to come would be decided by results in a series of races across Europe, and eventually the world, to become what we now know as MotoGP. That gives an indication of how important victory was to Moto Guzzi, especially as the pre-race favourite had been Tazio Nuvolari riding a Norton TT. Norton was the bike to beat and Nuvolari the rider to beat, yet newcomers Moto Guzzi and Mentasti had managed it. To back it up, Moto Guzzis also finished second and fourth: as the Secretary of the International Federation wrote, 'The dominating Moto Guzzis, so unorthodox compared to other [British] motorcycles, prove the importance of the Italian motorcycle industry.'

Yet there had been considerable drama in the Moto Guzzi camp in the hours running up to the Nations Grand Prix. Mentasti took a remarkable gamble to make the most of Monza's fast, open layout. Dramatically deciding to remove the gearbox and hand-change, Mentasti relied on the primary gear alone, getting more power to the back wheel but rendering the C4V a single-speed racer. The gamble paid off handsomely, with victory in the 249-mile (400km) race taking a little over three hours at an average of 81mph (130km/h). When Pietro Ghersi

The poster artwork for the races was highly stylized and arguably better than would be achieved today. A HERL INC.

won the German Grand Prix at the end of September 1924, Moto Guzzi weren't just famous in Italy, they were a benchmark across Europe, and could justly lay claim to being a major force in motorcycling. The C2V and C4V's strong visual link to the road-going Sport, which most customers were buying, was either canny marketing or, more likely, proved the inherent brilliance of Carlo Guzzi's original concept. It would also allow future production road and racing models to adopt proven developments from the factory racers. As the C4V evolved into the 4VTT for 1927, with needle roller big-ends that would become another Moto Guzzi standard, it amounted to a customer version of the previous year's factory racer. There was also a Binks twist grip-style throttle, with bigger wheels and a bronze alloy cylinder head replacing the old

The C2V raced by Valentino Gatti to victory in the 1923 Circuito del Lario.

cast-iron item. The TT was in turn tweaked to become the 1929 4VSS, which finally brought a front drum-brake to Moto Guzzi and the factory racer's oil tank above the fuel-tank layout to a production model. Although intended as a racing motorcycle, the 4VSS could be ordered with a horn and lights, as could its 250 counterpart, the SS250. These motorcycles were, however, unlikely to see use on an open public road, and the need for lights and a horn was more closely linked to these being requirements for races such as the Motogiro d'Italia and Milano–Taranto.

Advances by the Competition Brings a Change of Direction

Early in 1928, Moto Guzzi announced they would withdraw from racing, although the production of racing models was actually increased. Privately entered Moto Guzzis were

providing all the publicity the factory needed, and although production was around 3,000 motorcycles a year, providing almost 400 jobs, development on both the road and racing motorcycles was overdue. Bianchi's Freccia Celeste was showing more than just promise and would win the Circuito del Lario outright in 1929 and 1930, aided by the towering talent of Tazio Nuvolari. The Bianchi's bevel-driven double-overhead cams helped it make 25bhp, despite displacing just 348cc, but Carlo Guzzi was more concerned about an engine that would go on to dominate motorcycle road-racing right up to the present day.

In the early 1920s, a pair of young engineers, Carlo Gianni and Piero Remor, realized the perfect racing engine could be a transverse 4-cylinder unit. With exhausts facing forward to cool the exhaust valves, the low reciprocating weight of pistons, conrods and valves would allow plenty of revs. Although a single-cylinder engine like the Moto Guzzi might provide plenty of torque – the turning effort that ultimately spins the rear wheel – it is how often the torque is produced by combustion that provides ultimate power. The smaller components in a four allow it to spin faster and so provide more power, and the smaller individual cylinders mean a much smaller flywheel is needed to even out the power pulses. The big Guzzi flywheel might smooth out power pulses, minimizing vibration and improving tractability, but its inertia meant this was at the expense of acceleration. A big flywheel, along with the big, strong crankshaft needed by a 500cc single, also eats into the weight advantage a single should have over a multi-cylinder engine.

Gianni and Remor persuaded Count Bonmartini to fund development of their ideas under the umbrella of a new company that used the first letter of each of their names – GRB. Their first 490cc engine made 28bhp at 6,000rpm, immediately out-powering the Moto Guzzi 500, despite revving no higher than Guzzi's 250 single-cylinder racers. Recapitalization and a new business partner meant renaming the company OPRA (Officine di Precisione Romane Automobilistiche), but by 1928 the engine was developing 34bhp. This was the engine that would ultimately evolve into the dominant Gilera and MV Agusta 4-cylinder racers, so Carlo Guzzi was right to keep an eye on development and to believe his single-cylinder racers would ultimately be unable to compete. Even so, he was mistaken about how quickly the singles would be pushed aside and how long it would take to marry the power of multi-cylinder engines to the mysteries of motorcycle handling. In fact, 500cc single-cylinder motorcycles would remain competitive, even in world-class racing, until the early 1970s, and to this day, engineers find it harder to make a motorcycle handle well than to make it more powerful. It is this lack of balance between handling and power that would lead to the failure of perhaps the most famous Moto Guzzi of all time, the V8 racer, and Carlo's next project, his very own 4-cylinder engine.

Innovations, Including 3- and 4-Cylinder Engines

In many ways, Carlo's 1931 Quattro Cilindri was a case of something old, something new, something borrowed. Twin Bosch magnetos and a Cozette rotary supercharger were bought in and the position of the supercharger above the gearbox, which sat vertically behind the crankshaft as on modern sports bikes, showed original thinking. Triple roller bearings supported the crank, and needle bearings the conrods, ideas that were as up-to-date as the lubrication system. The very over-square layout, with a 56mm bore and 50mm stroke, was also something today's engineers would recognize as good practice in an engine designed for outright power. The four individual cylinders lay almost horizontally, mimicking the Guzzi singles, which could be justified in terms of packaging and cooling. Yet the pushrods driving overhead valves, and the hand-change, three-speed gearbox, seemed old-fashioned ideas in 1931. Moto Guzzi's works 250 racer was fitted with a foot-change for 1930, and Velocette had introduced the first positive foot gear-change (the system still used on most motorcycles) in 1928. This freed a rider from having to let go of the handle-bars to change gear, using a lever by the side of the fuel-tank. Now a rider could change gear with a single flick of the foot, thanks to a groundbreaking system designed by Harold Willis. Debuting on the KTT, it helped make Velocette a dominant force at the TT, despite the 348cc, single-cylinder, four-stroke making just 20bhp. Naturally, Velocette patented their new gearbox, but they were happy to sell the KTT to the public.

The Velocette also weighed a flyweight 265lb (120kg), where the Moto Guzzi Quattro was closer to 365lb (165kg), so despite producing 40bhp at 7,800rpm, it seems the power and weight would have proven more of a liability than an asset on all but the smoothest race-track. Tested and raced at Monza in 1931, the Quattro's only race was at the Nations Grand Prix in 1932, where three of them were entered by the factory. Terzo Bandini rode to great effect, challenging the winning Norton for the lead for much of the race. Yet all three Quattros failed to finish, and despite the considerable extra power they offered compared to the competition, they showed no great promise in the race. The Norton International that won was a new long-

stroke sohc design that produced just 29bhp from 490cc. In theory, the Moto Guzzi's 30 per cent horsepower advantage should have allowed riders to pull out uncatchable leads along the straights, but there were mitigating circumstances.

First, the Nations Grand Prix wasn't held at Monza, Moto Guzzi's home track, for the three years between 1932 and 1934. Instead it was hosted some 370 miles (600km) further south at Rome's airport, the so called Pista del Littorio. This was a much shorter, slower circuit than Monza, although the winning rider still averaged 105mph (170km/h). That the winning rider was Piero Taruffi also meant Bandini had nothing to be ashamed of – Taruffi would go on to win an F1 Grand Prix for Ferrari, as well as the last-ever Mille Miglia in 1957. Perhaps this was the reason Carlo persevered with Quattro until the end of 1932, working with test-rider Siro Casali, who would go on to manage a workshop within the factory. The frame of the Quattro was also a disappointment, and was incapable of allowing riders to take advantage of the power available. Designed by Carlo's brother Giuseppe, who had officially joined the factory in 1927, the frame introduced innovations that not only Moto Guzzi, but many other factories, would adopt in the future. Dural plates ran below and behind the engine, joining a conventional tubular chassis at the front to the headstock, and a triangulated rigid rear-end. Dural is the trade name for an aluminium alloy that becomes stronger over time after quenching, and had been developed in Germany for use first in airships and subsequently in aircraft. Besides bringing another aviation technology to motorcycling, Giuseppe's use of Dural plates also simplified engine removal and absorbed vibration. Sadly, the Quattro's chassis lacked the innovation that racing motorcycles desperately needed: rear suspension. A rigidly held rear wheel skips and jumps, especially on the crude road surfaces of 1920s Italy. Every time a rear wheel leaves the road, it denies the rider control and the engine of the means to transmit power to the road. The problem was widely acknowledged and, in America, for example, Merkel and Indian had dabbled with rear suspension as early as 1910 and 1913, respectively. But racing motorcycles had stuck with the rigid rear-end, so that even in the early days of motorcycling, just as now, conservative motorcycle buyers resisted innovations that hadn't been proven on the track. Ironically, as Moto Guzzi quietly dropped the Quattro, Carlo reinstated many of his ideas for the racing engine in a prototype 3-cylinder road-bike that did feature rear suspension. Only a handful of these 25bhp, 352lb (160kg), 495cc, megaliths were built, with the intention of offering a beautifully finished grand tourer to the discerning motorcyclist. Yet again, however, Carlo had misjudged the worth of

The sole surviving Tre Cilindri roadster. Astonishingly advanced for a 1932 road-going motorcycle.

complexity in a motorcycle and buyers ignored the 3-cylinder road-bike. Despite the triple's 19mph (30km/h) top-speed advantage over the 13bhp Sport, motorcyclists were not prepared to pay the 50 per cent premium Moto Guzzi were asking over the price of the Sport, and still failed to see the worth of fitting rear suspension to a motorcycle.

Giuseppe Guzzi, universally known as Naco, had learnt this the hard way. He was, if anything, even more of an introvert than Carlo, but still persuaded him and Giorgio Parodi of the value of rear suspension. Yet they proved to be men ahead of their time, and the idea was now tainted by the failure of the triple. Such false starts had left Moto Guzzi's racing programme on the back foot and, despite Carlo Fumagalli winning the 1932 Milano–Taranto on a 4VSS, this was still, in essence, a ten-year-old motorcycle at a time of huge technological progress. The fact that the Milano–Taranto had been reinstated after a seven-year hiatus as the Mussolini Cup, might also make this the time to wonder how Moto Guzzi could pay for such developments at a time of desperate economic woes for not just Italy, but most of the Western World.

There is no evidence that anyone at Moto Guzzi supported the fascists, and the Guzzi family were probably too private

and the Parodis too astute to comment publicly on political matters. Nonetheless, the factory benefited from substantial orders from the public sector, although, as today, it seems inevitable that government departments would be mindful of placing orders with businesses that were the lifeblood of a particular region, as Moto Guzzi undoubtedly were. Carlo Guzzi also remained committed to Moto Guzzi becoming a mainstream motorcycle manufacturer, and made amends for drifting into 3- and 4-cylinder backwaters with a new range of lightweight motorcycles. These 174cc to 232cc singles not only sold well, they also looked more closely related to Guzzi's incredibly successful 250 racers.

In fact by this point most of Moto Guzzi's racing success came from their 250, which had debuted in 1926, although from 1934 the 250 was only made available to factory riders. By then it was making 18bhp, equivalent to 72bhp a litre, which at the time was a phenomenal figure for a normally aspirated engine. In 1926, Moto Guzzis won sixty-two races, fifty of which were down to the 250. The Nations Grand Prix of 1928 saw Guzzi 250s take the first five places, so although these racers shared nothing with the road-bikes beyond a basic layout, the broadly similar silhouettes must have helped sell an awful lot of P250s and its siblings. Initially, the racer bore the 250TT moniker, hinting at the factory's ambitions for success on the Isle of Man. The TT was now undoubtedly the most important motorcycle race in Europe, if not the world, and a win on the island would pretty much guarantee world-wide success for a manufacturer. In 1922, a class for 250 machines had been added to the TT's programme. Geoff Davison was the first winner on a Levis, averaging some 50mph (80km/h), ironically the last victory for a British two-stroke on the island. Wal Handley set the fastest 250 lap by a whisker on an OK Supreme. 1922 also saw a new absolute lap-record for Alec Bennett on a Sunbeam in the Senior at 59.99 mph (96.52km/h), the last TT win by a side-valve machine.

The roll-call of British names highlighted the problem for manufacturers keen to win on the Isle of Man circuit – it took time to learn not just the layout, but also the nuances of various microclimates. The 1922 TT was also famous for the first-ever Manxman, Tom Sheard, winning the 350 race on the admittedly magnificent AJS. By 1920, the mountain course had pretty much settled at its current layout and 37-mile (60km) length, with a mix of climbs, fast open straight and tight corners, which created an incredible array of variables for a rider to commit to memory. The stone walls, trees and buildings

that line the route also make the TT lethally unforgiving of the smallest mistake, even by the standards of 1922. Remarkably, Pietro Ghersi managed to finish second on the Guzzi 250 at the 1926 TT, although he was disqualified simply because he had needed to change the spark plug during the race and his spare was not the same brand as the homologated original. Failure of his 500 single to finish the Senior might have left Moto Guzzi disappointed but it did prove they had potential, and led to one of the finest Moto Guzzis of all: the 500 Bicilindrica ('twin-cylinder').

When Carlo Guzzi thought again about beating the OPRA 500/4, his inspired solution was one that would influence Fabio Taglioni's creation of the Ducati V-twin forty years later. Finally recognizing power alone didn't win races, Carlo simply doubled up his winning 250 single to create a 120-degree V-twin with bevel-driven overhead cams. Power was just 43bhp, even using the cocktail of petrol and alcohol that pre-war racers were allowed, well below the 60 or so horsepower of the OPRA, but the narrow frontal area meant that almost 130mph (210km/h) was within reach. The bike's 120-degree firing order and twin big-ends (Ducati conrods share a single big-end) allowed Carlo Guzzi to design the engine so that the pistons need never travel in the same direction: as one piston rises,

The TT250 racer from 1926.

RIDING THE BIKES | **500 BICILINDRICA**

Trials legend Sammy Miller had considerable success road-racing before switching to the dirt. He was so impressed when he rode a Bicilindrica that he commissioned a replica for his New Forest museum.

Asked why the Bicilindrica didn't have more success, and why Moto Guzzi felt the need to replace it with the V8, Sammy Miller's view is typically forthright: 'They'd never any time for development, the Italians'. Sammy was road-racing with the Italian Mondial factory when the Bicilindrica got pensioned off, but hadn't ridden one until a few years ago when he sampled an original at Jurby in the Isle of Man. He was obviously taken with it, because he persuaded the owner to lend it to him for a few demonstration runs at his New Forest museum. Would he have pushed aside the Bicilindrica with the V8, which he has also ridden? His answer makes it seem unlikely: 'Development is key in racing. If you've got something that works you need to bring it along, not keep starting all over again.'

The Bicilindrica's long career might make Sammy's opinion that Moto Guzzi 'had no time for development' seem odd at first, but he has got a point. During its six-year career, Carlo Guzzi and Giorgio Parodi tried to replace the Bicilindrica with a triple, a four, a single and finally the mighty V8. Sammy was a world-class road-racer during this golden age, and his museum is proof that he understands engineering and history better than most.

Famous as the most successful trials rider of all time, and for creating the finest motorcycle museum in the UK, Sammy was also a gifted road-racer. Actually, better than 'gifted' – he won the first road-race he entered – the Irish Cookstown 100, in fact – and was a works rider for Mondial. He was also part of the first Ducati team to enter the TT, riding the 125 Desmodromic racer there in 1958. Sammy had become a victim of the Italian factories' withdrawal from road-racing at the end of 1957, and although Ducati were starting out in international competition, there were simply not enough rides to go around.

'Sometimes I think I should have scratched around and then made some money when the Japanese came onto the scene. Mind you, we could be losing one rider a week [through fatal accidents] so maybe it was for the best.' Sammy found the switch from successful road-racer to unbeatable trials rider easy; 'It's all throttle control. If you've got good throttle control then they're all just motorcycles', which seems to make him the perfect judge of the Bicilindrica. Especially since not only did he see the Bicilindrica race, he's ridden an original along with the impressively authentic replica recently commissioned for his museum. So what's it like?

Trials legend and accomplished road racer Sammy Miller demonstrates the Bicilindrica at his New Forest museum.

It's a very, very good bike. Smooth (even with the 120-degree cylinder splay) and easy to ride. Those things would have been important. I've no doubt at all that this is the bike that Taglioni copied when he built the Ducati bevel twins. Guzzi got there – how many years earlier? – anyway, long before Ducati.

The fact that evolutions of Taglioni's tribute to the Bicilindrica are still winning races today suggests that Sammy is right, and success in racing is about development, not reinventing the wheel. And he should know, he did enough winning in his time, much of it off the back of his own development of his famous 500cc Ariel HT5, GOV 132.

Sammy fitted modern carbs for the original Bicilindrica's time in the UK ('You can mess around with old carbs forever' he warns) but the rear Dell'Orto's position, down by the rear tyre, looks like the one bad idea on the bike, even though the engine definitely has a pre-war bits-and-pieces look. The engine might have changed surprisingly little down the years, although the chassis was constantly evolving. Despite only modest development, the Bicilindrica was winning races right up until the end of its career. Just as impressively, when Sammy rode one, he immediately commissioned a replica of his own, alongside the more predictable and crowd-pleasing V8. The Bicilindrica is that important in the annals of motorcycle history.

ABOVE: **A later Bicilindrica, with the fuel tank extended to create a fairing and improve aerodynamics, a Moto Guzzi obsession that led to building a wind-tunnel at the factory.**

LEFT: **Sammy Miller's convincing Bicilindrica replica.**

SPECIFICATIONS	MOTO GUZZI BICILINDRICA 500 (1933–51)

Layout and Chassis

Twin-cylinder four-stroke racing motorcycle

Engine

Type	120-degree V-twin
Block material	Aluminium alloy
Head material	Cast iron (later magnesium alloy)
Cylinders	2 in 120-degree V
Cooling	Air
Bore and stroke	68 × 68mm
Capacity	494cc
Valves	4 valves sohc
Compression ratio	8.5:1
Carburettor	Dell'Orto
Max. power	41–44bhp@7,000–7,800rpm
Fuel capacity	4.1 gallons/20 litres

Transmission

Gearbox	Four-speed foot-change
Clutch	Wet multiplate
Final drive	Chain

Chassis

Front	Brampton girder forks initially (later telescopic)
Rear	None originally, later swingarm
Tyres	3.00–21in front, 3.25–20in rear

Brakes

Type	Drums front and rear

Dimensions

Wheelbase	57.4in (1,390mm)
Unladen weight	332lb (151kg)

Performance

Top speed	Over 112mph (180km/h)

the other falls, making it more like a flat-twin BMW boxer engine than Fabio Taglioni's Ducati L-twin (Taglioni apparently hated people calling his engine a V-twin). The Bicilindrica's engine changed surprisingly little down the years – the bore and stroke remained square at 68mm by 68mm – although the chassis was constantly evolving.

The new Bicilindrica's first in a long list of victories came on 10 December 1933 at Via Caracciola, an unremarkable 0.75-mile (1.2km) street circuit in Naples. These early Bicilindricas were hardtails (i.e. lacking rear suspension) with girder forks, but compared to the competition, the Bicilindrica was light and handled adequately, aided by a low centre of gravity. Such qualities were relative: taking the Bicilindrica's first big win in the 1934 Spanish Grand Prix, Stanley Woods thought the handling evil enough to christen his bike 'the monster'. Yet a month later, Tenni and Moretti made the Italian GP a Bicilindrica one–two, Tenni going on to win the Italian championship. Badini then used his Bicilindrica to win the Milano–Taranto, a huge relief

for Guzzi after their disastrous 1933 effort. But the win that still eluded them was the most important event on the calendar: the Isle of Man TT.

Omobono Tenni and Stanley Woods were two of the greatest riders of their generation, perhaps of all time: Italian racing historian Mick Walker certainly felt Woods deserving of that title. By the time Woods agreed to race for Moto Guzzi in the 1935 Isle of Man TT, he had already won there six times previously, mainly for Norton, and had a string of other victories, including Grand Prix wins, to his credit. All Woods apparently needed was a motorcycle capable of allowing his talent to shine. It fell to Giuseppe Guzzi to design the Bicilindrica a sprung frame for 1935, with an unusual swinging arm layout that relied on springs hidden in tubes alongside the back wheel, and friction dampers that could be adjusted on the move. Weird or wonderful, the new set-up worked and, having already taken the 250 Guzzi to a win in the Lightweight TT, Woods then took the Bicilindrica to a Senior TT victory,

One of Italy's finest riders on one of her finest motorcycles. Omobono Tenni leaps his Bicilindrica over Ballaugh bridge in the 1948 TT. He was killed riding an Albatros 250 a few weeks later. A HERL INC.

The Tre Cilindri racer with Guglielmo Sandri in 1940. MOTO GUZZI

winning by just four seconds. The race was held in terrible weather, yet Woods averaged almost 85mph (137km/h) while setting a new lap-record on his way to what still stands as the closest ever TT win. It was also the first big win for an Italian manufacturer on UK soil, and turned Moto Guzzi from just another bike-builder into a world-wide brand.

Tenni fared less well, a terrifying practice mistake earning him the nickname 'Black Devil' as he ploughed along a grass bank to recover and finish the lap covered in mud. Tenni was only entered on the 250 in the Lightweight TT, but crashed in fog while lying second to Woods in the race. Less than a month later, Tenni won the 1935 Milano–Taranto on his Bicilindrica, and yet Carlo Guzzi still worried about the supercharged competition. He set to work on a supercharged, 3-cylinder, water-cooled replacement for the Bicilindrica, once again favouring a fresh start over fine-tuning.

The war brought an hiatus to racing, and when the brave new world arrived, pool-petrol and a ban on supercharging reprieved the Bicilindrica. Despite Carlo's concerns, the Bicilindrica would carry on winning races right up until the end of its career. Sometimes change was gradual – wheel sizes shrunk, forks got changed – and sometimes more radical, especially the final spine frame that must have also caught Taglioni's eye, and the curvy bodywork-cum-fuel-tank that reflected Guzzi's first lessons in aerodynamics. Despite new alloy cylinder heads, postwar 72 octane petrol meant less power, although the new frame and telescopic forks brought improvements to the handling,

The Tre Cilindri racer survives in Moto Guzzi's museum.

The Bicilindrica being run at Spa Francorchamps.
DG SPORT BIKERS' CLASSIC

as did the rear suspension's hydraulic shocks slung below the engine. The unique bodywork allowed riders to tuck in to make the most of the available 42bhp, and a lightweight Hydronalium (a German alloy that added small amounts of magnesium and nickel to aluminium) rear frame completed the main central frame beam and doubled as an oil tank. In 1947, Tenni won the Italian Championship on this Bicilindrica; then, in 1948, he used it to set the fastest lap at the TT – sadly, ignition failings robbed him of victory. The glorious final flings for the Bicilindrica brought Bertacchini victory in the 1948 Italian Championship and for Lorenzetti in 1949. Lorenzetti even won the Senigallia Grand Prix in 1951, beating Pagani and Milani's Gilera 500/4s. Fergus Anderson won a rain-lashed 1951 Swiss GP, with team-mate Enrico Lorenzetti third.

At the end of 1951, Moto Guzzi abandoned the 500 Bicilindrica to build their own 4-cylinder 500. Unfortunately, in choosing a designer for the Bicilindrica's replacement, Giorgio Parodi, who had become chairman when the company became Moto Guzzi S.p.A (Società per Azioni – effectively a company incorporated by share value), decided to look outside his own workshops. In theory, Moto Guzzi had a distinct advantage in the shape of Italy's youngest and brightest graduate engineer, who had joined them in 1936, the brilliant Giuliano Cesare Carcano. From 1947, he would run the Moto Guzzi racing department and become most famous as the designer of Moto Guzzi's V8 Grand Prix racer; but in 1951, he was ignored.

Another 4-Cylinder Dead End

So Parodi overlooked in-house engineer Carcano and commissioned Carlo Gianni, co-designer of the OPRA 500/4 that was the genesis for the dominant Gilera 500/4, to design a Bicilindrica replacement. Umberto Masetti had used the Gilera to win the 1950 500cc World Championship (making him the first Italian to win the blue riband class) and repeated the achievement in 1952. Geoff Duke would then use the Gilera to secure the title from 1953 until 1955, when what amounted to the same motorcycle racing under the MV Agusta banner dominated the championship until the early seventies. Parodi's admiration for Gianni was, therefore, understandable.

However, it proved misplaced, although there was much to impress in Gianni's design. Moto Guzzi's new wind-tunnel was ready for 1952, and had already been used to streamline the single-cylinder racers. The new Moto Guzzi four had the cylinders aligned longitudinally, rather than across the frame, to minimize frontal area. Unfortunately, this really necessitated shaft drive and, in turn, an engine speed clutch, just like the later road-going Moto Guzzi V-twins. Gear-changing could, therefore, be a hit-or-miss affair and, combined with the torque-reaction of the crankshaft spinning along the centreline of the bike, impacted on handling. To further minimize width, a form of mechanical fuel-injection, fed by a single carburettor tucked away on the right just above the gearbox, was used rather than fitting four

LEFT: **The wind-tunnel in use: the wide fairing gives away the V8's presence.** MOTO GUZZI

BELOW: **The ill-fated longitudinal 4-cylinder racer.**

carburettors to one side of the engine. Yet the two valves per cylinder, with double-overhead cams gear-driven from the crank, were set 90 degrees apart, identical to the Gilera. This was appropriate for the old supercharged engines but, with forced induction banned, this looked wide for a post-war design – Guzzi's racing singles were down to 60 degrees, as Carcano appreciated that narrower included valve angles were a key to gaining horsepower. There were some ingenious ideas on Gianni's four, but most of them were aimed at keeping the engine short enough to fit in a racing motorcycle, and preventing widening a layout selected for its inherent low frontal area.

The final difficulty was that the 500/4 was built at Gianni's base in Rome, over 400 miles (600km) from Moto Guzzi's factory, where fine-tuning and race preparation was carried out. With water-cooling, the Guzzi 500/4 weighed in at 320lb (145kg), considerably more than the air-cooled Gilera and MV Agusta fours, although with 55bhp at 9,000rpm, the Guzzi's power was comparable. However, despite initial promise and a turn of speed aided by its aerodynamic advantages, the Guzzi 500 was neither reliable nor rider-friendly. It was also aiming at a moving target and, when MV and Gilera undertook major redesigns that increased power to over 60bhp (ironically increasing included valve angles) alongside new fairings, Moto Guzzi's hopes of success with a 4-cylinder racer were dashed. A blessing in disguise, the demise of the Moto

Guzzi four handed the initiative back to Carcano. Assisted by one of Guzzi's greatest riders, Scotsman Fergus Anderson, both men accepted Guzzi's expertise lay with racing single-cylinder engines. However, it would be the 1954 Hockenheim race before Parodi was convinced that they were right, when Ken Kavanagh, following team orders and drafting Anderson on the Guzzi four, was inadvertently handed the race win, when Anderson's rear tyre delaminated at 155mph (250km/h). Anderson was unhurt but was convinced that unnecessarily powerful motorcycles made racing even more lethal than it already was.

A Return to Single-Cylinder Racers

Returning to single-cylinder race bikes would also reinforce the link to the motorcycles Moto Guzzi were trying to sell. There was another facet to this that pre-dated the war, when race organizers had realized entries were falling dramatically, as factory-supported exotica, such as the 4-cylinder bikes,

came to dominate the results. The solution to getting more racers onto the grid was seen as what we would now call production racing; although initially this amounted to simply insisting entries had lights and a stand. But Moto Guzzi were quick to realize that between their prosaic road-bikes and exotic racers there was room for an over-the-counter production racer to sell to these gentlemen racers. The first of these had an overhead valve engine, initially christened the Nuova C (for Corsa – 'new racer'), a motorcycle that won the 500cc class on its debut at the 1938 Circuito del Lario. By the time the production racer went on sale, the moniker had become GTCL (Gran Turismo Corsa Leggera – colloquially 'Lightweight Racing GT') and for 1939 it became the Condor. This production model was also much improved over the Nuova C and a world away from the mainstream 500S/GTS. The road-bikes' cast-iron heads and barrels were replaced with aluminium alloy, and crankcases were magnesium alloy. Just as importantly, the Condor shared the road-going 500V's four-speed gearbox with a foot shift. With a 7:1 compression and a monstrous (for the time) 32mm Dell'Orto carburettor, even the customer bikes had a claimed 28bhp.

A Sport 15DL tried for size by a Moto Giro competitor in Sicily.

RIDING THE BIKES | GTC LEGGERA

A rare early Moto Guzzi racer on the road came to its current British home via Libya and India, but the journey was worth it, according to Moto Guzzi owner, rider and dealer Gordon de la Mare.

Gordon de la Mare first got the Guzzi single bug back in 1967 during a motorcycle tour of Italy. Riding to a camp site in Rimini, he found himself escorted by a couple of Falcone-riding Carabinieri, and was struck by the odd (to English eyes) engine layout and overall design. The Guzzi single was unlike anything he had seen before, and had a charm and character all of its own. Right there and then, Gordon decided he needed to find a Moto Guzzi single to call his own. It just took him twenty-eight years, although he did have a Le Mans II in the meantime. In fact, the Moto Guzzi bug has gripped Gordon so firmly that he's a director of West Country Italian motorcycle dealers and period Moto Guzzi specialists, Moto Corsa.

Until recently, finding a Moto Guzzi big single in the UK was difficult, simply because so few of the 500s were originally imported, and it would be 1995 before Gordon finally bought a Falcone. But at this point in the story it's his oldest Guzzi that is of most interest, an ultra rare 1938

GTC/L; the L stands for Leggera (Light), the GTC/L weighing only 320lb (145kg) with the optional lights, compared to a standard GTC's 350lb (160kg). Gordon takes up the story.

I first came across the bike during the 75th Moto Guzzi anniversary weekend at the Mandello del Lario factory in 1996. It had a great history. Built in 1938, before returning to the factory in 1939, when it was rebuilt in Condor form and shipped to Addis Ababa in Abyssinia [now Ethiopia]. At the time this was part of the Italian empire, so the bike went straight to the local Moto Guzzi distributor where it was appropriated by a captain in the Indian Army. After World War II he had the GTC/L shipped back to India and sold it to a Maharaja. Forty years later a British guy on assignment spotted it being ridden around a local market, and in short order was the proud new owner.

To avoid the cost and difficulties involved in exporting a complete motorcycle, the GTC/L was simply dismantled and, over a period of time, departed India in suitcases. By 1993, everything was back in the UK and in one piece again.

LEFT: **Gordon de la Mare starts his beautiful and rare GTC/L.**

BELOW: **Proof that the GTC/L is road legal; it has a horn...**

Continued overleaf

RIDING THE BIKES

There was clearly no attempt by Moto Guzzi to keep production costs down judging by the quality of their work. Note Dondolino in the background, identifiable by a brake with no external mechanism.

However, the GTC/L is loud, so has a baffle plate that can be closed by a cable while on the move.

The 1937 GTC was Moto Guzzi's first over-the-counter racing motorcycle, based on the GTV. Although reliable, it was handicapped by its roadster origins and swiftly replaced with the GTC/L (also known as the Nuova C), an interim model incorporating lessons learned from the factory's supercharged 250 Grand Prix racer, including frame design and magnesium alloy components. Although the GTC/L was lighter than the GTC, its successor, the Condor, moved the process on, with aluminium alloy cylinder barrel and head, while the crankcases were in magnesium alloy. The result was a reduction in weight of some 44lb (20kg) over the GTC, the Condor tipping the scales at a mere 308lb (140kg).

The GTC/L won its debut outing at the Circuito del Lario in 1938, with Ugo Prini riding in the production class and setting a new lap-record. For 1939, the bike was officially the Condor, although the early pre-production version the factory entered in the 1939 Circuito del Lario probably retained the GTCL's cast-iron cylinder barrel and head. Ridden by Nello Pagani in the open class, the Condor was up against full-blown works Grand Prix bikes, including Dorino Serafini's supercharged Gilera four. Pagani won, despite having less than

half the Gilera's horsepower, and proved the Condor's potential. Just sixty-nine Condors were built before war ended production in 1940. Pagani had also shown his potential, and would be inaugural 125 World Champion in 1949. He even almost beat Les Graham to the 500 title, scoring more points, and the pair both winning two rounds. Unfortunately, Pagani was denied the championship by dint of the scoring system then in use, which required riders to drop their worst two results. But at least he had helped prove what a fine work-in-progress the Moto Guzzi GTC/L had been. The last word on this enchanting motorcycle must go to Gordon.

I do ride the GTC/L around the local roads as well as in classic events where it gets quite a bit of attention. The main challenge is that being so original it has no speedometer despite being capable of 105 mph, so some caution is needed. At least when asked 'Do you know how fast you were going, sir?' I can honestly answer that I simply don't have a clue.

SPECIFICATIONS	MOTO GUZZI GTC/L (1937–39 GTC)

Layout and Chassis

Single-cylinder four-stroke racing motorcycle

Engine

Type	Horizontal single
Block material	Magnesium alloy
Head material	Aluminium alloy
Cylinders	1
Cooling	Air
Bore and stroke	88 × 82mm
Capacity	499cc
Valves	2 valves sohc
Compression ratio	7:1
Carburettor	32mm Dell'Orto
Max. power	28bhp@5,000rpm
Fuel capacity	4 gallons/18 litres

Transmission

Gearbox	Four-speed foot-change
Clutch	Wet multiplate
Final drive	Chain

Chassis

Front	Girder fork
Rear	Swingarm

Steering

Tyres	2.75–20in front, 3.00–21in rear
Brakes	Drums front and rear

Dimensions

Wheelbase	58in (1,470mm)
Unladen weight	285lb (129kg)

Performance

Top speed	103mph (165km/h)

Post-War Development

The Condor's evolution from the GTC had a final flourish in a chassis that owed more to Moto Guzzi's supercharged 250cc factory racer than any road-bike. Magnesium alloy brakes and aluminium rims kept weight down to just barely more than 300lb (140kg), even in full road trim. Here was a motorcycle that could beat the supercharged Gilera four on the track, win the 1940 Milano–Taranto and yet was also flexible enough to be used as a police motorcycle. The only real challenge came from the new Gilera Saturno in 1940, but then racing came to an abrupt end as war burned through Europe. Just sixty-nine Condors had been built when Moto Guzzi ended production and switched to building products more attuned to the needs of a country caught up in a bloody conflict.

When peace returned, Carlo Guzzi set to developing the Condor into a Gilera Saturno beater. This was to be dubbed the Dondolino ('rocking chair'), some say reflecting the slightly suspect handling, even though it seems odd that Moto Guzzi would abandon their habit of naming motorcycles after birds and switch to using less-than flattering nicknames. So there are those who wonder if the Dondolino name was simply reflecting Norton's labelling their racing frames 'Featherbed'.

The post-war economic climate ruled out a major redesign, so the 1946 Dondolino amounted to a much-improved Condor, featuring a number of magnificent detail changes. The obvious visual difference was the aerodynamic rear mudguard, which replaced the Condor's more conventional fitment, yet so many Condors were upgraded by adding Dondolino components that this is far from a certain guide. Perhaps the most telling sign of Carcano's attention to detail is the beautiful magnesium alloy 260mm front brake, with internal levers to gain a tiny aerodynamic advantage. Carcano's famed obsession with saving weight is highly evident on the Dondolino with, as on the Condor, crankcases among the many components cast from magnesium alloy. In passing, it's worth noting that, although magnesium alloy is often called Elektron, that name is a trademark of the German company that developed magnesium alloys for aircraft use in World War I. They never made parts for Moto Guzzi.

In many respects the Dondolino shared much with Carlo Guzzi's original Normale, although tuned and improved by over twenty years of racing. Certainly many dimensions remained the same, notably bore and stroke, although compression was now up from even the Condor's 7:1 to 8.5:1, perhaps surprising given the quality of post-war petrol. The Dell'Orto SSM carburettor was also bigger than the Condor's at 35mm. The chassis, however, was much the same, although with a single spring (as opposed to the Condor's pair) for the rear suspension, hidden in a box under the engine. Dondolinos were assembled in small batches by the race department, individual bikes inevitably having minor differences from their namesakes. Coupled with the upgrading of racing Condors to Dondolino specification, telling them apart today is an expert's job. With 33bhp propelling just 282lb (128kg) in race trim, they were also an expert's racing motorcycle, and immediately competitive against all-comers.

As soon as Gilera got wind of the Dondolino, they released a 35bhp Sanremo version of their Saturno. Even so, a Dondolino finished second to a Saturno in the 1946 Circuito del Lario, and then won the Spanish Grand Prix. But the rugged Dondolino's real strength was in true road-racing, and especially the gruelling Milano–Taranto. Either an upgraded Condor or a Dondolino won that race every year from 1950 to 1953, often in style: in 1951 Moto Guzzi took six of the first seven places, split only by the fifth placed MV Agusta 500/4 race-bike – with lights. In 1955, Gilera tried the same trick, running two riders, Bruno Francisci and Orlando Vadinoci, on 500/4s to secure victory for Francisci. But by then a 500 single with its roots in 1921 needed a major redesign to remain competitive. Only fifty-four Dondolinos were built between 1946 and 1951, retailing at double the price of its more prosaic GTV/GTW Moto Guzzi siblings, but the achievement of those few bikes proved that they were worth every lira.

During 1946, Carcano developed a Dondolino for development rider Nando Balzarotti, dubbed the Gambalunga – 'long leg' – on account of the lengthened stroke. With an 84mm bore and 90mm stroke, the Gambalunga was the first significant Guzzi to be under-square. This reduced pressure on the big end, although power was up 2bhp from the Dondolino to match the Gilera Sanremo. The most significant feature of the Gambalunga was Carcano's favoured leading link forks and, although by the standards of the age it seemed a dated and under-powered factory racer, its light weight (just 276lb/125kg) and easy manners made it a favourite for national championships

ABOVE: **Sante Gemiani showing the commitment required to race in the Milano–Taranto. This is passing through Ferrara in the 1950 event on his Condor, uprated with Dondolino parts including the aerodynamic rear mudguard.** A HERL INC.

BELOW: **Guido Leoni also with an uprated Condor.** A HERL INC.

and road events. A Gambalunga won the French Championship every year from 1949 to 1951, and the Hungarian Championship as late as 1953.

RIDING THE BIKES | DONDOLINO

Who better to comment on the bookend evolution of the Condor than a rider who owns both its predecessor, the GTC, and its successor, the Dondolino?

The owner of the GTC Leggera featured previously discovered the hard way that once you start on the Guzzi singles 'train', you soon get sucked into wondering what else might be available. Having caught the bug, Gordon de la Mare decided there were two big holes in his life: an enormous one that would need a three-wheel Ercole to fill and a much sleeker void that was crying out for a Dondolino, the motorcycle many consider to be the ultimate gentleman's racer of the singles era. Inevitably both vehicles took some time to find.

Gordon was by this time a member of the Moto Guzzi Classics Club of Schio, near Vicenza, and had already ridden on a couple of their holiday tours. When he asked the club's president if he knew of any genuine Dondolinos for sale, the emphasis was on the word 'genuine' because, although the factory only built fifty-seven Dondolinos, there are probably more people claiming to own a Dondolino today than the factory ever built.

Eventually Gordon found himself in Schio during March 2004 on the trail of not one, but two, apparently genuine Dondolinos. One had just returned from Argentina (amazingly the frame number only one digit adrift from the Dondolino in Sammy Miller's Museum) but it was in a very poor state. The second bike was being sold by a gentleman who raced vintage Ferraris and was in very good condition, as well as holding ASI (Automotoclub Storico Italiano) documentation to validate it as genuine. The records showed it to have been built at the end of 1946, then sold by a dealer in Milan. Later, as was common with racing machines, the engine was replaced with a 1951 Faenza version of the Dondolino engine, with strengthened crankshaft bearings and Gambalunga valve gear to improve its competitiveness. Once Gordon had decided he wanted to buy the Dondolino, the next big challenge was affording it – these things are expensive.

BELOW: **The Dondolino. The magnesium alloy front brake had internal levers, part of Carcano's obsession with aerodynamics.**

INSET: **Attention to detail was another obsession.**

Gordon prepares to parade the GTC/L.

Continued overleaf

RIDING THE BIKES

Several weeks later, monies having been transferred, a massive pantechnicon arrived in the lane next to Gordon's home, and then there was this wonderful old racing machine leaning against his garage doors. Despite it being about seven in the morning, Gordon immediately settled on starting the Dondolino – just for fun – by bumping it down the road. Gordon grins at the memory: 'I remember thinking, "Wooah, is this thing loud".' The big problem with the Dondolino has proved to be that it is not just loud: it is very loud. Gordon again: 'I borrowed an Environmental Heath Inspector's sound measuring device and measured the exhaust noise at 125dB.' This is far above the level allowed at even 'noisy' track days and so, sadly, Gordon concluded that his pride and joy wasn't going to get a lot of outings in the UK.

Even so, the Dondolino has managed a few demonstration runs, including the Dunsfold Aerodrome's Wings and Wheel event and Gordon was fortunate enough to be a participant in the 2005 TT Parade. Sadly, he didn't get very far on race day – merely the end of the grandstand. The flywheel sheared off the locating key, unwound itself and then left the bike. The engine started running a bit erratically, followed by the flywheel overtaking the bike (a facet of the engine running 'backwards') on the opposite side of the road. The Dondolino still bears the scars of this today, which Gordon insists is patina. The good news is that he did get a treasured TT medal. The bad news was that the flywheel required a significant amount of repair work, including a new cone made by fifties Guzzi racer Trevor Barnes.

Since then Gordon has ridden the Dondolino at the 2007 post-TT event on the Southern 100 Circuit and also at the 2012 Cholomondeley Pageant of Power. He's fully aware that it could be more widely paraded if fitted with a silencer, but feels that would

The Dondolino again. The lower, forward filler is for fuel; the second cap is for oil.

Like most Moto Guzzi singles and the Bicilindrica, the rear suspension springs are below the engine and the mechanism either side of the back wheel is for damping.

physically degrade the original nature of the bike. Instead he's happy to just use it where the sound is tolerated and let people experience the thunderous glory of a true 1940s racing motorcycle.

SPECIFICATIONS   MOTO GUZZI DONDOLINO (1946–51)

Layout and Chassis

Single-cylinder four-stroke racing motorcycle

Engine

Type	Horizontal single
Block material	Magnesium alloy
Head material	Aluminium alloy
Cylinders	1
Cooling	Air
Bore and stroke	88 × 82mm
Capacity	499cc
Valves	2 valves sohc
Compression ratio	8.5:1
Carburettor	35mm Dell'Orto
Max. power	33bhp@5,500rpm
Fuel capacity	4.2 gallons/19 litres

Transmission

Gearbox	Four-speed foot-change
Clutch	Wet multiplate
Final drive	Chain

Chassis

Front	Girder fork
Rear	Swingarm

Steering

Tyres	2.75–21in front, 3.00–21in rear
Brakes	Drums front and rear

Dimensions

Wheelbase	58in (1,470mm)
Unladen weight	282lb (128kg)

Performance

Top speed	105mph (170km/h)

Developing the Racing 250 and Beyond

The Moto Guzzi 250 single-cylinder racer evolved into the Albatros for 1939 and when, post-war, the 1947 prototype 250 twin failed to live up to expectations, especially after the death of Tenni, subsequent Guzzi quarter-litre racers were always singles. Stripped back to just 265lb (120kg), the Albatros remained competitive for many years, despite production ending in 1949. Privateers particularly relished the Albatros, despite a price tag comparable to a Dondolino's and a production run of just thirty-four bikes. Many were subsequently upgraded to a later specification that came about by a happy accident to create the Gambalunghino – 'little long-leg'. After a towing accident almost destroyed factory rider

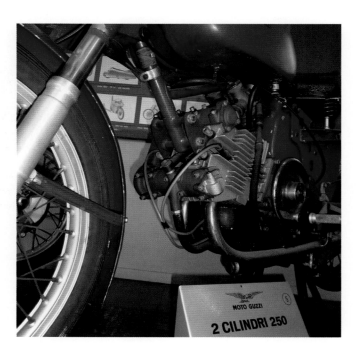

Despite being innovative the 250 Due Cilindri was not an improvement on the single.

Although Tenni practised on the Due Cilindri for the Swiss Grand Prix in 1948, he died riding the single-cylinder Albatros 250, despite many sources claiming he lost his life on the twin.

Enrico Lorenzetti's Albatros just prior to a race early in 1949, the 250cc engine was hastily installed in the Gambalunga's leading link fork chassis. Lorenzetti not only won his race on this 250-in-a-500's frame, but the unlikely combination of a big bike with a little engine was developed to allow him to win the Italian 250 championship.

It was these sorts of achievements that Ferguson and Carcano felt they could build on by developing the singles, and they set to improving the Gambalunghino. Carcano had built a new 350 single-cylinder racer for 1950, but Maurice Cann preferred a 310cc version of the Gambalunghino for the 1950 Junior TT, despite it failing to finish. The British rider was something of an unofficial development rider for Guzzi, his home-brewed dohc 250 as fast as the single-camshaft factory Gambalunghino's on the Isle of Man in 1951. By now the new wind-tunnel at Mandello del Lario was bearing fruit with lessons learnt, providing sometimes less than elegant – but nonetheless effective – aerodynamics that first benefited the Gambalunghino's 1953 overhaul. Stretching the engine as far as possible, a 72mm bore and 78mm stroke gave 317cc and 31bhp – the same as the earlier 350. Easily winning its first race at Hockenheim, a delighted Anderson entered the '317' in the Junior TT, where a third place convinced Carcano to pursue the 350 World Championship. Despite a late start, and reliability problems, Anderson went on to win the 1953 350 title for Moto Guzzi, as well as finishing fourth in the 250 Championship and ninth in the 500 class (behind Kavanagh in fourth, after a late

season switch from Norton to Guzzi). Enrico Lorenzetti took runner-up spot in the 350 class and third in the 250s. A remarkable achievement, helped by substantial funding, largely courtesy of the 65cc Guzzino's sales success, but still representative of the creative genius that flowed when Carcano and Anderson were paired. Yet despite a Moto Guzzi 250 also winning various national championships in 1953, including in Britain and Italy, the results were disappointing to the Guzzi board, who decided they would focus on the 500 class in future.

Enrico Parodi, Giorgio's brother and now taking control of Guzzi, offered 1954 works contracts to Kavanagh and Anderson, along with three Italian riders: Ruffo, Lorenzetti and Montanari. Carcano had a seemingly unlimited budget, making the team possibly the best-funded in the circus. Riders got a basic salary of £3,000 a year, which might be ten times a working man's income, plus prize money and expenses. By mid-season, Guzzi's riders had all abandoned the 500 four in favour of the single that bore an embarrassing similarity to the classic Moto Guzzi road-bikes. Leading-light of the works Guzzi riders, Ken Kavanagh, said what made the single good was its streamlining (1954 was the first year for the dustbin fairings) and light weight: he then damned it with faint praise by saying it had a much wider powerband than the Norton single, 'like a touring bikes'. Moto Guzzi's 500 four was finally buried for good, unloved by riders, although with four carburettors and a subsequent lift to 750cc, it became the Giannini G2 motor, finding success in Giaur racing cars.

RIGHT: **The Gambalunghino in Sammy Miller's museum.**

BELOW: **The Arthur Wheeler Moto Guzzi 250 ridden to victory in many events, including the 1954 Italian GP and North West 200.** Believed to have begun its life as a 1948 Albatros it was sold to Fergus Anderson to be reconditioned by the factory. It was collected by Wheeler in early 1952. In 1959 the bike passed to Trevor Barnes who began his racing career on the machine. He was soon winning on a regular basis and gained several wins and lap records. Barnes sold the bike in almost standard Gambalunghino trim (bar a Norton front end) to finance buying Arthur Wheeler's later Reynolds frame machine. It was then sold to and raced by Arthur Lawn before being fitted with Arthur Wheeler's first Reynolds frame from 1958 and installed on this bike by Arthur Lawn in 1964.

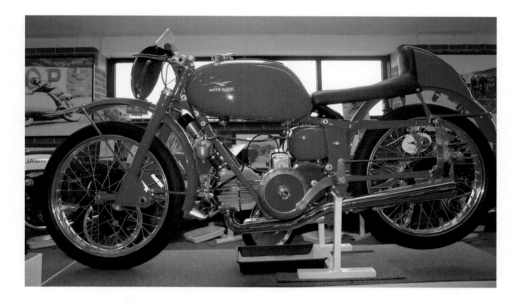

LEFT: **Gianni Leoni racing a Moto Guzzi 250 in 1950.** MOTO GUZZI

RIGHT: **By 1953 the 250 had the alloy 'bird beak' fairing. This is Enrico Lorenzetti.** MOTO GUZZI

As 1954 progressed, success came for Moto Guzzi in the 250 and 350 classes, yet the new 500 single proved too fragile, with components failing simply because they weren't substantial enough – an inevitable side-effect of Carcano's fixation with saving weight. Adopting the usual Guzzi single layout – horizontal cylinder, external flywheel and such – the latest 500 in fact owed much to the 250 Gambalunghino. With a dohc cylinder head, the 500's weight was comparable to the MV Agusta and Gilera fours, yet with around 45bhp it was some 20bhp shy of the multi's power output. Despite full dustbin fairing, developed in the wind-tunnel and beaten from magnesium alloy, the Guzzi could not match the speed of the fours. With rumours circulating that the FIM would ban streamlining and so destroy the Moto Guzzi single's only real advantage, a radical solution was needed. Ironically only full enclosure 'dustbin' fairings, which Guzzi had been best able to develop as the only manufacturer with a wind-tunnel, weren't banned until late 1957 when Guzzi chose to withdraw from racing. Even then, 'dolphin' fairings, leaving the front wheel uncovered, as seen on today's race bikes, were still allowed.

By the penultimate round of the 1954 Grand Prix season at Monza, the year's results were pretty much set in stone. Ray Amm's Norton would finish the year in second place with Kavanagh in third for Guzzi. Duke's Gilera was the runaway winner, but Kavanagh had beaten five other Gileras and both works MV Agustas. The Guzzi results hadn't been helped by breakages, and results weren't even up to 1953s mediocrity. Kavanagh also felt he was a potential World Champion with a better motorcycle under him, and seemed likely to jump ship. So just after the Monza's GP, a crisis meeting was held between the engineering team of Giuliano Carcano, Enrico Cantoni and Umberto Todero, with riders Ken Kavanagh and Fergus Anderson sitting in. They set to thrashing out ideas for a 500 that could beat all-comers, as well as showing off Moto Guzzi's

engineering expertise to the buying public. Carcano reasoned that a water-cooled V8 would fit the bill perfectly, being narrower yet more of a *tour de force* than the air-cooled fours that the opposition were using. He also believed a transverse four was too wide for a dustbin fairing, both in terms of aerodynamics and ground clearance. Carlo Guzzi still held out for development of his beloved 500 single but Giorgio Parodi, having branded the Bicilindrica project an 'antique', was unlikely to consider such a project prestigious enough. His brother and fellow director, Enrico, also supported Carcano. The V8 was coming.

The Most Famous Moto Guzzi of All – the Fabulous V8

The project was kept secret from anyone who wasn't part of the racing team. Carcano did the draft drawings and Enrico Tantoni the details. Todero was part of the project but was mainly committed to developing the 350 for 1955. At the beginning of February 1955, Fergus Anderson controversially announced the V8 project and might have jumped the gun because other members of the team had thought it was still supposed to be a secret. Anderson's star fell further when he destroyed the V8 prototype during its first test at Modena in April 1955. Inevitability some connect this to his subsequent retirement, but Anderson was now forty-five with a passion for golf, so wouldn't have needed much persuasion to go – especially since the V8 turned out to be such a monster to ride.

Once given the green light to build the V8, it took Carcano a mere eight months to deliver the first complete bike, which, in fully faired record-breaking trim, broke the 187mph (300km/h) barrier. But although top speed was impressive, reliability and handling were poor. Lap-records fell to the Guzzi,

RIGHT: **A V8 built from a mix of old spares and new parts using Moto Guzzi's plans by Giuseppe Todero.** SPIKE

BELOW: **Giuseppe Todero starts his V8. His father was a member of Carcano's original design team.** SPIKE

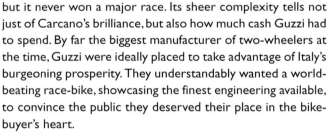

Packaging the V8 meant stubby exhausts, minimal frame and batteries to run a total loss ignition system.

The V8 certainly filled the fairing.
SPIKE

but it never won a major race. Its sheer complexity tells not just of Carcano's brilliance, but also how much cash Guzzi had to spend. By far the biggest manufacturer of two-wheelers at the time, Guzzi were ideally placed to take advantage of Italy's burgeoning prosperity. They understandably wanted a world-beating race-bike, showcasing the finest engineering available, to convince the public they deserved their place in the bike-buyer's heart.

So Guzzi persevered with the V8. The engine was developed rapidly during 1956 and by 1957 power had risen from 68 to 72bhp, a considerable advantage over the Gilera and MV fours. Total loss ignition required two batteries, eight coils and four sets of points on each cambox. The timing gear also drove the water pump of the unpressurized cooling system, and eight 20mm Dell'Ortos fed the cylinders. These accommodated valves too small for collet groves, so 5mm stems flared out to retain two-piece collets. The bottom end of the engine was similar to a straight four's, with wide crankpins carrying two conrods apiece. This complexity led to much that could go wrong, or at least not run perfectly. Bill Lomas once said, only half joking, that 'the best Guzzi ever managed was running the bike as a V7…once'.

Lomas was referring to Dickie Dale's ride on the Isle of Man in 1957, when Dale reported that the V8 was constantly mis-firing and ran most the race on seven cylinders, ironically making it much easier to ride. Dale finished fourth, which was impressive. He was clearly exhausted after the race. Sound-recordings of the V8 during that TT tell that the bike was not running cleanly, oddly similar to today's racing motorcycles that can cut ignition to improve traction.

By contrast to the engine's cutting-edge complexity, the V8's chassis was rather basic and little more than a scaled-up 350 frame. Leading link Girling forks housed a 19in front wheel, with a 20in rear. Total dry weight was just 330lb (150kg), helped by Carcano's refusal to paint the bike – like the dustbin faired sin-gles, the green 'paintwork' was actually simply an anti-corrosion treatment to protect the magnesium alloy. With no room for silencers, eight stubby exhausts, venting unequal firing intervals and 12,000rpm, made a sound like no other.

Although stable in a straight line, the V8 hated fast curves and almost killed a number of riders. Dickie Dale felt the prob-lem was with the front end, and abandoned the dustbin stream-lining in favour of a dolphin fairing for the 1957 TT. Bill Lomas thought the problem was weight distribution, and raced with

Dickie Dale on the V8 in the 1957 Senior TT. Dale preferred to ride with the dolphin (rather than the full 'dustbin') but was still estimated to be doing around 170mph when this photograph was taken at the bottom of Bray Hill. A HERL INC.

Australian Keith Campbell on the V8 in 1957, the year he won the 350 championship for Moto Guzzi. A HERL INC.

lead weights on the swingarm. Looking for vindication, Carcano asked Stanley Woods to test the bike and was delighted when Woods declared the handling perfect; but Woods was now fifty-three years old and riding at well below race pace.

Development might not have helped with the handling, but reliability gradually improved and a win eventually came for Giuseppe Calcagno at an Italian championship round in Siracusa in Sicily. But it was too little, too late. The V8's final race was the season closer at Monza in 1957. Lomas and Dale were already ruled out by injury and when Campbell fell in practice at Curve Ascari, breaking his pelvis, Guzzi had exhausted their supply of riders. Australian Keith Bryen was offered the ride, but after trying the V8 in practice, declined to race it.

Soon afterwards Moto Guzzi, along with Gilera, MV Agusta and Mondial, decided to withdraw from racing and the V8 was gone. Fast and fragile, the bike's real weakness was its handling.

With enough development the V8 might have become unbeatable, yet perhaps the V8's finest achievement was proof of how engineering genius can blossom if circumstances are just so. This ended Guzzi's involvement in racing until the V-twins appeared a decade later, but those were modified road-bikes racing in classes intended for such motorcycles. When the Italian manufacturers left the Grand Prix circus, the curtain fell on a golden age and the race series would become a benefit for MV Agusta who reneged on their agreement. How different the history of Grand Prix – and the Italian motorcycle industry – might have been if all the players had remained at the heart of the sport.

LEFT: **The Moto Guzzi museum has a spare engine on display along with the original racer.**

BELOW: **The V8 is so pivotal to Moto Guzzi's history it is still used in publicity material. Note poster of Dr John's racer, an equally important touchstone.**
MOTO GUZZI

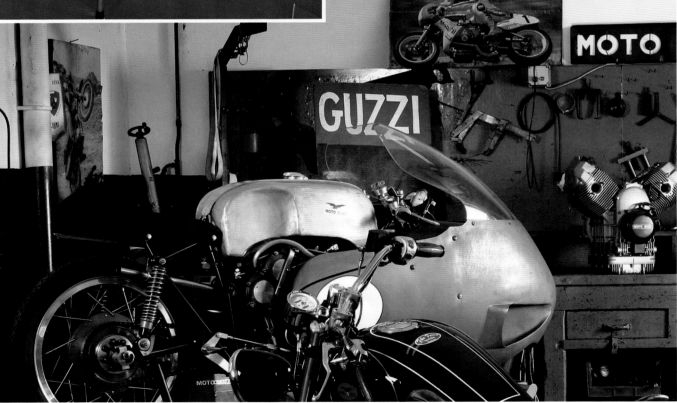

THE 250 AND 350 RACERS

The supercharged 250 Compressore from 1938, used for setting records as well as racing.

It might be understandable to focus on the bigger racers, but it was Moto Guzzi's 250s and 350s that brought the silverware home, especially post-war.

During 1925, Carlo Guzzi's thoughts turned to designing a 250 racing motorcycle. This was a comparatively new class, races traditionally having been divided into 350, 500 and, occasionally, unlimited categories. But in 1922, the Auto Cycle Union introduced a Lightweight TT for sub-250cc motorcycles. At the time this British-dominated event was undoubtedly the most important race in the world, and if Moto Guzzi were to prove they were building world-class motorcycles, the Isle of Man was where they had to prove it. Carlo's intentions for his latest motorcycle were made obvious when it was presented in the spring of 1926 as the TT250.

The design was pretty much what was expected from Moto Guzzi: a horizontal single with a unit construction three-speed gearbox and external flywheel. The specification didn't seem particularly exotic, with a cast-iron cylinder head

and barrel attached to aluminium alloy crankcases. But inside the engine, the chase for horsepower – and engine revs – was obvious. The square 68mm bore and stroke was unusual in an era when stroke was typically larger than the bore, and Velocette paid Carlo Guzzi an enormous compliment when their long-stroke 350 and 500 racers were joined by a 68mm × 68mm 250 in 1933. The 250TT also had crankshaft roller bearings, rather than the plain items of the 500, allowing lower oil pressure and less internal friction. The valves were set with an unusually small included angle for the time, although the head had just two valves rather than the four of the factory's 500cc racers. The claimed result was 15bhp at 6,000rpm, an output-per-litre even higher than the similarly bevel-driven overhead camshaft Norton and Velocettes. The level of specific power was comparable to Bugatti racing cars, which relied upon supercharging. Little wonder the design was immediately dominant and would remain competitive for nearly forty years.

Continued overleaf

THE 250 AND 350 RACERS

Moto Guzzi were quick to update the 250, and even before arriving in the Isle of Man for June's 1926 TT, it had a Binks-style twist-grip throttle, similar to that on modern motorcycles, rather than the thumb lever more often used at the time. Pietro Ghersi's moral second place in the Lightweight TT (he was disqualified by partisan organizers for having a non-standard spark plug) would be followed over the years with three World Championships (for Bruno Ruffo in the inaugural 1949 series and again in 1951, and for Enrico Lorenzetti in 1952). Other achievements included seven class wins at the TT, the Grand Prix of Nations sixteen times and the Circuito del Lario nine times. In 1938, Pagani finished second overall in the Milano–Taranto on a Moto Guzzi 250 at a pace that would have beaten the winning Bicilindrica 500 the previous year.

To achieve this continuing success, the 250 was never far away from its next update and was often reserved for factory riders only. In 1930, the gear-change became foot-operated, and the chassis gained superior British Brampton forks. 1934 brought a four-speed gearbox and a saddle fuel-tank above the top frame tubes; and by 1935, there was rear suspension. Shared with Moto Guzzi's Bicilindrica 500 (in essence a doubled-up 250 V-twin), the twin shock swingarm helped Moto Guzzi break the British dominance at the Isle of Man TT and convince the racing community of the value of rear suspension. 1938 saw Moto Guzzi getting really radical: by adding a Mandello-built Cozette-type supercharger, power soared to 38bhp (45 on methanol). Riding this '250 Compressore', Omobono Tenni set an endurance record at over 112mph (180km/h). For a 250 single without any aerodynamic aids that was a remarkable speed in 1938.

For 1939, new racing classes favoured production motorcycles, organizers envisioning enthusiastic amateurs racing their everyday motorcycles. Carlo Guzzi had other ideas and, working alongside his new protégé Giulio Cesare Carcano, designed the Albatros, essentially his Grand Prix racer minus the supercharger and fitted with lights. An all-alloy engine with one-piece crank and straight-cut gears in the gearbox told of the racing ambitions and the price – comparable to the 500 racers – told this was no everyday machine. With a 30mmm Dell'Orto carburettor (later

Memorial to Omobono Tenni, every bit as famous in Italy in his time as Valentino Rossi is today.

32mm), it gave 20bhp and, although the lighting and electrical equipment meant it weighed 297lb (135kg), this was still competitive.

Post-war, Carlo Guzzi felt things needed moving on and charged a new engineer Moto Guzzi had hired during the war, Antonio Micucci, to design a twin-cylinder 250. Again using square dimensions (55mm bore and stroke), the double-overhead cam Due Cilindrica (Two Cylinder) made extensive use of new alloys and an interesting cooling-fin layout. Combined with steeply inclined barrels, it certainly looked radical, but despite leading the 1948 Lightweight TT, it was a disappointment. Power was not all that was hoped for (possibly because of compromises to allow it to run with or without a supercharger, as their abolition was still uncertain) and riders complained of a lack of stability. Tenni must have had doubts about the Due Cilindra, despite initially riding it in the practice session at Berne for the Swiss Grand Prix. At the end of the practice session he decided to take out the Albatros to compare it with Micucci's twin, which was still in development. It started to rain, seemingly at random, around the circuit. Eymatt curve was part of a wet section that prevented Tenni holding his chosen line. Drifting wide, he left the road and hit a tree, the Albatros bouncing back onto the circuit. A following rider rushed back to the Moto Guzzi pit to get help but by the time they reached him, Tenni was already dead. Tenni was hugely loved in Italy, not least by Carlo Guzzi. His loss probably influenced Carlo's decision on the future of Moto Guzzi's racing 250, because a few weeks after the TT, the twin was consigned to history.

So Carlo decided the future lay with further development of the pre-war 250 single, although its final incarnation was the result of a happy accident. A towing incident meant hastily rebuilding Enrico Lorenzetti's 250 using all the factory had to hand – a 500 Gambalunga's rolling chassis. When he won the next race on the long and low Gambalunghino (little Gambalunga), a new Moto Guzzi works racer was born. By now the 250 engine might have had its roots back in 1926, but with an 8.5:1 compression and 35mm Dell'Orto SS carburettor, power was up to 25bhp at 8,000rpm.

Development now focused on aerodynamics, aided by Moto Guzzi's new wind-tunnel, which had been built during 1950. Streamlining was initially an enlarged rear mudguard, but grew to include a fuel-tank incorporating a front fairing pointing the way forward to the 350's full enclosure. So successful was the Gambalunghino that many privateers converted their Albatros. A final glorious fling came in 1953, impressively in the 350 class. Stretching the engine as far as possible, a 72mm bore and 78mm stroke gave 317cc and 31bhp, and the engine was fitted into the faired chassis of the new 250 Bialbero. With Fergus Anderson aboard, the hybrid won its first race at Hockenheim. Anderson then used the 'super Gambalunghino' to take third in the Junior TT and go on to win the 350 World Championship with Lorenzetti runner-up.

Unsurprisingly, given that the 250 engine could trace its origins back to 1926, by 1950, Carcano was working on a new 4-valve double-overhead cam design. This became the factory racer for 1953, but with a two-valve double-overhead cam ('bialbero') head, and still very much an evolution of the original 27-year-old design. An additional 0.4mm of bore increased capacity from 246.8cc to 248.2cc,

compression was up to 9.5:1 and the carburettor was now a giant 40mm Dell'Orto. There was the option of a fifth gear and weight remained at the Gambalunghino's 268lb (122kg). This was despite a hand-beaten magnesium alloy fairing, an odd bird-beak item that flowed into the fuel-tank. This design from the wind-tunnel was also fitted to the 350 and 500 singles, the latter debuting the full 'dustbin' fairing by the end of the season.

ABOVE: **Bill Lomas winning on the fully faired 350 in 1956.** MOTO GUZZI

BELOW: **Duilio Agostini and Dickie Dale on Moto Guzzi 350s at the Strubben curve at the Assen TT in 1956.** A HERL INC.

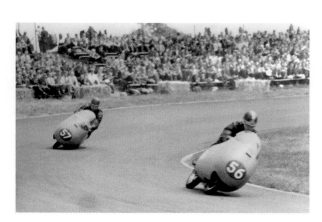

Continued overleaf

THE 250 AND 350 RACERS

NSU were now the dominant force in the 125 and 250 classes, but Lorenzetti still used the Bialbero to take third behind a pair of factory NSUs in the 1953 250 World Championship. Behind him in fourth to sixth place were Anderson, Montanari and Kavanagh aboard factory Guzzis, with three other riders scoring points aboard a Moto Guzzi 250. From 1954 to 1957, when Moto Guzzi withdrew from racing, the 250 was ever more neglected as Carcano focused on the 350 and especially the 500 class. Even so, Moto Guzzi took nine of the twenty placings in the 1954 Championship, with highest placed rider, Arthur Wheeler, in fourth, making Moto Guzzi once again the highest placed non-NSUs. For

1955, Cecil Sandford and Bill Lomas took second and third places in the 250 Championship behind a victorious NSU. By 1956, MV Agusta were starting their rule of Grand Prix racing, but Lorenzetti still managed third place in the Championship to split the first three MVs home, and Moto Guzzi remained dominant in the 350 class. The final year of Italian hegemony in racing was 1957, and while Moto Guzzi retained the 350 title, the much newer 250s from Mondial, MV Agusta and Gilera, coupled with their copycat dustbin fairings, meant that Lorenzetti could only manage ninth for Moto Guzzi. That stands as a remarkable swansong for the factory's final year of Grand Prix racing with a design that was over thirty years old.

More remarkable still was that the design was the basis for 350 and 500 double-overhead cam versions. While the single-cylinder 500 could not hope to compete with the Gilera and MV Agusta fours, the 350 did just that, winning the 350 Championship every year it was entered. Giving away that it was developed from the 250 was a very over-square (80mm × 69.5mm) bore and stroke that, with 349.2cc, came as close as possible to the 350cc class limit. Carcano's weight-saving obsession meant that at 280lb (127kg) it was barely heavier than the 250 and, coupled with advanced aerodynamics, the 350 was able to beat more powerful multi-cylinder opposition. This allowed Anderson to repeat his 1953 World Championship in 1954, with Ken Kavanagh and Lorenzetti fourth and fifth, respectively. Duilio Agostini, who later established the Moto Guzzi dealership in Mandello del Lario that carries his name, was seventh, up from tenth the previous year. The 350 Championship results in 1955 had Bill Lomas and Dickie Dale in first and second place, with Kavanagh and Cecil Sandford managing fourth and fifth. Agostini was again seventh and there were two other Moto Guzzis in the points. Lomas and Dale repeated their one–two the following year, with Kavanagh down to sixth place. The 1957 finale ended with a brace of Australian Keiths, Campbell and Bryen, in first and fourth place, and two other Moto Guzzis in the top ten.

Alongside this astonishing superiority, the roll-call of Moto Guzzi riders shows how open-minded the factory was in choosing its riders. That so many riders could achieve

Bill Lomas's title wining 1955 350. A Moto Guzzi 350 won every round of the championship that year.

success on what was, even at the end, a two-valve, single-cylinder, overbored 250, proved the integrity of Carlo Guzzi's original design. With 35bhp in 1953, rising to 38 by 1957, it was hardly powerful, yet the 350 filled riders with confidence. In the end that is the most important quality a motorcycle can pass on to a rider, and one that the smaller Moto Guzzi single-cylinder racers delivered in spades.

ABOVE: **This series of photographs is from an old album found by Peter Lockwood, but the photographer ('me', above) is unnamed. A shame, but clearly a Moto Guzzi fan.** PETER LOCKWOOD

ABOVE: **As it says, Anderson on the 250. Note the full fairing and 'biscuit tin' fuel tank above the engine.** PETER LOCKWOOD

LEFT: **The 1954 500 at the TT.** PETER LOCKWOOD

Continued overleaf

THE 250 AND 350 RACERS

WORKS MOTO GUZZI 500cc.

69

T.T. 1954

The 500 again. The circular fuel tank boosted capacity to 30 litres (6.6 gallons), useful on the Isle of Man.
PETER LOCKWOOD

WKS M.G. (MOTO GUZZI)

CECIL SANDFORD SILVERSTONE 1955.

EX WORKS MOTO GUZZI

72

CECIL - SILVERSTONE 1955.

ABOVE: **Cecil Sandford was provided with a 1954 works 250 for 1955, as Moto Guzzi did not officially compete in the championship that year.**
PETER LOCKWOOD

LEFT: **Sandford himself. Lorenzetti and Colombo were similarly provided with 1954 250s.**
PETER LOCKWOOD

CHAPTER THREE

THE ROAD-BIKES FACE DARK DAYS, WAR AND BOOM

Moto Guzzi's preparedness to invest in racing tells of a highly profitable, confident and successful motorcycle manufacturer. They were quick to spot opportunities, and when economic woes swept the world in the 1930s, Carlo designed a range of lightweights much more in keeping with the needs of ordinary motorcycle buyers. Guzzi were also quick to alter tack and take advantage of Mussolini's taxation changes, which made lower capacity motorcycles much cheaper to buy and run. Starting with the 174cc P175 single in 1932, Guzzi quickly enlarged this to the 232cc P250 in 1934, when the tax breaks evaporated for motoleggere (literally 'lightweight motorcycle', but then meaning the taxation class for bikes below 175cc). These new

An early (c.1933) P250.

motorcycles stuck to the traditions of Moto Guzzi singles, while premiering ideas that would find their way onto the 500. At last there were overhead valves, rather than the exhaust-over-inlet arrangement on the 500, and the crankcases had a more coherent aesthetic than the workmanlike, rather piecemeal, appearance of the bigger engine. Yet the P175 and 250 were still horizontal singles, albeit angled upwards slightly to give a more sporting air and additional cooling to the exhaust valve. The long-stroke P175 made just 7bhp, compensated for a little by the low 253lb (115kg) weight. However, when the P250 arrived, weight remained the same, and the newly over-square engine gave 9bhp at 5,500rpm. Just as importantly, it brought the first foot-change gearbox to a road-going Moto Guzzi. When the PE250 joined the range, with rear suspension (indicated by the E – *elastico* – prefix) Moto Guzzi were once again ahead of the market demands. Eventually the 250s grew to 247cc and were joined by the pressed-steel framed PL250, which reduced costs further. There was even the option of faster S versions. These lightweights would sell over 7,000 units by 1939, and go some way to explaining how Moto Guzzi funded their race team.

In the dark days leading up to the conflict, Moto Guzzi had also found favour with the fascist government, almost certainly by simply being in the right place at the right time – and building the right product. Providing much needed and often skilled work in a backwater of Italy would have made Moto Guzzi a prized national asset, especially when the country's leader, Benito Mussolini, was a keen motorcyclist and a big fan of Moto Guzzi's 500.

Fascism is something often airbrushed from Italian history, but in fact started there with the term coming from the Italian word *fascio*, which means bundle, and alludes to the symbols of authority used by the Romans. The traditional Roman fasces were bundles of wooden rods, tied together and often including an axe, representing the power of the Roman Empire. Somehow in the nineteenth century, 'fascist' came to mean a radical political movement, usually with a broadly socialist agenda. Growing out of the aftermath of World War I, the popularity of Italian fascism soon led to Mussolini being elected as leader of the country (calling himself Il Duce – the leader, a word now removed from the language) and then to the creation of a new political dictatorship in 1925.

While fascism is considered to be an extreme right-wing movement, Italian fascism initially had aspects of left-wing doctrine. It promoted nationalism and modernity in an aggressive style that idolized heroic pain and even death. So it should come as no surprise that Il Duce was a keen motorcyclist and especially admired the sport of motorcycle racing. So while the economic woes of the country led to the Milano–Taranto being abandoned after the 1925 event, Mussolini thought the bravery and stamina of the riders who participated represented values that could make Italy great again. That fascism was widely admired is often forgotten and, by way of example, Count Bonmartini, who funded the OPRA 500/4 racing project, is on record as being a supporter. Italians were in any event never subjected to Nazi-style propaganda, so that they remained relatively open-minded and less than willing participants in

1942 Moto Guzzi Alce 500 used in the Libyan conflict. Complete with correct military details and the original military number plates.
NORTH LEICESTER MOTORCYCLES

the war that would eventually burn across Europe. It is also worth pointing out that it was 1937 before Adolf Hitler persuaded Mussolini to adapt his views on the future of fascism to the regime that came to be known as Nazism.

Mussolini's 'leadership' was often carried out from the back seat of an Alfa Romeo, another firm beloved of the dictator, based in Milan not far south of Mandello del Lario. When Hitler came to tour Italy, Il Duce had a Lancia Astura coach built as an open tourer. Perhaps understandably there are not many photographs of these cars being used but the outriders in the handful that remain clearly show them aboard Moto Guzzi 500 singles. The police forces and military bought many, many, Moto Guzzi 500 singles, and Mussolini had one himself. During this time, economic expansion was being nudged along by government-backed infrastructure programmes. The autostradas are the most famous of these, but one of the biggest projects was recreating idealized Italian towns, both at home and as part of an expansion into new colonies in North Africa. Ostensibly intended to resettle farmers or workers from poorer regions, these new towns might have actually been useful backwaters for relocating politically difficult Italians. At least thirteen such settlements were built and the fascists made much of them, especially the five farming villages moulded from the swamplands south of Rome. These were particular favourites of Mussolini, and he would sometimes ride down to visit them. Local legend has it that if you visit them, you can still hear him ride by on his Moto Guzzi.

Whether or not anybody at Moto Guzzi had any sympathy with the fascists is unknown, and the Parodi and Guzzi family were discrete and cautious business people; it is possible that this made them wary of adopting a particular political stance. The facts make it seem unlikely they had any strong leanings because, although Moto Guzzi fitted German Bosch magnetos, they used more British products, and the Guzzi's had English blood on their mother's side. Moto Guzzis came with Dunlop tyres, Amac and Amal carburettors all of which were British, as were the Brampton girder forks fitted to some of the racers: indeed, some of the riders they supported were British. Mussolini was not a fan of the British, and he especially despised their Empire even as he tried to build his own in North Africa. Despite this, Mussolini's admiration for Moto Guzzi, regardless of their relationship with the British, was understandable. World-beating racers and utterly reliable and wieldy road-bikes were admirable enough on their own, but the factory's isolated position at the very north of Italy meant it recruited from a loyal, largely rural, local population, teaching them skills and looking after employees in a quite radical way for the time.

Eventually, generation after generation of families would work at the factory, and when Carlo reached old age, employees carved him out a tunnel in the rocks around the factory to ease his walk into work. Unemployment was always feared in Italy, both by men with families to provide for and by governments wanting to be seen as a force for good. Moto Guzzi would have been supported and cherished, regardless of partisan politics, as providers of employment wealth and social opportunity.

Innovation and Adaptation: Rear Suspension, Military Applications and Three-Wheelers

So Moto Guzzi had what might be called a 'good war'; their pre-war designs adapting to military use remarkably well. Moto Guzzi's first government contract was for a motorcycle often deemed a failure, or at least ahead of its time. Giuseppe (Naco to the family and friends) Guzzi had designed the innovative, fully suspended Moto Guzzi Gran Turismo (GT) in 1928, which, although failing to win the hearts of motorcycle enthusiasts, became the prototype for this first military order. In essence the GT was a 500 Sport with a swingarm, making it arguably the first swingarm-framed motorcycle to be sold. The lower bracing bars on the swingarm pulled a pair of rods running below the engine to compress four springs housed in a steel box below the cylinder. The parallelogram-style arrangement visible on either side of the rear wheel was actually damping. This system offered more suspension travel than previous attempts, along with much improved comfort and control. Moto Guzzi would stay loyal to the principle for forty years or so, but 1928 was simply too soon, and perhaps the GT would have sold better had the idea appeared on a racer before being offered on what was a heavy, touring machine. Weighing 44lb (20kg) more than the Sport, it was based upon limited the GT's performance to an extent unacceptable by the late 1920s. Eventually seventy-eight GTs were built over a two-year period for private buyers; yet slightly modified for military duties, 245 were sold to the government, and this version would evolve into the Italian wartime staple, the Alce ('Elk') and Super Alce. There would even be a three-wheel version – the Trialce – and in total over 14,000 Alce variants would be built. Naco's own prototype led an interesting life (including being hidden during World War II when the authorities were requisitioning motorcycles) and is still held in the

ABOVE: **Moto Guzzi owners just want to have fun. A 1970 Ercole.**

LEFT: **1929 Moto Guzzi Sport 14 with coach-built sidecar.** NORTH LEICESTER MOTORCYCLES

Moto Guzzi collection. Giuseppe even rode his GT to the Arctic Circle by way of development and promotion, a journey of around 3,700 miles (6,000km). The expedition ran though much of Norway and led to later GTs being called Norge (pronounced Nor-gay, Italian for Norway), a title still applied to Moto Guzzi's latest touring motorcycles.

Moto Guzzi's management seemingly enjoyed a happy knack of spotting opportunities everybody else had missed. All the building work of Mussolini's expansion required goods and materials to be moved, yet trucks were expensive and city streets narrow. Guzzi's solution in 1928 was the Type 107 Moto-carri, a 500 Sport with the rigid rear-end replaced by a pair of leaf-sprung trailer wheels. This supported a timber and steel open crate, which could be ordered with a canvas cover over a loop frame to create a small truck. Far more manoeuvrable than any truck or sidecar combination, the Motocarri could still be converted back to a solo motorcycle in short order. This was a feature absent from the three-wheeled Harley-Davidson Servi-Car, which commenced production in 1932, and was surely inspired by the Motocarri. So successful was the concept that Motocarri, despite literally translating as 'motorcycle cart' and being introduced to the Italian language by Moto Guzzi, now colloquially means any motorized three-wheeler. In one form or another, the Moto Guzzi Motocarri remained in production until 1980, by which time it was called the Ercole (Hercules), and must have contributed significantly to the total number of over 10,000 Sports built between 1928 and 1939. To put that into some kind of perspective, Moto Guzzi's entire production, from its establishment in 1921 until the outbreak of war in 1939, amounted to just over 50,000 motorcycles, including those delivered as Motocarris. Right through World War II these three-wheelers, especially the Trialce, were valued as being easier to ride, especially in difficult situations or with inexperienced riders, than a conventional motorcycle. Post-war the Motocarri were perfect for rebuilding the nation and, unlike many compatriots, Moto Guzzi's factory survived largely unscathed and was able to

swing into post-war action without a hiccough, whether fulfilling government contracts or planning for the future. Government contracts were a lifeline for many factories in Italy, assuming they had survived Allied bombing, destruction by retreating Nazis or the battles fought by liberating armies. Certainly during this era there is anecdotal evidence of government departments ordering motorcycles they didn't need if factories claimed they needed to make workers redundant, or even just halt recruitment. This explains why old police or military motorcycles are found in Italy with only a few kilometres on the clock: why would riders bother to fix a puncture or other minor failing when there were plenty of brand-new motorcycles lying around waiting to be ridden?

Yet while government departments might have carried on buying large-capacity motorcycles, the general public certainly didn't: in fact, they rarely had. Before the war Italy had been unusual on mainland Europe for viewing motorcycling as an extreme sport – motorcycles were seen as dangerous and complex machines for enthusiasts, where elsewhere they were seen as basic transport, a step up from a bicycle. Italy had long loved cycling and cycle racing, in the wealthier north at least, so there was no great pressure to move up from a bicycle. It had also been true that most factories were in cities and so had a large prospective workforce within walking distance; in the countryside people typically worked in their own village,

So passionately do Italians feel about Moto Guzzi, that this couple were delighted when the Milano–Taranto revival stopped at their wedding.
MOTO CLUB VETERAN
SAN MARTINO

farming or in a trade associated with rural work, with little reason to travel beyond a small patch of land their family had known for centuries. In essence there was no need for mass transportation and even a bicycle was a badge of prestige.

After the war everything changed. Factories lay in ruin, infrastructure had been destroyed and disastrous economics left ordinary people with worthless savings and little hope of self-sufficiency. Italian food, so praised and often so expensive today, was born out of a need to turn a few basics into food for a large family; figs, pine-nuts, mushrooms and herbs could be foraged, rabbit and boar hunted, pasta made with eggs from hens living on scraps. Foraging, hunting and pasta-making might be time-consuming but they are cheap and require little capital outlay. Today's elderly Italians aren't short for genetic reasons, they're short because they survived on next-to-nothing as children. Post-war Italy became desperate for cheap transport that could navigate war-ravaged roads to find work in the surviving, or rebuilt, factories, often surrounded by the rubble that was all that remained of past employees' housing. This was a nation fighting for survival. Paolo Campanelli, explaining his reasons for racing in the often lethal long-distance motogiro, said 'We never thought we were risking life and limb because if you didn't race you just died of hunger. If you didn't have a profession things were very hard. You tried to get out of poverty by racing. You tried to get a good result, to earn some money.'

Racing aside, the more conventional route from poverty was to find work in the factories that would be Italy's post-war salvation. For the largely rural population this necessitated transport that would cope with pot-holes and the hard, stone tracks Italians call *strade bianche* (white roads), while covering distances that a cyclist could only dream of, and costing little to buy and run. The traditional motorcycle manufacturers, like Moto Guzzi, Gilera and Bianchi, were caught on the back foot with ranges centred on 500cc single-cylinder sports motorcycles built for an enthusiast market that had all but disappeared. Suddenly the competition was not from traditional motorcycle manufacturers, but a raft of newcomers.

The New Scooters

First and foremost of these was the Piaggio Vespa scooter. Established in 1884 by Rinaldo Piaggio, after the war the firm's fortunes were inextricably linked to the Vespa scooter. The inspiration for the Vespa dates back to pre-World War II Cushman scooters built in the United States and imported into Italy in significant numbers by the liberating forces, who used them as simple everyday transport. The original Piaggio MP5 prototype debuted the enclosed drivetrain, fan-cooled engine, but the leg-guards had a tall central section, meaning that it had to be straddled like a motorcycle. Enrico Piaggio wasn't impressed, and like many others had condemned motorcycles as bulky, dirty and unreliable, but could see potential. Piaggio needed ideas, because the firm had been aeronautical engineers, an area of manufacturing that was prohibited in Italy by the Allies for a decade after the war. Bringing in one of Piaggio's most brilliant thinkers, Corradino D'Ascanio, to redesign the scooter changed the world's view of motorcycling overnight. Leg guards with an open space between them allowed women to ride in skirts, and a twist-grip gearshift meant boots weren't needed for a clumsy foot-change, or control sacrificed to reach for a tank-mounted hand-change. Wheels were interchangeable, and a spare carried, with mountings and suspension that allowed wheels to be easily changed. The monocoque construction (one of the first such motor vehicles produced) was aimed at mass production, also keeping road and engine dirt from the rider. The rear hump enclosing the engine and rear wheel looked like the abdomen of a wasp – *vespa* in Italian, giving the scooter its name, although some say the buzz of the two-stroke motor is what made the name stick. Here was something that every motorcycle wasn't: user-friendly, clean, cute and highly versatile. And cheap – although sales were initially disappointing, when a buy-in-instalments scheme was introduced the success story began. 60,000 Vespas were sold in 1950, and when the Vespa co-starred with Gregory Peck and Audrey Hepburn in *Roman Holiday* in 1952, sales hit 100,000 a year. The motorcycling world would never be the same.

Even worse news came in the form of clip-on motors designed to turn bicycles into mopeds, most famously Ducati's Cucciolo. Ducati had been a high-end electrical and camera manufacturer, with a range of world-beating products, but the factory had been destroyed by allied bombing and were grateful for a contract to produce a 48cc four-stroke engine designed by Aldo Farinelli. Nicknamed Cucciolo (Puppy) by its designer after a yappy exhaust note, the motor was initially put into production by automotive engineering firm SIATA, who quickly realized they couldn't keep up with demand, so approached Ducati to assist with production. Ducati soon abandoned plans to rebuild their pre-war business, and were building 240 Cucciolo engines a day by 1947. Ducati were far from being the only newcomers: other aircraft manufacturers, such as Aermacchi and MV, were switching to lightweight motorcycle production with huge success. If Moto Guzzi were to survive they needed to not only take on, but beat, this new wave of competitors.

Miniature Two-Strokes and Truly Mass Production

Fortunately, Enrico Parodi, brother of Moto Guzzi co-founder Giorgio and now in charge of the company, understood that the rules of successful motorcycle manufacturing had changed. Initially, engineer Antonio Micucci, who had joined Guzzi as a two-stroke specialist during the war, was called upon to design

John Britten, undoubtedly the most innovative motorcycle designer of modern times tries out a Guzzino. He's at the Fossatti hotel close to Monza and posing with members of the hotel owner's family. The Guzzino and its two-stroke relatives sold phenomenally well, and funded Guzzi's racing in an era before sponsorship. FOSSATTI HOTEL

a clip-on engine like Ducati's Cucciolo and Garelli's Mosquito. However, everyone at Moto Guzzi soon realized that this would be little more than a catching-up exercise and hardly what was expected from Italy's largest motorcycle manufacturer. What happened next not only secured Moto Guzzi's future, but made Moto Guzzi unique amongst the pre-war 'big five' Italian manufacturers as they continued to grow, rather than slide into decline. Today Gilera, Bianchi, Garelli and Benelli are either forgotten or minor players in motorcycling, but in 1945 they were, along with Moto Guzzi, the great names and major players in Italian motorcycling. The names that have taken their place today, names like Ducati and MV Agusta, were not even motorcycle manufacturers in 1945. The fact that Moto Guzzi still stands alongside them is down to one motorcycle: the Guzzino ('Little Guzzi').

So Antonio Micucci, overseen by Carcano, was instructed to abandon his 38cc two-stroke motor (nicknamed the Colibrì – Humming Bird) and design a complete motorcycle that would be a distinct – but affordable – step-up from the cyclomotors that were overrunning Italy. His answer was based around a 64cc rotary valve two-stroke that would give 2bhp, even on poor-quality fuel. Traditional Guzzi qualities included gear primary drive and a three-speed gearbox, and the all-alloy unit proved astoundingly reliable. Housed in a chassis that offered full suspension front and rear, and far more stability than a bicycle with a clip-on engine, the Guzzino was an instant hit when launched in 1946. Weighing in at a mere 100lb (45kg), the diminutive motorcycle was capable of 30mph (50km/h), which was just about enough for the market at which it was aimed. Production updates involved little more than renaming the bike Motoleggera 65, and astute re-engineering that allowed the price to be reduced some 30 per cent by 1949, meaning the complete motorcycle cost less than twice what Ducati were asking for a 48cc motor alone. The baby Guzzi also transcended class, being bought by everyone from young people riding to work in a factory to doctors out on their rounds. Around 50,000 were built in the first three years of production, a record for an Italian manufacturer. Such was their popularity that Moto Guzzi organized a street party for owners, asking them to visit the factory on 5 June 1949. Nearly 15,000 people turned up and Moto Guzzi claimed to count 12,660 Motoleggere 65 in attendance, bringing chaos not just to Mandello del Lario, but to neighbouring Lecco as well. The 65 even managed to survive a rule-change in 1951 that required such lightweight motorcycles to be registered and display number plates. At this point the 65 became the Cardellino (Goldfinch) with styling closer to a sporting lightweight motorcycle, including a pillion

Zigolos leaving the factory, and funding the racing.
MOTO GUZZI

Galettos in the museum...

seat. Over the years the capacity grew to first 73cc and then finally in 1962 to 83cc before production ended in 1963. By then almost 215,000 variants had been built and the design licensed overseas, a phenomenal number of motorcycles by Italian manufacturing standards. But in the final years, sales were slowing dramatically, perhaps unsurprising for what was in essence a twenty-year-old idea, but the main reason was that the motorcycling world had moved on again, and this time Moto Guzzi was in danger of failing to spot it. As affluence grew in Italy, buyers wanted a more sporting motorcycle with racing connotations, and again newcomers Ducati and MV Agusta were one step ahead of Moto Guzzi.

In the meantime there was another handful of lightweights that brought Moto Guzzi success, and perhaps a dangerous complacency. The Zigolo (Bunting), designed to be a step up from the Cardellino, was the first fully enclosed motorcycle to sell in significant numbers. Launched in 1953, a full five years before the remarkably similar Ariel Leader, the Zigolo was powered by a three-speed horizontal single-cylinder two-stroke, initially with a 98cc displacement increasing to 110cc for 1959. The pressed-steel bodywork hinted at similarities with the Vespa scooter, but in fact hid a more conventional chassis. Like the Guzzino and Cardellino before it, the Zigolo's price steadily reduced, as did its popularity, although by the time production ended in 1965, almost 130,000 had been sold. More innovative still was Carlo Guzzi's four-stroke Galletto scooter, of which more later on.

...and Galettos are still being enjoyed around Lake Como today.

Four-Strokes

The 246cc Airone (Heron) was in essence a revised 1934 P250, even down to the PE chassis numbers and exposed valve springs on early versions. Even so, the Airone outsold the Guzzi 500 singles fourfold, and the entire production run exceeded 27,000, almost exactly the same number as its replacement the Lodola (Skylark) would sell. Gradually tweaked for the post-war world, its gentle charms were soon lost on customers who were obsessed with racing glory, much of it fuelled by Guzzi's own racing programme. Initially, the Airone could muster less than 10bhp to pull a dry weight of 297lb (135kg), and even by the time production ended in 1957, the Sport version could rustle up no more than 14bhp. Today the Airone is perhaps the nicest of the Guzzi lightweights to ride but, as when it was new, by far the most expensive of the smaller Moto Guzzis to buy.

The Airone's biggest problem was that the market for sub-250cc motorcycles in Italy was very much being driven by racing, and the Motogiro d'Italia in particular. The Giro, like many races, limited entries to a readily available motorcycle with a maximum capacity of 175cc, and so new manufacturers were in an arms race to built production motorcycles that gave the maximum horsepower from that capacity. When Ducati debuted an engine with a bevel and shaft-driven overhead cam for the 1955 Motogiro, Laverda withdrew, protesting that such an engine would never be put into mass production. Yet it was, and the dominance of the Ducati in racing led to a huge sales success for their road-going bevel singles. The 1957 Ducati 175 Sport gave an incomparable 14bhp, and the pre-war giants had no answer: Bianchi's Tonale 175 might have had an overhead cam but produced less than 10bhp and, despite Giro success, boardroom squabbles meant Bianchi had little racing glory to reflect onto their road-bikes. Gilera's offering in the 175 class only had 150cc and relied, like Moto Guzzi, on high-profile Grand Prix racing to sell.

Moto Guzzi's response was dangerously close to suffering from the same failings as Bianchi's Tonale. Famously, the 175 Lodola (Skylark) was the last Moto Guzzi designed by Carlo

SPECIFICATIONS — MOTO GUZZI AIRONE (1939–61)

Layout and Chassis

Single-cylinder four-stroke road-going production motorcycle

Engine

Type	Horizontal single
Block material	Cast iron
Head material	Cast iron
Cylinders	1
Cooling	Air
Bore and stroke	70 × 64mm
Capacity	246cc
Valves	2 valves ohv
Compression ratio	6:1
Carburettor	22mm Dell'Orto
Max. power	12bhp@5,200rpm
Fuel capacity	2.3 gallons/10.5 litres

Transmission

Gearbox	Four-speed foot-change
Clutch	Wet multiplate
Final drive	Chain

Chassis

Front	Telescopic fork
Rear	Swingarm

Steering

Tyres	2.25–19in front, 3.00–19in rear
Brakes	Drums front and rear

Dimensions

Wheelbase	54in (1,370mm)
Unladen weight	297lb (135kg)

Performance

Top speed	62mph (100km/h)

RIDING THE BIKES | AIRONE 250

The most affordable of the early Moto Guzzi singles might actually be the nicest to ride, especially in modern traffic.

Brian Rogers's conversion to Moto Guzzi was almost accidental. Like so many he was seduced into Ducati ownership by the clear affection the motorcycle press have for the marque, but found the reality disappointing. His Ducati Darmah 900SD was supplied and fettled by Three Cross Motorcycles in Ringwood, Hampshire, but despite being importers for Ducati (along with most other Italian manufacturers at the time), they couldn't stop the trail of niggles with Brian's Darmah. Deciding the grand old Duke had to go, Brian's long experience with British motorcycles meant they ought to have been the default choice when it came to changing bikes, but by the late seventies that option was severely limited. Almost in desperation, Brian decided

to test ride a Moto Guzzi 850T3 sitting in the Three Cross showroom, and was immediate smitten. Although the T3 is long gone, Brian has become a long time and loyal member of the Moto Guzzi owners' club, and his garage is home to a trio of the Mandello motorcycles, of which this 250 Airone Sport is his favourite.

The Airone can trace its roots back to the P250 of 1934, and bears little relation to the 250 racers beyond the basic layout. Introduced in 1939, and remaining in intermittent production throughout the war, the original tubular frame soon reverted to a pressed-steel frame similar to the PE250s. Brian's version is the Sport with 12bhp, which although down on the 13.5bhp of earlier bikes, is still a handy 30 per cent more than the original Airone, later rebranded as the Turismo. What makes it so pleasant to ride is the lack

Brian Roger's beautiful Airone. Despite being expensive (prohibitively so in the UK) this was Italy's best selling 250.

of vibration compared to the bigger singles, and great suspension and brakes. The 200mm drums are 20mm bigger than the Turismo's and actually pretty much identical, along with the wheels and tyres, to the 70lb (32kg) heavier Falcone 500. As Brian says, 'It's just such a lovely bike to ride'.

RIGHT: **Although the Airone shared nothing with the Albatros racer, the similar profiles must have helped sales.**

BELOW LEFT: **The quality of alloy castings was much higher than most other 500s, so as a 'mere' 250 the Airone was very upmarket.**

BELOW RIGHT: **Brian's Airone wears its original Dell'Orto carburettor.**

Continued overleaf

RIDING THE BIKES | AIRONE 250

The Airone also has a finish and specification that reflects its original status as a prestige machine. While smaller Guzzis were two-strokes, built as cheap ride-to-work machines, the Airone Sport had alloy castings and Borrani rims, generous rubber grips and footrests, and plenty of expensive chrome plating to give it the demeanour of the even more expensive and prestigious Moto Guzzi 500s. The name – Airone means Heron – also makes clear the link to Moto Guzzi's 250 racer, the Albatros. Actually more expensive than the 500 Condor racer, the Albatros was designed by Carlo Guzzi and Giulio Carcano in 1939 as an over-the-counter racer for events restricted to amateurs riding production motorcycles. In essence, the Albatros was the factory's supercharged Grand Prix bike minus the supercharger, and hugely successful. The reflected glory made the Airone Italy's best-selling 250 and, although it was officially imported into the UK, it was as expensive as a Triumph Speed Twin, so unsurprisingly failed to find a market.

Brian's Airone was imported with the help of Ian Ledger, the UK's Moto Guzzi owners' club singles expert. It was first registered in Italy in 1955, six years before production ended, and since then it has either been fastidiously cared for or restored. 'It's been no trouble at all,' avows Brian before admitting that curiosity once got the better of him and he now checks certain bolts in the engine regularly. But then it is a single, although the rider is blissfully unaware of vibration. Brian's Airone is clearly his keeper, the last motorcycle he'd sell. 'It's fast enough, and it doesn't vibrate like the Falcone. It's a lovely sunny afternoon bike' but beware of nightfall, because 'the lights are the worst thing about the bike. I've got a bicycle LED light that clips onto the handlebars.' Which proves the bike gets ridden, surely the greatest testament to the gentle charms of a motorcycle that is still able to inspire a desire to get out on British roads sixty years after it was built on the sunny shore of Lake Como.

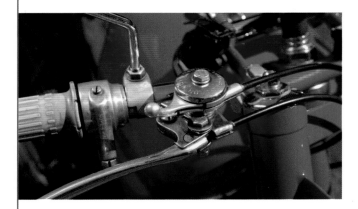

ABOVE: **Other quality fittings include a Super Pratic throttle.**

RIGHT: **Although the early Airones had a tubular frame it was quickly superseded by a part pressed steel, part tubular item.**

himself, dragged from retirement for a final session at the drawing board, although the new 175 bore little resemblance to Guzzi's of old. The cylinder was only angled forward by 45 degrees, rather than being horizontal, although it still made the engine look like nothing else. The large flywheel hid behind an alloy cover to make the engine look more like the competition's offerings, and yet the Lodola still lacked their sporting air. More importantly, despite the overhead camshaft hinting at sporting intent, the Guzzi made just 9bhp. Unsurprisingly, then, it seems a Lodola was never entered into the Motogiro. But then a twist of fate gave the little Guzzi an unexpected helping hand when the Italian Government banned racing on public roads, following an accident in the 1957 Mille Miglia, when twelve people died as a result of Alfonso de Portago's Ferrari crashing into the crowd. The Motogiro, along with the Milano–Taranto, simply ceased to exist and the importance of the 175cc class was instantly diminished. Moto Guzzi decided, as did Ducati, to increase the capacity of their lightweight challenger, although unlike Ducati they chose not to take the opportunity to increase performance. Instead the Lodola reverted to the more old-fashioned (if easier to maintain) overhead valves and the revised 235cc Lodola gained the title Gran Tourismo. Despite softening the engine's level of tune, the increased capacity gave 11bhp. However, surprising competition success then came to the Lodola as 'regularity' (regolarità) events became popular. These were typically 2,000km trials designed to test the ability of motorcycles away from the tarmac. Their rise was probably not unconnected with the banning of the Motogiro but, like the Giro, using such events to prove the capabilities of small-capacity production bikes was brilliant marketing. So Guzzi took the 235cc ohv Lodola and converted it for regolarità use, which happily made it competitive in international six-day trials (ISDTs). Having abandoned the 175 Lodola's overhead cam when relaunching the bike with 235cc, Moto Guzzi retrofitted the ohc head for ISDTs, with some works bikes even getting 247cc and a five-speed gearbox. So armed, and running along-side similarly improved Stornellos, the Guzzi team ran away with the 'Silver Vase' at the 1963 ISDT in Czechoslovakia.

SPECIFICATIONS — LODOLO GRAN TOURISMO

Layout and Chassis

Single-cylinder four-stroke road-going production motorcycle

Engine

Type	Inclined single
Block material	Aluminium alloy
Head material	Aluminium alloy
Cylinders	1
Cooling	Air
Bore and stroke	64 × 68mm
Capacity	235cc
Valves	2 valves ohv
Compression ratio	7.5:1
Carburettor	22mm Dell'Orto
Max. power	11bhp@6,000rpm
Fuel capacity	2.6 gallons/12 litres

Transmission

Gearbox	Four-speed foot-change
Clutch	Wet multiplate
Final drive	Chain

Chassis

Front	Telescopic fork
Rear	Swingarm

Steering

Tyres	2.5–18in front, 3.00–17in rear
Brakes	Drums front and rear

Dimensions

Wheelbase	52in (1,314mm)
Unladen weight	264lb (120kg)

Performance

Top speed	65mph (105km/h)

RIDING THE BIKES | **LODOLA GRAN TOURISMO**

Richard Varley might have spent a great deal of effort restoring his Lodola, but he's far from precious about using it.

The 1956 175cc Lodola was the final Moto Guzzi designed by Carlo Guzzi, and was also the first Moto Guzzi four-stroke to abandon their trademark horizontal cylinder layout. Even the traditional external flywheel was hidden behind an alloy engine case. The Lodola might then seem to mark a point where Moto Guzzi's self-confidence faltered, since the steeply sloping cylinder also lacked the visual arrogance of competitors like Ducati, Mondial and Moto Morini's 175s. It also lacked their performance, despite featuring Moto Guzzi's first mass-produced overhead-cam engine. Initially, traditional Moto Guzzi fans took fright, especially since the overhead-cam layout complicated decokes. By 1959, Moto Guzzi realized their mistake and reinvented the Lodola with a 235cc pushrod version of the engine, which nonetheless retained the dome in the valve gear cover for the overhead cam; this was to prove fortuitous when the overhead cam was retrofitted to the 235cc Lodola factory racers that were entered into International Six-Day Trials.

For everyone else, the 235 Lodola was re-styled to reflect its lack of Motogiro ambitions as a lightweight Gran Turismo, and for most riders, this was a worthwhile upgrade. The 235 feels much more relaxed to ride than the 175, since the capacity increase was achieved principally by increasing stroke: the 175's bore and stroke is 62mm × 57.8mm,

while the 235 uses 64mm × 68mm. With a compression ratio of 7.5:1, power was a modest 11bhp at a gentle 6,500rpm, offering excellent fuel-consumption along the way.

Richard Varley bought his 1959 235cc Lodola to restore (actually he bought a pair of them, which does simplify checking originality and getting hold of spares). The Lodola was used for touring, most impressively competing in the 2011 Tour des Cols. This involved trying to ride thirty-four *cols* (passes) in eight days, including climbs to over 8,000ft (2,500m) and the infamous Stevio pass, which gives its name to another Moto Guzzi. Richard summarizes why he likes the Lodola so much and rides it so often, despite also having a recent model Ducati Monster and a classic Morini 3½.

With just a gentle prod on the kick-start it bursts into life. It is virtually vibration free, needs refuelling every 280 to 300 miles (450–480km) and is very relaxing to ride. Yes, it only does 65mph (105km/h) but it will do 55mph (88km/h) until it runs out of fuel, which is much longer than I want to ride. It is light, manageable and easy to fix.

Richard's 2,000-mile (3,225km) continental adventure brought only minor mishaps, despite tough climbs and torrential rain. Most of the problems experienced he puts down to failing to take enough trouble over assembly and not reading the handbook – this advises different carburettor settings when the air temperature is over 23°C. The altitude probably didn't help either but, like most riders out on a limb, Richard found himself imagining that the resulting vibration was something terminal, like failing main bearings. It wasn't and, just as the owner's handbook promised, dropping the carburettor needle one notch fixed the problem permanently. Sadly, the Lodola did break down on his way back to the

Richard Varley and his beautifully restored and much ridden Lodola GT 235.

The traditional large Guzzi flywheel was hidden for the first time behind the Lodola's left-hand engine casing.

UK, although this might be blamed on having to run with the lights on at all times – a piece of European legislation Carlo Guzzi could be forgiven for failing to foresee over fifty years ago. The only problems Richard could identify when the Lodola was recovered to England were a failed coil and a stripped thread on one of the dynamo's drive belt pinch bolts. Having found the rear brake more effective than the increasingly noisy front on mountain descents, he also had them skimmed and trued. The Gran Tourismo averaged 90mpg (3.1ltr/100km) and used (or leaked) less than a litre of oil. Some days Richard rode almost 300 miles, by which point the Lodola's generally excellent comfort was tested *in extremis*. More to the point, his trip highlighted the level of overkill modern motorcycles often amount to, and how a Lodola can do pretty much anything a rider might reasonably ask of their mount. Travelling light and at a more modest pace also means you are more likely to interact with people, and Richard wonders whether the electrical system may even have kept up with demand if he had used a battery charger each evening. No wonder Moto Guzzi sold over 26,000 Lodolas: they must have seemed a perfectly rational motorcycle when new, and still make a lot of sense today.

LEFT: **Although built to a price point, fittings and build quality on the Lodola were still high.**

BELOW: **The Lodola was a replacement for the Airone, and reflected demand for a 175. However, the 175 Lodola was not sporting enough to meet market expectations so was relaunched as a 235.**

The Stornello was also built in scrambler and Regolarita guise: this is the latter.
MIKE SCANLON

Stornellos on the production line. A Carcano design intended to be cheap to build and sell well. He succeeded on both counts. MOTO GUZZI

Mike Scanlon discovered this Regolarita in Malaysia, and it has a number of 'works' features, including magnesium alloy rear hub and special forks.
MIKE SCANLON

The Stornello 125 was introduced in 1960 to build on the eventual success of the Lodola. The all-new model was the work of Carcano, a four-stroke single designed to be cheap to manufacture and that would hopefully sell as well in the USA as at home. Over 58,000 would be built before its demise in 1974, outliving the cull of Moto Guzzi lightweights that took

place in 1965. But the Moto Guzzi from this era that had the greatest potential and was the most avant-garde was the Galletto (Cockerel). Even though 71,000 were sold during its 1950 to 1965 production run, it deserved greater success. Powered by a four-stroke flat single, there were many similarities to the pre-war Guzzis, including an external flywheel and over-square dimensions, initially giving 160cc but growing to 175 when the three-speed gearbox gained a fourth ratio, and finally increasing to 192cc. Although designed with a scooter-like step-through pressed-steel chassis, wheels were 17in in diameter to offer motorcycle levels of stability, and for 1954 an electric starter was available. With a heel-and-toe gear-change, spare wheel and sturdy construction, the Galletto offered the sort of universal, user-friendly transport that deserved to sell better, especially given the reliability – you can still find many

The Stornello survived until 1974, gaining a 5-speed gearbox and 153cc (nominally 160) along the way.

Gallettos in regular use around Lake Como. The fact that it bore a remarkable similarity to the Honda Super Cub launched in 1958 might have more to do with the demise of the Galletto, and Guzzi's subsequent problems. The little Honda went on to become the world's best selling motorcycle (around 60 million variants over a fifty-year period), the Super Cub proving that the Japanese, and Honda especially, understood that great products alone were not enough.

The Japanese are Coming – and So Are Cheap Cars

The 'You meet the nicest people on a Honda' advertising campaign, backed up by investment in racing and dealerships, spoke of an ambition lacking just about everywhere else – and certainly not just in motorcycling and Italy – that allowed Japan's rise to become a global powerhouse. While Moto Guzzi were happy to be market leaders at home, with occasional forays into the American market, Soichiro Honda's first visits to the Isle of Man TT also included a trip to Germany as part of the itinerary. With Soichiro was Takeo Fujisawa, a man whose roots were in business rather than engineering and a trusted ally who would become Honda's vice-president in 1964 and retire with Soichiro in 1973: their relationship was that close. Fujisawa realized that companies could not rely on the post-war economic boom some countries were enjoying, but that you

had to grow your market both in terms of new products and countries you sold to. He spotted that in Europe people went from a bicycle, bought a clip-on engine and then moved on to a scooter, with the hope that they could eventually afford a car. A similar path was followed in America, and motorcycle manufacturers seemed happy to offer lightweight motorcycles and accept that they would quickly loose their customers to the car manufacturers. This was fine in a world with a growing population and increasingly affluent society, where new customers were easy to come by, but it did rely upon perpetual growth. By contrast, the motorcycle enthusiast was seen as a separate market, requiring high-performance, large-capacity motorcycles with a sporting heritage. The thought that the buyer of a small-capacity motorcycle might be turned into a motorcycle enthusiast with a loyalty to a brand and buy ever-bigger motorcycles from the same factory was a new idea. So not only was the Honda Cub intended to sell as a simple scooter, it was also intended to be the first step into the Honda brand that would see owners trade up to ever larger capacity motorcycles, each with the name Honda proudly emblazed across the fuel-tank.

This was revolutionary thinking. The launch of the Nuova Fiat 500 in 1957, at a price of 465,000 lira, was supposed to signal the death-knell for large-capacity motorcycles. This was little more than Moto Guzzi were asking for their 500 singles, and even the 250 Airone was almost 400,000 lira. Enrico Parodi, therefore, believed that Moto Guzzi should move even further downmarket, resulting in a move into sub-50cc two-stroke motorcycles and mopeds. Yet, perhaps more critically, he neglected the Falcone (Falcon) and Astore (Goshawk), which were now Guzzi's only big bikes, both 500cc singles that sold well, largely by basking in the glory of the racing Dondolino and Condor, and sharing many styling cues.

The Falcone: the End of an Era?

The Astore had been a stop-gap development of the earlier GTV and GTW 500 singles, only lasting two years before being replaced by the Falcone Turismo. The Falcone had been introduced alongside the Astore in 1950 as a more sporting alternative but it quickly became obvious that the Falcone's close association with the glorious racing Dondolino and Condor was the key to sales success, and so the Falcone became the Falcone Sport in 1952 and was joined by a hybrid Turismo that amounted to a Sport with an Astore's engine.

The engine was what made the original Falcone and Falcone Sport special. Although the Dondolino and Condor's magnesium alloy components were aluminium equivalents on the Falcone, and specifications such as the carburettor size and compression ratio were substantially reduced, in most respects the Falcone's engine was identical to the racing single's. This gave owners the tantalizing prospect of upgrading to Dondolino specification, raising the Falcone's modest power of 23bhp

(some 5bhp more than the Astore/Turismo) to over 30bhp at comparatively modest cost, given that the Dondolino was almost 900,000 lira, double the Falcone Sport's price. Yet, as delivered, by the mid-fifties the Falcone looked part of a bygone era. Weighing in at 387lb (176kg), it favoured long straights or sweeping curves, rather than city centres and torturous mountain roads. The considerably cheaper Ducati 175 was almost as fast and, with a far shorter wheelbase and 154lb (70kg) less to carry around, much quicker on real roads. The Ducati also bore

ABOVE: **Unusual but apparently original fuel tank on this Falcone Turismo.** MOTO CLUB VETERAN SAN MARTINO

LEFT: **A post-war 500 of the GT series ridden beside Lake Como.**

ABOVE: **Another Falcone on the Milano–Taranto revival.**
MOTO CLUB VETERAN SAN MARTINO

RIGHT: **The Zigolo 110 production line being used for later mopeds, probably the Chiù of the early 1970s.**
MOTO GUZZI

a strong similarity to the firm's racing motorcycles, at a time when Moto Guzzi could offer no road-going equivalents to their magnificent Grand Prix racers. The Falcone harked back to pre-war racers and, given its popularity as a police motorcycle and evolution into the utilitarian 1969 Nuovo Falcone, any residual glamour evaporated. Moto Guzzi's belief that big motorcycles were a thing of the past, combined with an inability to compete with Vespa and the Japanese in the scooter and moped market, quickly led to serious financial difficulties. With hindsight, these were serious and avoidable mistakes and the problems that followed were inevitable.

The Parodi family had lost father Emanuele, and others, in the war, and Giorgio died in 1955. By the early 1960s, Carlo Guzzi had lost any influence over the factory that bore his name after a series of bitter disagreements with company directors

LEFT: **And another Falcone. That so many are still ridden regularly is a testament to the design and quality components, although Italian weather must help.** MOTO CLUB VETERAN SAN MARTINO

BELOW: **It's a similar story on the Moto Giro. A Falcone is flanked by a Guzzino and 850GT.**

ABOVE: **Out in the countryside on Guzzi 500 singles.** MOTO CLUB VETERAN SAN MARTINO

RIGHT: **Some adjustment is inevitably required occasionally. Note Benelli 500 Quattro on the right, which would have been built at the Moto Guzzi Mandello factory.** MOTO CLUB VETERAN SAN MARTINO

over the future direction of the business. He died following a short illness in 1964, two years after his brother had passed away. That left Enrico Parodi as the only member of the original families who had founded Moto Guzzi and was clearly gifted and experienced, having joined the business in 1942. Even so, a series of disastrous investments had frittered away the family fortune, and Moto Guzzi would also disappear without drastic action.

ABOVE LEFT: **A 1938 Guzzi 500 in Bregenze.** MOTO CLUB VETERAN SAN MARTINO

ABOVE RIGHT: **The styling of the Falcone Nuovo (1971–76) was less successful. This is the version based on the Military Falcone.**

LEFT: **Old-fashioned paint and chrome, along with period extras, improves the look of the Falcone Nuovo enormously.** NORTH LEICESTER MOTORCYCLES

CHAPTER FOUR

BIRTH OF THE V-TWIN

The 1960s saw a rapidly shrinking market for motorcycles in general and Moto Guzzi in particular, yet Moto Guzzi employees still enjoyed very generous pay and conditions. There were subsidized housing, canteens, a medical centre and library, even a rowing club – the factory rowing eight had travelled to England in 1948 as the Italian national team, winning a Gold Medal at the Olympic Games. Mirroring Moto Guzzi's history, they would be a dominant international force for nearly a decade. Moto Guzzi also had overseas subsidiaries in Spain and Turkey, as well as holiday resorts. Staff loyalty is perhaps best illustrated by workers creating a tunnel during their free time to ease Carlo's walk to his office as old-age crept up on him. Carlo was, however, now gone, and while production had peaked in the 1950s at 30,000 motorcycles a year, using cutting-edge facilities, those days too were long gone. And yet employing 1,500 people, mainly local, Moto Guzzi was too big to fail. The creditors were circling, but if they simply foreclosed and sold off the assets not only would they never see their money back, they would also ruin Mandello del Lario and many people's lives. This was an era when the market was changing rapidly, and although the Italians, largely thanks to import control, bought the best part of 250,000 home-grown mopeds and small commuting motorcycles each year, the market for larger and sporting motorcycles was shrinking rapidly. The Japanese were already established as world market-leaders and even the smallest of the Japanese 'big four' manufacturers, Kawasaki, were building many more units than the entire Italian industry put together. Names that had enjoyed tremendous prosperity comparatively recently were folding. Mondial, the marque Soichiro Honda most admired, failed (although the name remained on motorcycles using imported two-stroke engines) and Bianchi and Parilla also ceased motorcycle production. The industry giants, Moto Guzzi and Gilera, only remained because the government stepped in, taking the view that Italy's prestige and prosperity depended on

businesses such as these. The future looked bleak indeed for the Italian motorcycle manufacturers.

In 1966, Moto Guzzi was put into receivership and almost exactly a year later was reborn in the ownership of SEIMM (Società Esercizio Industrie Moto Meccaniche – something along the lines of 'motor mechanical industries management society' in English), a state-backed vessel intended to hold on to Moto Guzzi until it could be returned to the private sector. The new managing director, Romolo de Stefani, came with a solid pedigree, having worked with Ducati and Bianchi. Journeyman engineer Lino Tonti joined him, the two having worked together at Bianchi, Tonti abandoning his Linto 500 Grand Prix project to do so. Unsurprisingly, there was cost-cutting and the shock departure of Carcano, who has always remained silent on exactly why he left. He moved on to designing sailing boats and would never design another motorcycle, but then he had become besotted with Moto Guzzi as a boy. Carcano's father had owned the ferry that Moto Guzzi hired to take their motorcycles across Lake Como to the Circuito del Lario when Carcano was still little. Allowed to join the race team on the ferry, the racers and mechanics had taken the wide-eyed young Carcano to their hearts and filled his head with dreams. Dreams that would be realized in motorcycles as disparate as the fabulous V8 racer and the super-simple – and super-profitable – Stornello. Yet he still had one more legacy to bestow on Moto Guzzi, an engine he had been working on a since the demise of the V8 in 1957: a sturdy, powerful but simple, pushrod V-twin.

Carcano's Leaving Present: a 90-Degree V-Twin

Carcano had been dreaming of building the ultimate road-going motorcycle when he penned the early sketches of a 90-

degree V-twin, although his original 1950s design never made it off the drawing board. Once the V8 project was dropped, he revisited the idea, thinking a basic V-twin might find a market as a stand-alone engine to drive things like water pumps on remote farms, a device with multiple uses: a 'utilitarian engine' as he called it. Instead, Moto Guzzi management once again overlooked Carcano's genius and again set about developing more small, two-stroke motorcycles. A Moto Guzzi V-twin looked less and less likely, and for many years it seemed that Carcano's ideas of building a motorcycle with such an engine would remain a project to fill his spare time, solely as an intellectual challenge.

Carcano had bought one of the Nuova 500 Fiats that he liked very much, and almost on a whim decided he would fit his prototype V-twin into the Fiat. Returning to Mandello from Milan one day, flying along at some 90mph (140km/h), he was spotted by a journalist from a car magazine who could not believe how quick the Fiat was compared to his own Alfa Romeo. Making a note of the licence plate, the journalist tracked the little Fiat down to 'Ing. Carcano of Moto Guzzi fame'. He understandably assumed there was something going on between Fiat and Guzzi, an opinion often repeated since. In fact, there wasn't – Carcano was just having a little fun.

In the end, the first production Moto Guzzi 90-degree V-twin was for an army contract that needed a motocarri-style vehicle for mountain troops. This looked a smart move, given the fantastic success of Motocarri three-wheelers: the Ercole version sold nearly 40,000 units between 1945 and 1975, inspiring a 192cc Ercolino that would sell almost 30,000 Galletto-based trikes. It was the Guzzino's designer, Micucci, who sketched out a 754cc V-twin for military use in a vehicle that could do the work of the army's mules in the mountains. Fan-cooled, the engine had little in common with Carcano design beyond basic architecture. In any event, the half-tank, half-motorcycle, V-twin christened 3×3 failed to find favour, despite looking the part. There were caterpillar rear-tracks and substantial dimensions, partly due to the sizeable motor buried below the rider's seat. Complexity, and concomitant handling problems, led to this V-twin project being still-born and just 200 or so 3×3s were built. Moto Guzzi still needed a home for Carcano's leaving present.

Taking a cue from Carcano, Moto Guzzi wondered if there might be merit in redesigning his V-twin as a retro-fit for the Fiat 500. Much of the work on this project was by Umberto Todero, who had worked with Carcano on the V8 racer. This engine stayed true to the fundamentals of Carcano's original 500cc design but was enlarged to some 650cc with fan-cooling and a car-style gearbox and clutch. Moto Guzzi had built record-breaking cars before: pre-war, with a Bicilindrica-powered streamliner; and post-war, with 250 and 350 singles. However, Fiat showed no interest in the project, and given the lack of

Despite being a pre-war idea, the Motocarri was still selling in the 1970s. This is an Ercole from 1970.

funding at Moto Guzzi, the idea was quickly dropped. The Abarth tuning firm, in fact, became Fiat's sporting partner.

What happened next was a blessing in disguise, when Moto Guzzi were told that a major government contract they had expected to be theirs for the taking would be put out to tender. Almost since their introduction, Moto Guzzi 500 singles had been the automatic choice for the Italian police force and army, but in 1963, the opportunity to bid for a new contract was also offered to Gilera, Laverda and Benelli. Calling for a low-maintenance, long-lived but powerful motorcycle, the bid

was one Moto Guzzi could not afford to lose. The solution was obvious: Carcano and Todero redesigned the V-twin intended for Fiat to fit into a motorcycle.

Dubbed the V7 (reflecting the engine layout and capacity), the new Moto Guzzi not only won the police and army contracts, but a modestly tuned civilian model also wowed visitors to the 1965 Milan show. In a way, the new 704cc motorcycle was the polar opposite of Carcano's racing designs, being fantastically robust and built for reliability and comfort above pretty much all else. At 535lb (243kg), even the civilian version made

RIGHT: **An early US Police V7, inspiration for the California.**
MOTO GUZZI

BELOW: **A US Ambassador, again in Police specification.**
MOTO GUZZI

just 44bhp and could barely top 100mph (160km/h). But just as Carcano had ruthlessly chased horsepower for the design of the V8, he was equally single-minded when designing the V7. The design brief had called for an engine that would last 62,000 miles (100,000km) without major work and be easy to work on. Although such heroic reliability was rare in the motorcycle world, it was already expected by car buyers, and so Carcano adopted car practices where it made sense. A notable example of this was the big-end bearings: they were accessible by removing the sump, normally an integral part of a motorcycle's engine cases, because on the Guzzi, the sump unbolted as a separate casting – just like a car's. The other feature that looked brave, if not foolhardy, was complete reliance on an electric engine start, just like most cars. Even the Japanese, undoubted popularizers of the electric starter, would fit kick-starts as a safety net for owners who let their battery go flat, for at least another decade. Carcano instead specified a car-sized battery and generator. As it happened, along the wide-open spaces of North America, the V7 was the perfect travelling companion and, along with the Italian Government, the United States took the lion's share of the V7's 15,000 production run that would last until 1976.

Lino Tonti Fills Carcano's Shoes

When Tonti joined Moto Guzzi, he had immediately set to improving the V-twin. Unsurprisingly, the American market was clamouring for more performance and a hike in the rather

ABOVE: **V7 Special in rare UK sunshine.**

BELOW: **The original 'loop-frame' California.**
MOTO GUZZI

modest (by US – that is, Harley-Davidson – standards) cylinder capacity. So by the end of 1968, Tonti had increased bore and valve sizes to create a 60bhp, 757cc engine and, with a raft of other changes, the V7 also lost 33lb (15kg), allowing it to at least match the top-selling British bikes in straight-line acceleration. Named the V7 Special for most markets, the importance of exports was recognized with models destined for the United States being tagged 'Ambassador' and featuring American's preferred left-foot gearshift. Although the Ambassador was more expensive than the British, Japanese and BMW competition in 1967, they still displaced less than 650cc. The British and BMW offerings also lacked an electric start, and BMWs were seen as a little dull next to the glamorous Guzzi. The Guzzi also proved

The V7 brochure, demonstrating surprising off-road talent.

The brochure shots naturally feature Lake Como.

to offer exemplary reliability, unlike the increasingly fragile British twins, which was attributed to Moto Guzzi's unique shipping practices. Where other manufacturers saved on transportation costs by dispatching motorcycles partially disassembled, the big Guzzi was run for up to five hours on the test bench while carburetion, cable runs, brakes and such were set up to Carcano's specification by factory technicians. The V7 was then crated up and shipped out ready to run, a feature the Berliner brothers would use to gain valuable publicity in the USA. American road-testers from the top-selling magazines were invited to the importer's warehouse, directed to a wall of unopened crates and invited to pick one – any one. The chosen crate would then be opened in front of the waiting journalist, the motorcycle within started with the road test beginning right there. Unsurprisingly the resulting copy was positive, but then if the motorcycle had proven unreliable, the story would have been very different.

Despite appearances akin to the Harley 74, which was clearly one of the motorcycles with which the Ambassador intended to compete, in some eyes at least, Moto Guzzi seemed to have sporting potential. Despite the looks being called 'Elephantine' (complete with a photograph of the Guzzi behind an elephant) when tested by *Cycle* magazine, the overall assessment was flattering. The south-west Guzzi distributor, Bob Blair and George Kerker of ZDS Motors built a surprisingly competitive racer from an Ambassador, which, while looking nothing like the motorcycle Moto Guzzi had exported, was in fact surprisingly standard. Apart from some bracing, the frame was original, as was the bottom end of the engine. Conventional tuning, with racing camshafts, porting and Mondial pistons, was aided by Tonti loaning Kerker parts from his record-breaking V7s. Kerker even visited the factory and sampled some of Tonti's developments first-hand, when he tried out the development version of the Ambassador, looking incongruous with a sporty half fairing and clip-on handlebars the only obvious changes from standard.

Racing and Record-Breaking with the V-Twin

The ZDS Motors racer, on the other hand, looked little like the original Ambassador donor bike. Intended for Kerker (who would go on to establish Kerker exhausts) to race in the USA, its appearance was unique, with little in the way of bodywork beyond a Triumph race tank and seat, plus the obligatory fairing. Lightweight forks and a front disc-brake completed the

**The record breaking V-twins that were based on loop-framed bikes
but would prove to be part of the V7 Sport's development.**

transformation, with weight reduced to a remarkable 331lb (151kg) – 170lb (77kg) less than the road-bike – the bike was intended to enter the Daytona 200 in early 1970, by which time fuel-injection was planned. In the meantime, magazine road-testers were invited to try the bike with standard carburettors to gain valuable coverage for the Ambassador's potential.

The resulting write-ups were indeed positive, talking of the gearing now being far too short to realize the Guzzi's poten-tial. The Ambassador was only geared for 120mph (194km/h) and the hope was that closer to 150mph (242km/h) could be achieved, although altering gearing on a shaft-drive motorcycle

is not straightforward. Testers also cautioned that slow gear-changes were needed to allow for the heavy flywheel, although this would be less significant on the straights and banking of Daytona. The most telling thing about the Guzzi V-twin's latent racing pedigree was that it was banned from entering Daytona on the grounds it was too wide – an act of sheer protection-ism for Harley-Davidson. The American Motorcyclist Associ-ation (AMA) made the decision, along with rules that prohib-ited overhead valve engines (like the British twins) exceeding 500cc in certain (Harley dominated) events that allowed side-valve engines (like the Harley-Davidson's) to displace 750cc.

There would be more of this protectionism to come, as the United States sought to preserve its only large-scale motorcycle manufacturer.

In Europe, there were also individuals keen to unlock the V7's inner racer. By the late 1960s, endurance races, often run non-stop for 24 hours, became accepted as the true breeding ground for technical innovation. Small teams tried to convert standard road-machines into reliable racing motorcycles, often using innovative ideas unseen in other classes. The Dutchman Jan Kampen Senior, ran such a team, and when Moto Guzzi introduced the V7, he bought one of the first, tired of the poor reliability of his British twins. Kampen was a gifted tuner, having won the 1968 Dutch production championship with a Norton, and although he appreciated that a stock V7 was not really a racing motorcycle, he believed it had potential. When his V7 finished second in a 1969 six-hour race, he attracted the attention of the Moto Guzzi factory. Kampen soon became friends with Tonti and an integral part of the factory's development programme, which ultimately led to the V7 Sport and the 850 Le Mans. On a weekly basis, engines were shipped to the Netherlands to be tested and abused on Kampen's own dynamometer to see where and how they would break, and what power had been achieved. Careful dismantling of each broken engine led to detailed reports of suggested improvements, which were sent back to Tonti, together with the wrecked engine. Tonti repeated the tests at Moto Guzzi, and proven improvements ultimately found their way into the engine that became the V7 Sport.

Tonti had also developed a version of the V7 Special for record-breaking. Dramatically increasing carburettor size from the Special's 29mm to 36mm, and compression ratio to 9.6:1, were tricks that would reach production with the Le Mans. Similarly, dramatic weight-loss allowed the sporting promise of Carcano's V-twin to be realized. With a top speed of over 140mph (225km/h) when fitted with a dolphin fairing, Tonti's record-breaker took a clutch of rosettes with high-profile riders on board, including MV Agusta star Remo Venturi, Pagani, Brambilla and racing reporter Roberto Patrignani. These records included the 1000cc one- and twelve-hour records at averages of 135mph (218km/h) and 111mph (180km/h), respectively. This was despite the engine running at just 757cc and, with capacity slightly reduced, three 750 class records were also established. Encouraged by this, a few V7 Specials were entered in production races with mixed results, although in standard trim the Special was really too heavy to compete. Although the Guzzi's weight, marginal brakes and handling were not significant issues when competing against Harley-Davidson tourers, even compared to BMW's twins the big Guzzi's sporting credentials were harder to establish. Against the top-selling sports bikes, the Guzzi's failings were at their most obvious. British twins dominated the market with similar power to the Guzzi V-twin but, with far superior road-holding and around 132lb (60kg) less weight than the V-twin, the British bike's performance and racing success meant it ruled in the showrooms of Europe, America and Australia.

These were issues that Tonti was keen to address, harbouring racing ambitions for the V-twin and also mindful of the new wave of 'superbikes' on the way. From the British there was the Norton Commando and Triumph Trident, but more significantly, 1969 saw the arrival of Honda's CB750. This 4-cylinder, disc-braked phenomenon raised the bar considerably, both in terms of the buying public's expectations and every motorcycle manufacturer's plans for the future. This was a completely new leisure market that Honda's Takeo Fujisawa had imagined a decade before, creating a new breed of rider who enjoyed motorcycling as a sport in itself, rather than something briefly flirted with before cars, marriage and career moved traditional buyers on to other products.

Birth of the Superbike

Seizing the *Zeitgeist*, Tonti set about designing a completely new chassis to create the V7 Sport. Perhaps 200 (or maybe just 150 – accurate figures are unavailable) of the 1971–72 'Telaio Rosso' (Red Frame) bikes were hand-built, with chrome-molybdenum frames and lightweight 748cc engines identified by missing gearbox ribbing. These are perhaps the most undervalued Italian exotica: independent tests found that the bike would easily outperform any other 750, and make the V7 Sport arguably the finest sporting motorcycle of the early 1970s – truly a race-bred production bike. Thanks to Tonti's sporting ambitions, and the support of Guzzi's managing director Romolo De Stefani, the tall V7 Special became a low and lithe racer. Tonti removed the belt-driven dynamo between the V7's cylinders and replaced it with a Bosch alternator on the front end of the crank. This allowed space to run the twin top tubes of his new double-cradle frame from headstock to tail, doing away with the V7's loop frame, lowering the overall centre of gravity and improving handling beyond recognition. Front forks were cartridge-style, manufactured in-house but, although innovative, were a little lightweight and arguably the V7 Sport's only handling failing. Elsewhere components were exemplary, with Koni rear suspension, a steering damper and wide Borrani alloy rims, with a new design of tyre by Michelin. Although niceties such as air-filters were omitted (leading to failings in the chrome-plated bores that had proved trouble-free in the V7 Special with its substantial air-filter), other features delighted: there was a courtesy light under the seat, the rear mudguard

hinged up to allow the rear wheel to roll out and the bottom frame rails unbolted to facilitate engine removal. The new gearbox now offered five speeds, although the starter motor had barely more than half the power of the V7 Special's, which, although saving weight and space, would cause reliability issues.

The engine was comprehensively redesigned to both reduce weight and increase power. Additional external crankcase ribbing helped with the former (although on the original Telaio Rosso the gearbox was still a smooth casting as per the earlier V-twins) and a 9:1 compression ratio with the latter. The 30mm Dell'Orto carburettors had accelerator pumps, adding extra fuel when the throttle was opened quickly, but were only 1mm larger than the V7 Special's. The Sport's bore was actually half a millimetre down on the Special's, meaning a reduction to 748cc from 757cc, and so warning competitors that the Sport was intended to race in 750 class events. Yet when 844cc versions came third and sixth in the 1971 Bol d'Or at Le Mans, the potential for further development was clear.

Mike Hailwood was invited to test the new motorcycle. Quite unprompted, he said this was the best-handling road-bike he'd ever ridden, and immediate racing success said he wasn't just being his usual gentlemanly self. Homologation for production racing required at least 100 bikes to be built, and in

ABOVE: **Luciano Gazzola, Tonti's main test rider, on a V7 Sport Telaio Rosso during the 1972 500km race at Monza. Along with co-rider Carena, the standard V7 Sport finished fifth against a field of fully faired racing motorcycles.** A HERL INC.

RIGHT: **Australian Jack Findlay on a V7 Sport specially prepared by Tonti for the 200 Miglia di Imola in 1972. This was the race that made Ducati when their 750 V-twins finished first and second against arguably the strongest field in the world. Findlay was 10th, his team mates 8th and 11th. Note Lockheed discs.** A HERL INC.

RIDING THE BIKES | V7 SPORT

Richard Skelton's V7 Sport.
RICHARD SKELTON

The first big Moto Guzzi sportster – and, even today, Richard Skelton finds his V7 Sport impressively quick. In 1971 it must have been astonishing.

It's very easy to read the period road-tests of the V7 Sport with a bemused indifference now that 125mph (200km/h) can be wrought from a two-stroke 250 or a 600cc commuter. Yet in 1975, the V7 Sport's claimed 72bhp was in the same league as Grand Prix racers, and a measured 125mph top speed was only topped by exotic supercars costing ten times as much as the Guzzi. Even so, at £1,350 the V7 Sport was not just the most expensive motorcycle on sale in the UK, it was more expensive than most cars. Yet even today it stands out as a motorcycle built without compromise, and still feels fast. Richard Skelton's 1972 Sport came into his life as part of a deal that involved selling his 1976 Ducati 900SS and fond memories of a Le Mans.

I don't think the gear-change is as precise as the Le Mans – it feels like an old car where you push the stick into the H-gate and can't feel anything even though the gear goes in fine. Having said that my V7's never missed a gear-change. The brakes are a disappointment, although they come to you as the ride progresses. Maybe you get used to them or maybe they get better as they warm up. It's a fantastically fast A-road-bike: I rode a couple of hundred miles down to Norfolk, mainly on A-roads and it feels like a Le Mans, so steady in the corners. It's a cliché, but it really does feel like it's on rails, it's so planted. Really it's the motorcycling equivalent of an old fighter plane, with the V-twin sound and you just sitting in those long bends. It feels like you should have an old flying jacket on and goggles. A delightful feeling and my goodness it's fast, considering its age. My [modern Hinckley] Bonneville often feels like there's a lack of oomph, that it could really do with more power, but I never get that feeling on the Guzzi.

Attention to detail on the Sport extended to a rubber cover for the ignition switch, an underseat light and a hinged rear mudguard to facilitate rear-wheel removal. RICHARD SKELTON

Continued overleaf

RIDING THE BIKES | V7 SPORT

Just 2,643 V7 Sports were built, along with perhaps 200 of their hand-built predecessor, the Telaio Rosso, and 948 of the interim 750S that paved the way for the S3. Yet today they still fetch far less than the equivalent Ducati 750GT (4,133 built) or the later 900SS (over 6,000 built). Indeed, even Moto Guzzi's own first edition Le Mans is almost as valued, despite a production run of over 7,000 units and the fact that the equally numerous Le Mans II is all but identical and often refurbished to look like its predecessor. It is unusual for a motorcycle as rare and important to a marque's history to be so undervalued, so speculators might want to start collecting V7 Sports now in the hope they will follow

Ducati's bevel twins into the 'collector-investor's' consciousness. But that would be a shame, because the V7 Sport is just such a nice bike to ride, as Richard points out.

I think as I get older I'm drawn more and more to the Guzzi V-twins. They feel more relaxed, more enjoyable, than anything else.

In a world that's increasingly frenetic and performance-oriented, a motor vehicle that actually reduces stress levels doesn't seem like a forty-year-old design – it seems bang up to date.

Jan Kampen senior's V7 Sport at the inaugural round of the World Endurance Championship in 1980. Despite being almost a decade old the team finished tenth, making it the only V7 Sport to have won a world championship point. A HERL INC.

total during 1971–72 between 150 and 200 were hand-assembled at Mandello. All very impressive, especially when the new motorcycle went on to prove its worth on the race-circuits. The public's first view of the V7 Sport came when two were entered in the Monza 500km in June 1971, one shared by Vittorio Brambilla and Guido Mandracci, the other by Raimondo Riva and Pierantonio Piazzalunga. The latter pair held second for much of the race and finished third behind two other super-bikes of the day: a Honda CB750 and a Triumph Trident. Later that year, Mandracci and Brambilla took third at the Bol d'Or 24 Hour, despite a breakdown, puncture and crash. Other successes came during 1972–73, including three finishers in the 1972 Imola 200 in the hands of Brambilla, Jack Findlay and Mandracci (8th, 10th and 11th). Factory test-rider Luciano Gazzola, heavily involved not only in the V7 Sport's development but also that of the earlier 750 Special and the forthcoming Le Mans, put in many fine races. Abbondio Sciaresa won the Monza 500 in 1974, but by then the V7 Sport was looking shaky against the competition and development had begun in earnest on what was to become the now legendary Le Mans.

SPECIFICATIONS MOTO GUZZI V7 SPORT (1972–74)

Layout and Chassis

90-degree V-twin four-stroke road-going production motorcycle

Engine

Type	90-degree V-twin
Block material	Aluminium alloy
Head material	Aluminium alloy
Cylinders	2
Cooling	Air
Bore and stroke	82.5 × 70mm
Capacity	748cc
Valves	4 valves ohv
Compression ratio	9.8:1
Carburettor	Twin 30mm Dell'Orto
Max. power	70bhp@7,000rpm
Fuel capacity	5 gallons/22.5 litres

Transmission

Gearbox	Five-speed foot-change
Clutch	Wet multiplate
Final drive	Shaft

Chassis

Front	Telescopic fork
Rear	Swingarm

Steering

Tyres	3.25–18in front, 3.50–18in rear
Brakes	Drums front and rear

Dimensions

Wheelbase	58in (1,470mm)
Unladen weight	453lb (206kg)

Performance

Top speed	125mph (200km/h)

LEFT: **Ernesto Brambilla racing a factory Telaio Rosso in the Vallelunga 500km race near Rome in 1972. He finished second, behind a Laverda SFC.** A HERL INC.

RIGHT: **Twin discs became a V7 Sport option, as did a rear disc eventually. The former were also available as retro-fit items.**

Having helped develop the V7 Sport engine in endurance racing, Jan Kampen Senior was naturally one of the first to employ the new V7 Sport in some of the bigger long-distance races; on more then one occasion beating the official Guzzi factory team. In the 1974 24-hour race at Spa-Francorchamps, for instance, Guzzi's semi-official team included Gazzola and Martinek on an 844cc (the capacity the 850 Le Mans road-bike would inherit) works machine. They finished the race in ninth position, with the Kampen team up in sixth. The second factory entry, Sciaresa and Mulazzani (on another 850), retired with mechanical difficulties. Kampen even built a number of grasstrack-sidecar racers using tuned 750cc V7 Sport engines, winning national championships in Holland and Scandinavia. He stopped entering the V7 Sport in endurance races in 1975, the team's number one bike being converted for street use by Kampen's son. Eventually the motorcycle was parked up and forgotten in the corner of the workshop, until it was announced in 1980 that the first race in the inaugural Endurance Racing World Championship would be at Assen. Tempted by the thought of racing at home, the old Kampen team treated the forgotten motorcycle to a quick once-over, some new fibre-glass bodywork, but left the reliable yet powerful engine as it had been in the road-bike. With a brace of national championship riders aboard, the end result, after eight long, hard hours of racing, was a magnificent tenth place. Kampen's was the first private team to finish, putting a number of factory bikes and riders to shame. Their tenth place also meant a single world championship point, the only world championship point ever awarded to a V7 Sport.

In the early 1970s, the press and public were besotted with the V7 Sport, even if it was 20 per cent more expensive than the already pricey Ambassador and V7 Special, and the most expensive motorcycle on sale in Britain in the days before Harley-Davidson had an official importer. Here was a beautiful sporting motorcycle with a fabulous heritage (the metallic green paintwork a nod to the green chromatic coating Carcano had used on the 1950s racers) and, with a claimed 72bhp, the most powerful motorcycle on sale. Yet the specification also made the Sport potentially an all-day, everyday motorcycle with shaft drive, deeply padded dual seat and 'swan-neck' handlebars that could be set at a touring or racing stance – or anything in-between. Press reports were glowing across the globe, most testers achieving around 125mph (200km/h), significantly quicker than any other 750, including the Kawasaki triple, Honda four and the new twins from Ducati and Laverda. Track times were also superior, despite the Guzzi's comparatively hefty claimed weight of 453lb (206kg), which, when measured wet,

was closer to 503lb (230kg). Clearly Moto Guzzi was on to a winner, although equally clearly the Sport would never be commercially viable if it needed to be hand-built in small numbers. So for 1972, the design was productionized with a steel frame painted black for Europe and, initially, silver elsewhere, a new gearbox identified by external ribbing and assembly on a production line. This precluded the hand-finishing of various engine components on the original Telaio Rosso, although Guzzi did not admit to any reduction in power. Otherwise the Sport was much as before, even gaining indicators for the United States versions and, despite being priced as a premium product, over 2,000 were sold in 1972 alone. Having spent the 1960s building cheap little commuter bikes, and in the process allowing the world to forget Moto Guzzi's glorious racing history, suddenly motorcycle magazines around the world were heaping praise on the V7 Sport, as both the ultimate sportster and all-round big bike. On the back of this came retrospectives on Guzzi's history, in general, and the sonorous V8 racer of the late 1950s, in particular. Carcano's dream of building the ultimate road-going motorcycle looked to have been realized, and once again Moto Guzzi were regarded as serious bike-builders by enthusiasts.

Updating the Earlier Twins and De Tomaso's Arrival

Alongside the V7 Sport, the original 'loop-frame' was developed to share many of the Sport's engine upgrades, notably gaining the five-speed gearbox that made the most of the relaxed longer stroke engine, now displacing 844cc and giving 65bhp. Weight went up by 30lb (14kg), despite adopting the lighter ribbed crankcases of the Sport, although there were now also indicators. Encouraged by the United States importers, the famous Berliner brothers, who also acted for Ducati, North America accounted for half of Guzzi's V-twin sales. This was acknowledged by naming what Europeans bought as an 850GT, 'Eldorado' for the American market. The name resonated there as the mythical city made of gold, based on a Mexican story about a gilded chief; the word is Spanish for 'golden one'. Raising the capacity to 844cc also allowed Guzzi to compete for US police force contracts, and when they started usurping Harley-Davidsons as the police department's motorcycle of choice, people took notice. Although a large motorcycle by European standards, the Eldorado was a lightweight compared to the Harley Electra Glide it competed against, which was around 220lb (100kg) heavier than the Guzzi. This made the

Guzzi far wieldier than the Harley in cities, yet it was just as comfortable and adept at carrying the usual paraphernalia of a police motorcycle. The Eldorado also performed on a par with the new superbikes: *Motorcyclist* magazine discovered that in third-gear roll-ons, the Eldorado would romp away from BSA's new Rocket Three, despite the British 750 triple weighing 10 per cent less. Demand for a civilian version of these Harleyesque police bikes, with their black and white colour scheme and touring accoutrements, led to the California, a name today still applied to the latest and largest Moto Guzzi. Between them, the V7 Special/Ambassador and 850GT/Eldorado/California accounted for a production run of almost 18,000 motorcycles between 1968 and 1974.

It was this that brought famed motor industry entrepreneur Alejandro De Tomaso on to the scene in 1972, attracted by the sales of the V-twin, especially these older 'loop-frame' versions that were being bought in large numbers by both the Italian and American public sector. These sales and cash flow, along with Moto Guzzi's production facilities, made the firm an attractive addition to De Tomaso's portfolio. Guzzi's current proprietors, the state-owned SEIMM, believed the factory was now back on an even keel and their job was done, so they were only too happy to sell Moto Guzzi back into the private sector. De Tomaso had already acquired control of Benelli from the Benelli family in 1971, shortly after the factory had won the 1969 250 World Championship. Kel Caruthers had been the surprise victor after Benelli's number one rider, Renzo Pasolini, suffered a series of mishaps. Pasolini and Mike Hailwood, riders who enjoyed a tremendous international fan base, had also raced a 4-cylinder Benelli 500 in the 1968 World Championship. These factors ensured that the Benelli name was known and admired the world over, even if its sole big road-bike, the 650cc parallel twin Tornado, offered little to differentiate it from British twins and less performance than cheaper Japanese motorcycles. De Tomaso was thinking on a grand scale, talking of poaching Giacomo Agostini from MV Agusta to race a new Benelli 500 four, which would spawn a road-going 750, although nothing came of such bravado. Nonetheless it was fine publicity and spoke of De Tomaso's belief that the world-wide boom in motorcycle sales was something Italy could – and should – take a share of. In his mind this would involve following the Japanese model of investment in automation and moving away from exotic, low-volume, manufacturing. This latter course, he believed, was a dangerous path to tread, relying upon constant innovation in order to stay ahead of the Japanese. These were the days before the widespread acceptance of premium brands, where consumers were happy to pay extra in order to be

associated with a particular product; these were the days when consumers expected endless improvement and ever keener value for money. De Tomaso was not alone in thinking that a wide range of motorcycles with something for everyone was the future. Gerald Davison of Honda UK from 1968 until 1985, and a friend of Soichiro Honda, also felt the motorcycle industry was in danger of chasing the performance-oriented buyer, rather than offering a broad range of motorcycles that attracted new people into the sport. In the late 1960s, the Italian industry was so small that it wasn't even on Honda's radar, and Davison considered the British industry beaten. His view was that the only way the British, never mind the Italian, motorcycle industry could be saved was by going niche. This was something Harley-Davidson eventually realized with great success, although by the time they adopted this strategy, in the 1980s, the idea of premium brands was well-understood by business and consumers. However, there is no guarantee becoming a niche player would have worked in the 1970s, when even Harley were still trying to expand into the smaller classes by building two-stroke motorcycles in Italy for export.

There were certainly those at Moto Guzzi who felt that going niche was the answer, and that developing the V7 Sport as the premier sporting motorcycle for the discerning and moneyed enthusiast was a good place to start. So in 1972, hot on the heels of the 844cc version of the V7 Sports' success at the Le Mans Bol d'Or, a road-going replica was announced. Unsurprisingly, this development of the Sport was to be called 'Le Mans' and was first shown to the public in late 1972. With an engine upgraded to 844cc, visually it was a V7 Sport with a half fairing, 40mm carburettors, humped seat and triple disc-brakes. It was the brakes that provided the greatest innovation, being linked so that one front disc operated in harmony with the rear disc, controlled by the foot brake via a hydraulic splitter. When disc brakes first appeared, there was concern that the front brake would be too easy to lock, especially by a less-experienced rider in tricky conditions. This was especially true of motorcycles like the Guzzi V-twin with a low centre of gravity, where weight transfer tended to push the front wheel along, rather than compressing the front forks and increasing front tyre grip. However, at the time a low centre of gravity was still considered essential for a sporting motorcycle. Tonti's inspired solution to the potential braking issues this raised was to spread the braking force across both tyres.

When De Tomaso took control of Moto Guzzi during 1973 he was unconvinced that this uprated V7 Sport, innovative or not, merited putting into production, still believing that volume production was the only way to save the Italian motorcycle

Luciano Gazzola, Tonti's main tester, in a secret development trial of the 844cc Le Mans. This prototype was based on a Telaio Rosso. A HERL INC.

industry. While De Tomaso was happy to take the income from sales of the touring V-twins, the thousand or so annual sales the new Le Mans might generate would take up a valuable production line. In any event, he felt motorcycles with big twin-cylinder engines would be unable to compete in the 1970s marketplace. Travelling the world he saw people buying Japanese multi-cylinder motorcycles, and talking with excitement about their link to the race-track. Riders had for years pleaded with MV Agusta to build a road-going version of their 4-cylinder racers, something the proud Count Agusta refused to do until it was too late to fend off the Japanese. When a road-going MV Agusta 750 four finally went on sale in 1971, it was more than twice the price of the Honda equivalent and, even backed by the most evocative name in motorcycling, failed to sell as well as hoped. This was further proof to De Tomaso that he need-

ed to price his motorcycles at a level comparable to the Japanese. Yet he believed MV Agusta had one thing right, and that was to offer a range of motorcycles that evoked images of racing – motorcycles like the Benelli fours and the Honda sixes.

De Tomaso certainly intended his motorcycle production to be profitable and one of the attractions to him of Moto Guzzi was their huge factory, a far cry from Benelli's city centre facilities in the heart of Pesaro on Italy's eastern coast. There was, in De Tomaso's eyes, no reason to keep developing the Moto Guzzi V-twins, which were expensive to build and looked dated up against motorcycles coming out of Japan. Instead De Tomaso planned to badge a new range of multi-cylinder motorcycles as Moto Guzzis and Benellis, allegedly walking through the Guzzi factory immediately after he'd bought it and waving a sword while shouting 'No more stupid twins'.

RIDING THE BIKES | **850GT**

Surely the spiritual genesis of the new California 1400, the 850GT is big, heavy and a cosseting softy to ride. Brian Rogers test-rode a V7 that so impressed, the owner promptly changed his mind about selling it. Undeterred, he tracked down an 850GT instead.

Brian had already owned and sold two Moto Guzzi 850T3s by the time he sampled the V7 (the original tourer, not to be confused with Tonti's far sportier V7 Sport), but Brian was seduced by the more glamorous styling of the earlier models. Like so many Guzzi owners, he'd become disenchanted with Ducati, and in 2010 decided that his brace of Guzzi singles left enough space in the garage for another V-twin. 'I like the V7 and 850GT because they're nice and low: I'm quite short but I can easily get both feet on the ground, which is not that usual with such a big, comfortable, soft bike.' Brian also likes the originality of his GT, right down to the first supplying dealer's sticker on the mudguard. He's changed the indicators for the sake of more certain signalling and had the clutch rebuilt: a goodly proportion of the 35,169km on the odometer was accumulated by the previous owner, a family man with a sidecar, which did little for the Guzzi's usually robust clutch. Other than that the bike is exactly as it left Mandello in 1972, changed only in appearance by the patina of a life well-lived.

Brian's very happy with the way his GT rides and handles, and is even defensive about the big drum front brake: 'They're very good if they're properly set up, but they do have to be properly set up – it is a heavy bike. But I'll admit they take some getting used to if you're used to disc brakes. It is a surprisingly fast bike.'

Brian's GT was imported from Italy some years ago. It seems the original V7 and 850 never found their way to the UK when new, officially at least, and contemporary road tests in British magazines were imported from the United States. But then Moto Guzzi hadn't had much luck selling their lightweights in Britain, and their biggest offerings would have most probably been the most expensive motorcycles on sale in the UK, as the V7 Sport was when it finally arrived on UK roads. The British motorcycle manufacturers were still dominant in the home market, and even Harley-Davidson only managed to sell in the UK thanks to the enthusiasm of Warr's on the King's Road, who had been the spiritual home of Harley in the UK since 1924. One British magazine, when testing a V7 in 1971, wrote incredulously of a suggested asking price of over £900, feeling that even at £750 it would seem expensive against the competition: British and Japanese 750s were nearer to £600. Indeed the early 1970s were when those in the know were beginning to suspect the game was up for any motorcycle manufacturers based outside Japan, as the British industry turned multi-million pound profits into multi-million pound losses, and sales of Japanese motorcycles exceeded 8 million a year. Who would have guessed that Moto Guzzi would not only succeed in selling the V7 and 850GT, but that over forty years later would launch the new California 1400 to equal acclaim, this time accompanied by a belief that the bike would sell well, despite an unashamedly upmarket price tag.

An original California spotted in the UK with a pass for Swiss roads on the screen.

SPECIFICATIONS MOTO GUZZI 850GT (1971–74)

Layout and Chassis

90-degree V-twin four-stroke road-going production motorcycle

Engine

Type	90-degree V-twin
Block material	Aluminium alloy
Head material	Aluminium alloy
Cylinders	2
Cooling	Air
Bore and stroke	83 × 78mm
Capacity	844cc
Valves	4 valves ohv
Compression ratio	9.2:1
Carburettor	Twin 29mm Dell'Orto
Max. power	64bhp@6,500rpm
Fuel capacity	5 gallons/22.5 litres

Transmission

Gearbox	Five-speed foot-change
Clutch	Wet multiplate
Final drive	Shaft

Chassis

Front	Telescopic fork
Rear	Swingarm

Steering

Tyres	4.00–18in front, 4.00–18in rear
Brakes	Drums front and rear

Dimensions

Wheelbase	58in (1,470mm)
Unladen weight	517lb (235kg)

Performance

Top speed	112mph (180km/h)

The current V7 range seeks to mimic the look of the V7 Sport, but is based on Tonti's later 'small-block' engine.

MOTO GUZZI

CHAPTER FIVE

DE TOMASO AND DIVERSIFICATION

Having declared publicly and repeatedly that the future of Moto Guzzi was with a range of Japanese-style two- and four-stroke multi-cylinder motorcycles, the reasons for De Tomaso's prompt U-turn remain something of a mystery. For not only did the V-twins remain in production, they continued to be developed and the range extended. At least De Tomaso's change of heart seems odd, until you look at what was happening at Benelli at the time, and learn that all the Benelli four-strokes were actually built in the Moto Guzzi factory at Mandello del Lario. Similarly, all the 'Moto Guzzi' two-strokes from this era were designed and built at the Benelli factory in Pesaro. The plan was to develop this 'badge engineering' and mass produce near-identical models with different brand identities, as was normal in the car world De Tomaso had come from. Both Benelli and Moto Guzzi still had significant brand values, especially in Italy, with Moto Guzzi the higher profile, particularly overseas. So De Tomaso intended to build the four-strokes in the Moto Guzzi factory at Mandello del Lario, providing the Guzzi-badged bikes with a marginally higher specification (and higher retail price) than the Benelli equivalents. Similarly, all the two-stroke models would be built down at Pesaro, regardless of the tank badge they would ultimately wear. So about this time the Moto Guzzi story becomes inextricably linked with the Benelli story, which in turn plays a big part in the De Tomaso story.

Alejandro De Tomaso divided opinions like no-one else in the Italian motor industry. Some saw him as a modernizer who saved the Italians from themselves, but others claimed he was an asset-stripper who took government cash to replace workers with robots and feather his own nest. In the 1970s, he had owned Maserati, Ghia and his own eponymous sports car business, which allowed him to forge strong links with Ford, both in the USA and in Italy. Yet it was the Italian motorcycle industry he saw the greatest potential in, and

by the second half of the 1970s, was building 80 per cent of Italian motorcycles.

Born in 1928 to wealthy parents, De Tomaso's father was an Italian expatriate who had married into a moneyed Argentinean ranching family. De Tomaso senior's political nous allowed him to rise to become a minister in the Argentinean Government, only to die of a heart attack at the age of thirty-eight. This forced De Tomaso junior into leaving school at fifteen; he was expected to learn the family cattle business, but his passions lay elsewhere. Time away from the ranch usually involved racing cars or supporting an underground organization opposed to President Juan Peron. When an attempt to overthrow Peron was unsuccessful in 1955, De Tomaso looked implicated and fled to his father's homeland, Italy. Settling in Modena, a city between Bologna and Milan – the heart of Italy's motor industry – De Tomaso found work as a mechanic for Maserati. It didn't take him long to get himself a drive, racing for Maserati and OSCA. De Tomaso worked his way up to Formula One, marrying fellow racer and American heiress Elizabeth Haskell on the way. By 1959, he'd founded De Tomaso cars, which would go on to build the legendary Pantera, a car that combined Italian mid-engine style with America V8 reliability. The Pantera had its detractors, but that didn't stop Agostini owning one. Other four-wheeled ventures included buying coachbuilders Ghia, then infamously selling the name to Ford to denote a trim level on rather ordinary mass-produced cars. De Tomaso also rescued Maserati in 1975 with Italian Government assistance. Finance was often raised via his wealthy wife (having changed her name to the rather more Latin Isabelle) and her brother Amory. Those who met De Tomaso talk of a quiet, diminutive man with a charming ability to enthuse listeners and persuade doubters. In fact those who met both men comment that the person Claudio Castiglioni, who resurrected Ducati and MV Agusta, most reminded them of was De

Tomaso. And like Castiglioni, De Tomaso knew how to generate publicity. De Tomaso also spoke English fluently, something virtually unheard of in the Italian motorcycle industry at the time. The lack of English speakers, the language of most world markets, in the Italian motorcycle industry might partly explain why Italian factories were less reliant on overseas sales than the British industry. Italian manufacturers instead focused on a protected home market that limited imports to just 2,000 small-capacity motorcycles a year, barely 1 per cent of the demand. There were then steep tax barriers at 350 and again at 500cc, which meant that if the Italian industry was to expand into the bourgeoning big-bike market, they would have to focus on exporting as never before. But in the meantime they were almost immune to the Japanese, whose business model focused on building a reputation with small-capacity motorcycles that would generate a brand loyalty in riders, as they

A later 254, the first 4-cylinder 250 road bike. Like all the multi-cylinder 4-stroke badged as Moto Guzzi or Benelli it was built at the Mandello del Lario factory.

worked their way onto ever-larger models. De Tomaso saw huge possibilities in this concept and so, after selling many of his interests in the car industry, he moved into motorcycling.

4-Cylinder Racers and Road-Bikes

After buying 85 per cent of Benelli (the remainder stayed with the family) in 1971, De Tomaso almost immediately announced he would pay Giacomo Agostini 70 million lira if he would leave MV Agusta and race for Benelli. This was outrageous at the time, both in terms of the amount of money and the fact the offer was made as a public statement, but it was pure De Tomaso. A new racing 500 was shown to prove De Tomaso's intent, although sceptics believed it was a prototype that Benelli had been developing for some time. The promised road-going version was shown in 1973, just two years later, and Walter Villa raced an updated version of the double-overhead cam Benelli 350 four in the Italian Grand Prix at Monza the same year. But that was to be Benelli's final Grand Prix appearance, and the road-going 500 four looked to have no connection to the glorious Benelli racers of the past. In fact doubters pointed out that, with its single overhead camshaft, the new Benelli motor looked suspiciously like the Honda 500 Four engine that had arrived in 1971. Indeed, unusually for an Italian manufacturer, nothing was said of who designed the engine, instead much fuss was made of the fact that the styling of the new Benelli was by Paolo Martin of Ghia. Despite an impressive track-record with cars, Martin's work on motorcycles was less warmly received, although De Tomaso would stick with him for many subsequent Moto Guzzis, including the early Tonti-framed V-twin tourers and the Nuovo Falcone, probably because of Ford and De Tomaso's links to Ghia. The new Benelli 500 was also slightly underwhelming because instead of the fashionable front disc-brake sported by the Honda, there was an old-fashioned and costly Grimeca drum at the front of the Benelli, although this was probably more useful in the days when Japanese disc-brakes could be less than effective, especially in the rain. When the press tested the Benelli, with a simple '500 Quattro' (500 Four) graphic on the side-panel that even mimicked the '500 Four' logo on the Honda, the similarities were marked. The Benelli might have handled and stopped better than the Honda, but then it was a good deal more expensive. De Tomaso's plans to compete with the Japanese on price seemed to have been quietly shelved. Alongside the Benelli, a 350 four was launched, badged as a Moto Guzzi

350GTS. But like the Benelli Quattro, the 350GTS suffered poor sales and was perceived as an expensive re-imagining of the Honda equivalent. The historic names and taxation system undoubtedly helped these motorcycles sell in Italy, but overseas such things meant little or nothing. The superior dynamics of the bikes convinced some enthusiasts to pay a premium over the Japanese equivalents, but this was a time when straight-line performance was the most important aspect of a motorcycle's repertoire, closely followed by unquestionable reliability. These were things the Japanese understood well, and their model development followed these two rubrics above all others. So while the traditional, club-like, European and American motorcycle manufacturers tried to make do and mend with existing designs, while asking whether they could afford to develop completely new motorcycles that buyers might reject, the Japanese asked why not build the bikes your market research suggests will sell?

De Tomaso was almost alone outside Japan in both understanding this and being prepared to do something about it. He regularly gave interviews in English on his views and the problems the European motorcycle industry faced, which he felt varied from manufacturer to manufacturer. When he bought Benelli they had, in De Tomaso's words:

> *Big problems, but it was difficult to isolate them. The Japanese onslaught had destroyed the morale of too many people. The first thing I did was to change some personnel, then I spent money on equipment. I instructed the design of new models, 4-cylinder engines up to 500cc, and 6-cylinder for 750 and 900cc.*

Accusations that the bikes were straight copies of old Hondas were not countenanced:

> *Benelli was the first manufacturer to produce a four in 1938, so charges of plagiarism should be directed at Japan, not Benelli.*

In fact Belgian firm FN built a four in 1905, albeit fitted into the frame longitudinally, an idea taken up by Indian in 1928. Yet Benelli had shown a transverse 4-cylinder supercharged racer in 1939 (the war meant it was never raced), so De Tomaso did have a point. And his designers' modular approach, with many shared parts, was revolutionary. It also allowed, along with taking inspiration from the Honda 500 Four's engine, the team to produce a range of production-ready engines in a very short timescale. While certainly similar in many aspects to the Honda

Vittorio Fossatti of the Fossatti hotel aboard a Moto Guzzi 350GTS. His pillion passenger was a photographer for the Giro d'Italia bicycle race.
FOSSATTI HOTEL

500 Four, there were many differences in detail, which either proves that the Italian designers wanted to create something new and improved, or frustrates latter-day restorers wishing that the readily available Honda parts would fit the now classic Benelli multis.

Trying to Upstage the Japanese – the 6-Cylinder Italian Superbike

The smaller and middleweight motorcycles were essential for the lucrative and sheltered Italian home market, but overseas sales would need something far more adventurous. And so in late 1972 De Tomaso introduced a wide-eyed public to the world's first production 6-cylinder motorcycle, simply badged as the Benelli 750 Sei (Six). As soon as he'd gained control of Moto Guzzi, his intention was to produce an all but identical Moto Guzzi version, and the 6-cylinder prototype Sei with

Keith Martin, who won the 1974 500
production TT aboard a Kawasaki Mach I
for UK importers Agrati. When Agrati became
Benelli (but not Moto Guzzi) importers they
entered Keith in the 1975 TT on a Sei that was
surprisingly close to the standard model seen here.

Moto Guzzi badges has made guest appearances in the factory's Mandello del Lario museum. Some production Seis were also badged as MotoBis, the breakaway Benelli brother's trademark that was eventually absorbed back into the fold after developing a loyal following for a range of small-capacity, horizontal, singles not unlike mini-Moto Guzzis.

The Sei was to be, in De Tomaso's eyes, the premier Italian sporting motorcycle, selling on a world stage as a serious competitor to the Japanese, yet almost as soon as it was in production De Tomaso inexplicably returned to developing the V-twins as Moto Guzzi's future. The popular version of events is that Lino Tonti persuaded De Tomaso to stick with the twins for the Moto Guzzi brand, but a few simple facts challenge that story as incomplete, at least. Like much of Europe, Italy was fraught with industrial strife during the 1970s, and unusually for the Mandello del Lario factory, casting of the new Sei's cylinder head had been contracted out. Strikes delayed production, and although the Sei should otherwise have been on sale in 1973, in both Benelli and Moto Guzzi guises, instead near-complete 750s sat in Mandello del Lario, frustrating De Tomaso's attempt to gain credibility in America. It would be late 1974 before the Sei reached the United States, and 1975

Keith on the Sei in the 1975 Senior TT.
The non-standard pipes made a big
difference to performance, but other
than the bodywork the Sei is standard.
KEITH MARTIN

Keith in the production race, although the standard
pipes are hidden. Ground clearance was a major
problem. Keith never raced a Benelli again, although
Joey Dunlop did, including a Sei at the 1979 TT.
KEITH MARTIN

by the time the British importers could launch the bike in a blaze of publicity that included providing up-and-coming TT racer Joey Dunlop with a Sei to race on the Isle of Man. Sadly he failed to finish, with a broken crankshaft, a well-known problem with early Seis, caused by a manufacturing fault. But even if Joey had won, it seems unlikely it would have helped the Sei much, because between its public debut in 1972 and the Sei arriving in showrooms, the world of superbikes had changed beyond recognition.

When Honda launched the CB750 Four in 1969, it wasn't just European manufacturers who were taken aback. In Japan, Kawasaki had been on the cusp of launching their own 750, an even more outrageous device than the Honda with double overhead-camshafts atop 4-cylinders, just like Grand Prix racers. But instead of relying upon the superior specification to push Honda from the top step of the sales podium, Kawasaki upped the capacity to 903cc to launch the 130mph Z1 in 1973. Rumour had it that they secretly tested a 1000cc version with a US focus group, but feedback made Kawasaki decide that even for the power-obsessed Americans this was excessive. It also left Kawasaki something in the bag for a model update in 1977. Ironically, the Benelli Sei was designed to be upgraded to 900cc, but road-tests reported that smoke escaping from the silencers when the throttle was closed after high-speed runs was attributable to crankcase pressure caused by a design optimized for a capacity greater than 750cc. Unfortunately De Tomaso didn't sanction this upgrade until 1980, possibly wanting to be sure the Seis' crankshaft and gearbox failures were dealt with first.

By the time it was readily available, the 750 Sei had plenty of competition that hadn't been on the market when it was conceived. Tested at 124mph (198km/h), the Sei was not much faster than the Honda it was expected to comprehensively out-perform, especially given that the Italian motorcycle was dangerously close to twice the price of its oriental competitor in export markets. On the test strip, the Sei was trounced by the Z1, which was 25 per cent cheaper, even if the Kawasaki was dynamically inferior. Even Ducati's new 860GT was significantly cheaper, ironically also suffering poor sales due to unappreciated styling by another car-design studio, Giorgio Giugiaro's Italdesign. In fact, at the Sei's launch, only two other readily available motorcycles were more expensive: BMW's new R90S, with its distinctive handlebar fairing and smoked paintwork; and Moto Guzzi's latest sporting V-twin, the 750S3.

Despite De Tomaso's optimism, investment and best efforts, by the time the 750 Sei was replaced by the 900, barely more than 3,000 had been built. Although no sales targets were ever made public, De Tomaso's stated intention was to double production at Mandello del Lario by replacing the V-twins with the fours and sixes. Given that 3,791 V7 Sports and 11,806 850GT/Ambasadors were sold during this time, it seems reasonable that a figure in the region of 30,000 fours and sixes must have been the aim. Even the futuristically styled Moto Guzzi and Benelli 250 four (another world first) failed to sell, and occasionally these are still found in their original shipping crates. By any measure, despite being fine motorcycles, the Sei and smaller fours were a sales disappointment, and possibly a disaster that would have killed Moto Guzzi had the V-twins not continued to sell.

De Tomaso Plans for the Future with V-Twins

When De Tomaso arrived at Moto Guzzi, he believed it had few principal failings. Certainly he spoke of a lack of new models and ideas, especially in terms of styling. Moto Guzzi, De Tomaso decided, needed a stronger image. He claimed to change little other than to promote some people, but that was all. Yet even today, purists view De Tomaso with suspicion and contempt, especially his replacing the V7 Sport with the 750S and then S3 to slash production costs. But De Tomaso loved the Italian motor industry and loathed the Japanese, believing their reliance on exporting from a low-wage economy to a much more affluent Europe was a threat to a way of life. 'The Italian motorcycle industry is more powerful than the British ever were' he once boasted, 'but the Japanese are huge.' De Tomaso planned a new automated factory in Milan:

> ...run by robots – you don't have to pay wages, you don't have to pay for medical assistance and social security, all these things. Don't get me wrong, I approve of all this socialist legislation [despite often giving the impression he didn't] but it makes us uncompetitive... all the time the Japanese worker is working fifteen hours a day... but I don't want to work fifteen hours a day. So I want to see more import controls, not just in Italy, but in the EEC [now European Union]. It will make things more expensive, but will pay for our civilized social system.

Some of his remarks are disingenuous, and reflect the fact that most people had no idea of the investment in modern factories that was taking place in Japan, as had already been reported back to a sleepwalking British motorcycle industry by famous

Triumph designer Edward Turner. There was also Honda's declared policy of spending 2 per cent of its phenomenal turnover every year on research and development, something the European industry had almost forgotten about. Even so, in Italy detractors still felt De Tomaso was merely a wealthy man trying to get wealthier on the back of the Italian Government. For those doubters, bearing in mind the lack of investment in the UK during that time, De Tomaso's views on the death throes of the British industry make interesting reading.

If you [a government] give money to a company to buy more equipment and to produce in a more competitive way, I approve of that. But if you give money just to keep them treading water, just to keep alive, and they lose money on every single bike, then I'm against that.

That last remark might have also been a dig at Ducati, De Tomaso's biggest competitor in his home market, whose bevel-driven V-twins might have been magnificent motorcycles, but

The V7 S that replaced the Sport had twin front discs as standard, but a standard rear disc had to wait for the linked triple discs of the later S3.

were heavily subsidized by state grants and Ducati's own range of diesel engines. However, alongside the failure of the Sei and the lacklustre sales of the smaller fours, to prove De Tomaso's pragmatism – undoubtedly aided by some persuasion from head engineer Tonti – the V-twin range was rationalized, improved and left in production to fight another day. The loop-frame went and, in an act of brilliant rationalization, the superior Tonti frame was fitted across the range. The gear drive to the Sport's camshaft and oil pump was replaced by a chain, and the linkages to the gear shift were altered both to make them cheaper to produce and easy to change to the left-foot gearshift required in the USA from 1974 onwards. Ostensibly a safety measure that introduced consistency to the market, the American legislation was a thinly-veiled attempt to protect Harley-Davidson from British imports. Traditionally, European motorcycles had the gear-change on the right, but Harley-Davidson fitted them on the left; inevitably, European manufacturers had to follow suit, often via a less than elegant array of rods and linkages that did little for the smooth operation of the gearbox. However, this belated attempt by the US Government to protect its last remaining large-scale motorcycle manufacturer failed to recognize that by 1974, the fortunes of the British motorcycle industry were on the wane and the new challengers now came from Japan. In particular, from motorcycles such as the Honda fours and the Kawasaki Z1, which, like all Japanese motorcycles, had a left-foot gear-change as standard.

Fortunately, the design of the Moto Guzzi V-twin's car-style gearbox made adapting it for left- or right-foot gear-changing straightforward, which allowed European purists to keep their beloved 'racing' layout, while American's could have their Guzzi with left-foot shift. And although those same European purists grumbled that the later Sports were less exotic than the original Telaio Rosso, they were still outstanding motorcycles. The initial replacement for the V7 Sport was labelled the 750S and, despite suffering from plans to cut costs and double production, it was still superior to the final 750, the 1975 S3, which was in reality little more than a sleeved-down version of Moto Guzzi's 850T3 tourer with sportier styling. Indeed, the concept of keeping the S3's capacity at the original Sport's 748cc seemed perverse, when racing versions had run the T3's 844cc displacement since 1972. Despite this, and all the cost-cutting, the S3 was still one of the most expensive motorcycles on sale, particularly if you discount the almost unobtainable MV Agustas and – in Europe, at least – Harley-Davidsons. Only the BMW R90S was more expensive, yet road-tests were still full of praise, even if failure to match the Japanese and Germans in fit and finish, as well as switchgear, highlighted areas Guzzi

Another Police California, this time a T3 version, showing how close these were to production models. MOTO GUZZI

Remarkably original T3 California, now with the Tonti V7 Sport frame that allowed rationalization of the production lines as well as much improved handling.

would need to improve upon if they were to survive the relentless updating of Japanese motorcycles.

Broadening the appeal of the Moto Guzzi range could not simply involve phasing out the old loop-frame tourers, but

meant introducing a new range of V-twins with the frame from the V7 Sport. Not only did this reduce production costs and rationalize the range – again, a practice widespread in the car industry but rare with motorcycles – it led to Guzzi tourers that were exceptionally comfortable motorcycles, with handling comparable to the finest sports bikes. The best-selling T3 (nearly 12,000 built over a twelve-year run) was a 1975 update of the 850T (Interceptor in the USA), which had first married the Sport's Tonti-designed frame to a flexible 844cc update of the GT/Eldorado's engine. An excellent specification created a motorcycle that promised the reliability and simplicity of a BMW, with the traditional sporting prowess expected of Italian motor vehicles. The only shortcomings noted by testers of the 850T were the rather overworked single front disc, and less than inspiring styling, again by Ghia. The T3 introduced a California version to address the latter criticism, along with the triple-linked discs, which had first been shown on the 844cc Le Mans prototype in 1972. This was another Tonti innovation that provided for the footbrake to operate not only the rear disc, but also one of the front discs, making locking the front wheel almost impossible, despite motorcycles becoming heavier and their brakes more powerful. The front brake-lever operated the second front-disc and, although the system is often returned to the traditional front/rear control on Moto Guzzi's of this era by today's owners, at the time it was widely praised, particularly by the specialist press. More than anything it shows how innovative Tonti and De Tomaso were prepared to be. With a fine sales record that proved the multi-cylinder

engines had been a blind alley (5,300 850Ts were sold in its single year of production), Tomaso was persuaded that there was plenty of room for V-twins in Guzzi's future and gave the green light to the Le Mans.

The Magnificent Le Mans

Seen in the flesh and ridden on the road it seems unbelievable that the Le Mans stared out as a cost-cutting exercise, intended to be cheaper to build than the V7 Sport. Little more than the T3's 844cc barrels (with cast iron rather than chrome liners) plus 10.2:1 pistons yielded a big jump in performance. Despite the Le Mans even keeping the T3's touring specification cam profile, magazine testers regularly broke the 130mph (210km/h) barrier, an unbelievable figure in 1976, especially given that magazines were now using electronic timing equipment and exposing manufacturer's over-optimistic claims. It was, however, the styling that made the Le Mans a phenomenon. In essence an S3, a pretty enough but hardly groundbreaking update of the Sport by Paolo Martin of Ghia, the Le Mans was, for many, simply the best-looking motorcycle available. First shown at the 1975 Milan show, for the first time in a while, Moto Guzzi offered no styling credits and, rationally, little was changed.

Later version of the original Le Mans, identified by the separate tail light and dual seat. These seats had the 'cover' bonded to the foam and so it is rare to see an original item like this one today.

RIDING THE BIKES | LE MANS 850

August 1976 was key in forming the opinions of a certain generation of British Moto Guzzi fans: it was the issue of *Bike* magazine that featured an up and coming photographer's image of the original Le Mans alongside the strapline 'Falling in love again'. Richard Skelton was among those smitten.

Bob Carlos Clarke was a mature student when he was persuaded to do some photography for *Bike* magazine to bolster his portfolio. He would go on to create some of the strongest images of women during the 1980s and beyond, most frequently being compared favourably to Helmet Newton. After variously trying out journalism, the London College of Printing and gaining an MA at the Royal College of Art, he started as a photographer, simply to meet women. His uniquely voyeuristic style soon made him a hit with magazines and, years before Photoshop, he was fascinated by the possibilities of manipulating images. And that is where his Moto Guzzi Le Mans photograph comes in. Featuring a female rider at rest, goggles pushed up and a leopard skin one-piece outfit artfully cut back, the model stares into the distance as if contemplating the ride ahead. She seems oblivious to the camera or the fact that she seems to have stopped the Le Mans in a wood, in the dead of night.

Carlos Clarke hand-tinted the negative of this already striking image until it looked like nothing else, and certainly not the usual chap-on-a-motorcycle imagery that magazines typically used. Although, in theory, he could have applied these ideas to any motorcycle, he didn't, and the dark and oddly moving image perfectly suited the Le Mans, the black of night flowing from the matt black features that were unique to the Le Mans. The bight red paintwork – again, pretty much unique in the metalflake 1970s – was also used as a sample for an unearthly luminescence that lit the scene. This was underground press and album cover art in a

mainstream motorcycle magazine. No wonder so many people remember it. Not least Richard Skelton:

I had always been a Ducati fan. A friend's older brother had a 750GT. A lift on the back of that was almost a religious experience and I would sit in science lessons doodling orange Desmo singles in schoolbooks. Then in the summer of 1976 when I was counting down the days until I could get an FS1-E [Yamaha sports moped] I got [the August issue of] Bike magazine one day and went up to my room to read it. There was a Le Mans test in it and I can remember being transfixed by the Bob Carlos Clarke picture, and reading the test again and again. I kept returning to it. It was just such a stunning looking motorcycle. Arguably the best looking bike of the seventies along with the Ducati 900SS. I was 23 before I owned one; I'd been to the TT on my Honda 400 Four and on the Mountain the bigger bikes would overtake, weaving; but the Italians were rock steady and I fancied I'd be doing the same. When I saw a Le Mans for sale in Motor Cycle News in York it was just twenty miles from where I was living. I took a friend along who was a mechanic and did the deal.

Naturally it was an original red Le Mans. 'I stopped in a lay-by on the way home just to look at it,' grins Richard.

The Bob Carlos Clarke Le Mans photograph that appeared in *Bike* magazine and changed so many young men's view of Moto Guzzi.

SADLY THE ESTATE HAS YET TO DIGITIZE BOB'S EARLY WORK, BUT LATER IMAGES ARE AVAILABLE AS LIMITED EDITION GICLÉE PRINTS AT BOBCARLOSCLARKE.COM

Continued overleaf

RIDING THE BIKES | **LE MANS 850**

To ride, it was very low; and hard work. You had to be positive; put into a corner and then pull it back out. But while it was leaned over it felt absolutely solid; as if you could take your hands off the handlebars, just fantastic. You couldn't change gear quickly — well, you could but you needed everything to be just right, so it was better to take your time. But because there was so much torque it didn't really matter. Having said that, it wasn't the complete shock it might have been coming straight from a Japanese machine because I'd had a Triumph Bonneville before.

My best memories are riding it on the TT circuit to a Guzzi owner's club meeting, a really fast ride with two other Le Mans in tow. By the time we got to Glen Helen there must have been thirty or forty Le Mans parked up. And another time, I was on the M62 keeping a steady 100 for mile after mile, able to do that because it was a Sunday morning and traffic was light when I suddenly sensed all was not well and looked behind to see a police car. I rolled it off gradually but the copper pulled me and asked what speed I'd been doing. I said it was hard to say because these Italian instruments are all over the place. He said he was an ex-police motorcyclist and the Guzzi was a lovely bike. He looked it over admiringly and told me it had been a nice steady ton and then he said: 'Just slow down a bit and watch out for idiots in Allegros changing lanes without indicating. Off you go.' As he was getting back in his car I said cheerfully that the speedo was pretty accurate after all. He froze for several seconds with one leg in the car. Then he shook his head, sat down and closed the door. I was glad to slip away.

After five or six years I sold it for a Yamaha FJ1200 for two-up touring. And then I owned another one, it must have been twenty years later. It's worth saying that both were completely reliable and ownership was totally hassle free. And they're still fabulous looking bikes.

The re-styling actually amounted to little more than a new seat, side-panels, headlamp cowl and paintwork to create one of the most handsome motorcycles of all time. The silky black lowlights on the tank top and silencers made the chrome and metalflake, which had defined the first-half of the 1970s, look suddenly dated. Yet these were apparently born of necessity as Pat Slinn, then service manger of the UK Moto Guzzi importers, remembers from his complaints to the factory about the appalling quality of chrome plating on their motorcycles.

The factory is really only accessible by either the lakeside road or the train station that is right opposite. So emptying dirty electrolyte from the plating tanks would involve huge expense; they couldn't really just pour it into Lake Como!

The solution was to avoid chrome plating; this also reveals that, unlike many Italian manufacturers, and Ducati especially, Moto Guzzi made most things in-house; the front forks on a Le Mans have a beautiful engraving of the Moto Guzzi eagle — unlike the forks on later Benelli Seis, which are otherwise identical. Pat also remembers De Tomaso, and found him a charismatic man who behaved quite modestly and let people gravitate towards him. Years later, when Pat met Claudio Castiglioni, the person the latter-day Ducati and MV Agusta chairman most reminded him of was De Tomaso.

Debuting at the 1975 Milan show, the Le Mans (there was no 'Mark I': it was just Le Mans) initially had a solo seat with a padded racing hump for occasional pillion use and a tail light moulded into the rear mudguard. These soon gave way to a more practical seat and a tail light that would gradually appear on other Guzzis, a sign of De Tomaso's continued focus on modular production.

The press reviews for the Le Mans were ecstatic, especially after the mixed reception for the S3. Over 7,000 of the original Le Mans were sold in a three-year production run. Lighter flywheels made the Le Mans feel much sportier than its predecessors, and the bike was ready for anything from cross-country touring through to winning production races. Yet despite looking more exotic than anything else on the market, the Le Mans was surprisingly wieldy and all-day comfortable, with far lower running costs than its competitors. Oddly then, although possibly not helped by the more touring-stance of the 1978 Mark II, the Le Mans somehow failed to create the

SPECIFICATIONS — MOTO GUZZI LE MANS (1975–78)

Layout and Chassis

90-degree V-twin four-stroke road-going production motorcycle

Engine

Type	90-degree V-twin
Block material	Aluminium alloy
Head material	Aluminium alloy
Cylinders	2
Cooling	Air
Bore and stroke	83 × 78mm
Capacity	844cc
Valves	4 valves ohv
Compression ratio	10.2:1
Carburettor	Twin 36mm Dell'Orto
Max. power	80bhp@7,300rpm
Fuel capacity	5 gallons/22.5 litres

Transmission

Gearbox	Five-speed foot-change
Clutch	Wet multiplate
Final drive	Shaft

Chassis

Front	Telescopic fork
Rear	Swingarm

Steering

Tyres	100/90–18in front, 110/90–18in rear
Brakes	Linked triple discs

Dimensions

Wheelbase	58in (1,470mm)
Unladen weight	436lb (198kg)

Performance

Top speed	132mph (213km/h)

In 1976 Bob and Arlene McIlvaine flew from the USA to Germany to tour Europe on a BMW. When that motorcycle was stolen they took a train to Mandello del Lario and bought a Le Mans to continue their tour on. They then shipped it back to the USA and continued to use it for a decade. COURTESY OF THE MCILVANE'S GUZZI SPORT RIDING GRANDSON, CHRISTIAN CLARKE

kind of race-track mythology managed by the Ducati 900SS and Laverda Jota. Again, this may be connected to De Tomaso's businesslike dismissal of racing, plus the Le Mans initial racing success was modest and almost entirely due to the efforts of racer Luciano Gazzola, alongside factory mechanic and sometime racer Bruno Scola, supported by Tonti. There were modest achievements in endurance racing, with midfield placings,

perhaps more a reflection of how competitive and innovative the class was at the time, rather than any failings on Moto Guzzi's part. In fact today, if you want to win a classic endurance race, a Le Mans is probably the default choice, with the Spanish Moto-Box and French Moto Bel teams almost unbeatable with their big Guzzis, even against the 16-valve 4-cylinder Japanese bikes.

Racing the Le Mans

The Le Mans did rather better at racing in the UK and USA. The Le Mans won the 1977 Avon Production Racing Championship, a series supported by *Bike*, the UK's best-selling motorcycle magazine. The coverage that ensued made even entering the championship fabulous publicity and Slater Brothers, the British Laverda importers, took the series to their heart. They had persuaded the factory to build a highly tuned version of the firm's 1000cc triple, which initially was only available in the UK. Called the Jota, a musical reference reflecting the importers' interest in classical music, this was a motorcycle practically invented to win the Avon title. During its debut year in 1976, the Jota was dominant, setting lap-records at pretty much every circuit in England. The tested top-speed of 140mph (225km/h) made it the motorcycle that most racers coveted, and the Slaters were happy to support them. Numerous other wins followed, including the Avon Championship in 1978 and 1979. But in 1976, a young racer called Roy Armstrong instead bought a Le Mans on hire-purchase from Steve Wynne of Sports Motorcycles

Moto Guzzi ownership appeals to all sorts.
MOTO CLUB VETERAN SAN MARTINO

to race alongside Wynne's own rider, John Sear. While Sear had the rare factory (and so homologated for road or racing) 'PR' (production racing) tuning kit, which included pistons that stretched capacity to 944cc, Armstrong's bike remained standard. Armstrong wouldn't even get a set of 944cc pistons from the new Convert tourer until July 1976.

In 1977, the duo again raced their Le Mans, even allowing Steve Tonkin and George Fogarty (Carl's father) to borrow the bikes for the 1977 Production TT. This is where Armstrong met the Guzzi mechanic Scola, who with Gazzola had had success with the Le Mans in Italy. It should be pointed out that others with strong connections to the Moto Guzzi factory question this version of events, but the story goes that Scola spoke good English and was happy to help Armstrong develop his machine. Scola was a factory mechanic and Armstrong was bright enough to keep a notebook of his suggestions. Scola was particularly scathing of standard Guzzi fork dampers and Armstrong worked to improve what was undoubtedly the original Le Mans' greatest weakness. Like the V7 Sport before, Tonti had travelled a bridge too far in his search for weight-savings when he designed the forks, and the solution was to fit Ducati fork stanchions. John Sear also had the advantage of the PR kit's close ratio gearbox, which Roy didn't have until he bought one much later in the season. His diligence in improving the Le Mans, and patient wait for a PR kit (which only comprised the gearbox, 944cc pistons, a camshaft, valve springs and spacers) was to be rewarded. Against all expectations, Roy beat the Laverda Jotas and Ducati 900SS to lift the 1977 Championship for Sports Motorcycles and Moto Guzzi.

Across the Atlantic, others were having surprising success with the Le Mans in the United States. Reno Leoni was a tuner of repute, having been paid by Ducati to visit the United States in the 1960s to sort out problems the importer was having with the single-cylinder road-bikes. It would be decades before Leoni retired to his homeland, in the meantime building a reputation as the man who could get the most from Ducatis on the race-tracks of America. Developing first the desmodromic singles, then the bevel cam-drive V-twins, he was to be the first to prove to the Ducati factory that the later Pantah engine, conceived as a 500cc road-bike, could be re-engineered into a successful 748cc racer. Unsurprisingly, therefore, Leoni is remembered as a Ducati man, but in 1976, and again in 1977, Leoni was persuaded by Berliner, who imported both Moto Guzzi and Ducati into the USA, to turn his attentions to the Le Mans. Controversially, some claim Scola, not Leoni, built the successful motors and it is possible that particular bikes received Scola's attention before being shipped out to Leoni.

However, again those with strong links to Moto Guzzi doubt this claim. What is certain is that Leoni made sure only a trusted few ever saw the engine being worked on. It seems likely that the engine had a roller-bearing crank (as opposed to the plain bearings in production engines), allowing the engine to rev higher and for longer. There was also talk of sleeved cylinders to allow a wider bore and other special parts. The fact that the Le Mans used at Daytona was built in America and retained a plain-bearing crank tends to support the view that the roller-bearing crank originated in Moto Guzzi's own racing department at Mandello. In any event, Leoni was undoubtedly exclusively responsible for the racing Guzzis, once they reached him, and it was Leoni who ensured they were ready for riders Mike Baldwin and Kurt Liebmann at each circuit.

Kurt Liebmann and Mike Baldwin had been the men to beat in US club races on Leoni-built Ducatis in the mid-1970s, making the trio's collective switch to a bike based on a mild-mannered sports-tourer (shaft drive and all) look perverse. That they turned the Le Mans into an AMA Superbike winner took Leoni from being an admired club racer's engine tuner into a race-bike builder of national repute. The breakthrough win came at June 1976's Loudon Superbike round with Baldwin dominating the race on the Berliner Moto Guzzi. His 16-second lead by the end of the race stands as one of the largest margins of victory in AMA Superbike history, beating the previous nigh-unbeatable factory BMWs of Gary Fisher and Reg Pridmore. However, with just four rounds in the inaugural

series, a failure to finish one round and starting the year on road wheels and treaded tyres, Baldwin finished the championship in fifth.

Perhaps Leoni's finest moment was his Moto Guzzis finishing one–two at the 1977 Charlotte AMA Superbike race. Baldwin won by 23 seconds and Liebmann beat the Yoshimura Kawasaki of Wes Cooley back into third place. Once again, however, inconsistency would rob the team of the title, with Baldwin finishing the year in third place. Yet these wins were fantastic for Moto Guzzi, Leoni said proudly, because the Le Mans sold out in America and became a racing motorcycle of choice for up-and-coming racers. As so often when the fortunes of an Italian motorcycle manufacturer are concerned, victory on the track resulted in success in the showroom. When a certain Dr John Wittner started racing Le Mans in the USA in 1984, he would secure the sporting heritage of Moto Guzzi for an entire generation, but in the meantime, the factory had to broaden its appeal to keep the same customers, who so loved the Ambassador and Eldorado, coming back for more.

The Automatic Convert and Other Tourers

And so, alongside the Le Mans, Moto Guzzi launched one of the most revolutionary motorcycles of the time, and possibly of all time. Increasing their latest tourer's cylinder bore size

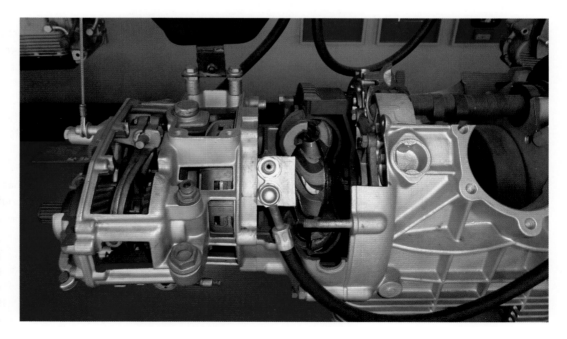

Cutaway of the semi-automatic gearbox in the Convert, with the vane of the torque-converter clearly visible.

raised displacement to 949cc (as used in the Le Mans PR kit) but the talking point of the resulting V1000 i-Convert was a two-speed automatic gearbox, and a radical bid to become the ultimate luxury tourer. Winning a top Italian design award in 1975, the Convert certainly addressed the Guzzi V-twin's biggest weakness: the car-style engine speed gearbox that required a patient foot, if smooth changes were to be achieved. The German Sachs torque converter (hence 'Convert') still required the rider to shift between high and low gear, simply because there was no room for the truly automatic shifting of an automatic car. The fact that such an idea reached production is a sign of De Tomaso's love and understanding of the car industry, as well as his unwavering self-confidence. Critics point to the Convert as proof De Tomaso was not a motorcyclist at heart, and yet Honda revealed the CB750A Hondamatic a year after the Convert appeared with an almost identical transmission set-up. However, both manufacturers had misread the direction of the market and neither sold well, although the Convert remained in production for a decade. In fact it provided one of Moto Guzzi's most surprising racing results in the hands of an eccentric French Moto Guzzi dealer, Charles Krajka.

Krajka was a man who loved bow ties and Guzzis, and for the 1976 Bol D'Or (still then held at Le Mans) he built a Le Mans racer with a much modified Convert gearbox. Racing under the moniker Guzzi Matic, in practice the bike was tens of seconds a lap slower than the works Moto Guzzi with a conventional

ABOVE: **The 'Guzzi Matic', an automatic V-twin racer based on the Convert and built by whimsical French Moto Guzzi dealer Charles Krajka to race at the 1976 Bol D'Or.**

LEFT: **When the Convert failed to sell as well as hoped, a version with a conventional 5-speed gearbox was offered as the G5.**

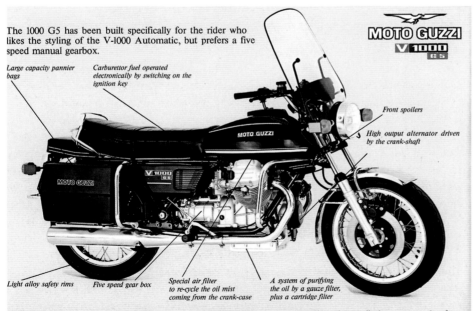

The 1000 G5 has been built specifically for the rider who likes the styling of the V-1000 Automatic, but prefers a five speed manual gearbox.

MOTO GUZZI
V 1000
G5

Large capacity pannier bags

Carburettor fuel operated electronically by switching on the ignition key

Front spoilers

High output alternator driven by the crank-shaft

Light alloy safety rims

Five speed gear box

Special air filter to re-cycle the oil mist coming from the crank-case

A system of purifying the oil by a gauze filter, plus a cartridge filter

The 1000 G5 is equipped with the integral braking system, patented by Moto Guzzi in 1975. This major contribution to motorcycle safety won presented by the German Automobile Club and is acknowledged as the safest motorcycle braking system by specialised press all over the world.

The Guzzi Matic finished well, despite poor lap times. It survives in the Moto Guzzi museum.

gearbox. Yet over 24 hours the Guzzi was barely slower than the works bike, finishing just one place behind it in sixteenth. Even so, the world wasn't ready for an automatic motorcycle, although Guzzi didn't give up on the idea of a luxury tourer. From 1978 they offered what amounted to the Convert with the T3's conventional five-speed gearbox, to produce the less than imaginatively labelled V1000G5 – a V1000 with five gears. Even a limited run of automatic Californias couldn't save the concept, and fewer than 2,500 Converts were built.

Alongside the G5, Moto Guzzi released another tourer, the Spada (Sword – or SP1000 in some markets) – with an innovative two-piece fairing clearly aimed at stealing sales from BMW's new fully faired sports-tourer, the 1977 R100RS. Much was made of using Moto Guzzi's legendary wind-tunnel to create the fairing, and certainly the idea of allowing the upper section of the fairing to turn with the handlebars allowed the screen to be near enough the rider to minimize turbulence, while remain-

ing rather more svelte than the enormous aftermarket fairings now sweeping the United States. It also allowed the Spada a more relaxed riding position than the BMW, which tucked its rider inside the fairing in a rather sportier riding position than the traditional BMW stance.

Updating the Le Mans

Clearly Moto Guzzi felt they were on to something with the split fairing, as a similar item appeared on the updated Le Mans, badged Mark II. The 1978 update also addressed the problem of the original model's rather lightweight front forks, one of a number of details on the first Le Mans that were sometimes compromised to save weight. The forks were the greatest symptom of this and the small battery another, which was an issue on a motorcycle without a kick-start, still considered a foolhardy omission by many riders of the era. Unfortunately, the updated Mark II lacked the purity of its forebear and was considerably heavier when weighed, despite factory claims to the contrary. Despite these niggling doubts, the Mark II just about managed to outsell the original Le Mans, proving the era's demand for sporting excellence. But a more successful motorcycle overall was the CX100, a shotgun marriage of the Mark II Le Mans and the Spada tourer, which allowed Moto Guzzi to continue to sell a sports bike in the USA. When the Le Mans engine failed to meet US environmental agency requirements in 1979, around 300 of the oddly named CX100 were built. Using the Spada's 9.2:1 compression and 30mm carburettors complete with air-filters (10.2:1 and open 36mm carburettors on the Le Mans), performance should have been considerably blunted. Yet, despite a weight penalty, the extra torque of the Spada's 944cc engine overcame the doubters and the influential *Cycle* magazine saw fit to make the CX100 a cover star with a suitably complimentary road test inside the magazine.

Any failings of the Le Mans II were comprehensively addressed by Mark III, which appeared in 1981. Introducing new square cylinders and more angular styling, which had debuted on the 500cc Monza in 1979, there was a sense of aggressive purpose about the Le Mans III that struck the perfect balance between classic racer and contemporary road-bike. This was probably the high point for the Le Mans, with details such as a classic white-faced Veglia tachometer and air-filters on the carburettors summing up Moto Guzzi's clever linking of the past to the future. Clever too was engine design allowing the Le Mans III to be sold in the USA, meeting all the clean-air regulations and yet still being the quickest accelerating of Guzzi's

An original Le Mans alongside a Mark III on the Motogiro revival.

850s, while matching the original Le Mans' top speed. Practicality was even enhanced by a larger fuel-tank. Clear links to the V7 Sport were underlined by modest success in endurance racing and, despite competing in the showroom with far more complex Japanese competitors, such as the new Suzuki GS1000 and 6-cylinder Honda CBX, this would be the best-selling Le Mans of all, with over 10,000 built. Sadly, Moto Guzzi failed to build upon this and, despite growing to 949cc, subsequent Le Mans were lumpen and followed fashion – especially the fashion for 16in wheels – too closely, generally failing to strike the right balance between what was a twenty-year-old concept and a marketplace dominated by Japanese technology. The final version was the Le Mans V of 1987, which really offered little or nothing over the 850s, and when an Ultima Edizione ('Final Edition') was announced in 1993, it was little more than a curiosity when compared to the Yamaha FZR1000 or Kawasaki ZZ-R1100. Moto Guzzi were not alone in having to build themselves a niche from which to compete with the now omnipresent Japanese, and Laverda and Ducati also struggled to find their

way as the ubiquitous 4-cylinder competition chipped away at the traditional Italian advantages of sporting charisma and fine handling and braking. De Tomaso's conviction that Moto Guzzi's future lay with the V-twin was emphasized as Benelli were allowed to drift on with old models until he finally closed down both the Pesaro factory and the Benelli production lines at Mandello del Lario in 1988. Instead there would be a new range of smaller, cheaper V-twins and a commitment to developing the Le Mans as a racer, along with building on the Moto Guzzi's V-twins traditional market as an American-style touring motorcycle. In the end Moto Guzzi had a very good 1970s, selling more large-capacity motorcycles than any other Italian manufacturer, and at least half as many again as nearest rival Ducati. The heydays as a volume manufacturer in the 1950s may have passed, but back then most Moto Guzzis had been small two-strokes for the protected home market. As the 1970s drew to a close, Moto Guzzi were selling high-value, large-capacity motorcycles to an increasingly appreciative world-wide audience.

CHAPTER SIX

BABY TWINS, AMERICAN CRUISERS AND RACING WITH THE DOCTOR

The Italian home market throughout the 1970s remained protected, partly due to import controls and partly due to lobbying by people like De Tomaso. De Tomaso was also busy trying to keep Honda from expanding a factory in Italy to circumnavigate import restrictions: since 1976 they had been assembling 125s and were keen to expand the operation. There was also a tiered value added tax system, which made 350 and 500cc motorcycles much cheaper than their bigger brethren in the home market. Despairing of the failure of the small-capacity Benelli and Moto Guzzi fours, plans to expand the range (there had even been talk of a 125 four) were abandoned and Tonti was allowed to develop an entirely new 500 V-twin he had developed to prototype form.

Unsurprisingly, De Tomaso had insisted that the new design should be even cheaper to produce than the existing V-twins, and that it should have the potential to be enlarged: indeed, the current 744cc V7 range can trace its roots back to Tonti's 1970s design. But given a clean sheet, Tonti also addressed many of the bigger engine's failings and weaknesses. The clutch was improved and, like the gearbox, it was no longer directly driven. This allowed the gearbox to be fitted lower than the crankshaft, lowering the centre of gravity, improving gear-changing and allowing primary drive to be easily altered. The latter point was particularly important, given that the engine was not only planned to be launched in both 350 and 500 formats, but to be developed into a larger capacity motorcycle. There was also attention to details, which would make ownership easier, with the oil-filter accessible without removing the sump, as on the older V-twins, a neat rear-disc design on the shaft drive-side of the swingarm to simplify wheel removal and, on early bikes, a brake-fluid reservoir under the fuel-tank, which was remotely operated to protect it from crash damage. The remarkable compact engine, soon known as the 'small block' to reflect the diminutive dimensions, also featured Heron-style combustion

chambers. The design was first proposed by aero-engine designer Sam Heron around 1918, who was quick to understand that an overheating exhaust valve was one of a four-stroke engine's greatest weaknesses, and that filling the valve with sodium reduced the problem greatly, ideas understood and adopted by Carlo Guzzi. Ironically, Heron was responsible for much research into semi-hemispherical combustion chambers while an engineer at the Royal Aircraft Establishment, but his name is given to designs that run inlet and exhaust valves parallel in a flat cylinder head with dished pistons accommodating the combustion chamber. The big advantage of this layout is much reduced manufacturing costs and the possibility of changing compression and squish by simply swapping pistons, rather than machining

The Fossatti family again, this time with their 350 Imola.
FOSSATTI HOTEL

the cylinder head. The practice was commonplace enough in the car world and introduced to motorcyclists with the 1971 Morini 350, which has become something of a cult classic. The disadvantage of the Heron design, in motorcycles especially, is that the exhaust and inlet tracts must be fairly torturously curved if the exhaust pipe and carburettor are to be conventionally placed. This, along with the necessarily heavy pistons, limits high rpm power, although offers good torque and fuel economy. Tonti, like Morini designer Franco Lambertini, felt these were acceptable compromises in a sub-500cc motorcycle engine.

The diminutive new engine led to an equally diminutive motorcycle. The new V50 weighed an astonishing 110lb (50kg) less than the 850T3 and was almost 44lb (20kg) lighter than the 4-cylinder 350GTS at 348lb (158kg), despite the V50 offering the refinements of shaft drive and linked brakes. Dimensions of the new bike were also closer to a 250's than other 500s, a deliberate ploy to make it attractive to riders stepping up from a lightweight. With a typically brilliant eye for publicity, De Tomaso launched the 490cc V50 and its smaller sibling the 346cc at the 1976 German Cologne Show to take advantage of the event's unusual lack of new model launches: indeed, the only other new models on show were Yamaha's XS250 and

The California II brought the squared off barrels to the touring range in 1981, raising capacity to 949cc. The chassis was also substantially different to the T3 California.
MOTO GUZZI

360 four-stroke parallel twins. Despite Guzzi claiming the V35 made 34bhp and the V50 46bhp, performance was hardly earth-shattering, although the latter was comparable to Morini's new 500, also featuring Heron combustion chambers. Unfortunately, with more performance-oriented offerings appearing at the same time, notably the Laverda Alpino, Ducati Desmo Sport and Honda CX500, the new Moto Guzzi would need to be priced competitively if it were to sell. Sadly, the new V35 and V50 were not as cheap to produce as had been hoped, and would be priced at a similar level to its faster compatriots at home and at half as much again as the Honda in export markets. A double blow was that, bowing to European Union pressure, the Italian Government was forced to abandon a tax regime that favoured indigenous manufacturers. The floodgates were open to the Japanese importers and Guzzi needed to up its game by building better motorcycles that were far more competitively priced.

Moving the Baby Twins into a Mini Factory

Part of the reason the V35 and V50 were proving costly to build was the crowded and dated facilities at the Mandello del Lario factory. In 1975, De Tomaso had acquired the more modern Innocenti factory in Milan. Originally manufacturing Lambretta scooters, Innocenti had expanded to build the British Mini under licence, selling out to British Leyland for around £3 million in 1972. When ambitious plans went unrealized, and troubles in the UK led to bankruptcy and nationalization for Leyland, De Tomaso stepped in with his customary eye for a deal. Although sales of the factory's cars collapsed, De Tomaso introduced a new Bertone-bodied Mini, which, although successful, left him with plenty of spare capacity. Refitting part of the factory with highly automated production lines permitted the V50's production to be relocated to Milan in 1979. This allowed the V50 to realize Tonti's efforts to produce a competitively priced competitor to the Japanese and, for most markets, the V50 was barely more expensive than the well-received and top-selling Honda CX500 V-twin. It was, therefore, pleasing, if unsurprising, that the V50 sold well, notably in export markets. Sadly, however, quality control at the Innocenti plant was poor or even non-existent, and while the big V-twins continued to enjoy a reputation for sturdy engineering, the new V50 for a time looked like it might become a warranty nightmare. Failings weren't minor either, with a former owner recalling investigating a dramatic loss of power to discover one

The fashion in the mid-1980s for fully enclosed motorcycles led to the Bimota DB1 and Ducati Paso. However, Moto Guzzi's interpretation, the Falco, did not reach production.

piston stuck at the top of the barrel and the remains of the gudgeon pin in the sump. Remarkably, the engine had continued to run on one cylinder. Most failings were less serious, but the baby Guzzi was quickly tarnishing the factory's long-held and hard-won reputation for reliability. Later bikes had extra crankcase ribbing to minimize distortion and so oil leaks, and at least proved Moto Guzzi were prepared to address problems. But, as seems inevitable with all Italian motor manufacturers, it was decided that what the V50 and V35 really needed to increase sales were racier, faster versions that would bring some glamour to the range.

The resulting 1979 Imola 350 and 1980 Monza 500 were indeed racy, with pitch perfect styling that would be developed for the Le Mans III. While such styling, and a name shared with a famous circuit, was entirely laudable for the race-proven, 130mph (210km/h) Le Mans, it looked less appropriate for the smaller bikes. The Imola, on the other hand, could barely reach 93mph (150km/h), which, although quick enough for a 350, was some 12mph (20km/h) less than most Japanese 400s. The Monza, while benefiting from more upgrading than the Imola, was faster at over 106mph (170km/h) but still well behind the typical 114mph (184km/h) that magazines were obtaining from Ducati's Pantah, despite the latter being hampered by over-gearing. For 1981, the Ducati would grow to become a nominal 600, and Moto Guzzi followed suit by showing a V65 at the Milan show late in 1981. The updated 643cc engine included a revised

bottom-end that hinted at 750cc potential, but again the Heron cylinder-heads limited performance. The compact nature of the bike also conspired with ungainly styling to make it seem to be a motorcycle with an identity crisis: neither a sportster nor a tourer. Some might have argued it wasn't even a true Moto Guzzi, being assembled at the Benelli factory in Pesaro, although the engines were still built at the Innocenti plant.

Seismic Changes in the Motorcycle Market

The motorcycle market was fragmenting, a process Moto Guzzi had been at the heart of by successfully offering the disparate styles of the Le Mans and the touring California, even though these were fundamentally the same motorcycle. Traditionally, few motorcycles had been focused on a single arena, although owners would often choose to accessorize their motorcycles to make them more suitable for a preferred style of riding. The aftermarket accessory market had exploded in the 1970s to reflect this, offering everything from huge Windjammer fairings and deep 'King and Queen' seats for the touring rider, to parts intended to create a racer on the road. The Japanese, as ever, had been carefully watching and learning. Honda launched the 1000cc Gold Wing in 1975, a water-cooled flat four with an initially confusing lack of purpose, even to importers who had wanted a performance bike to steal sales from Kawasaki's Z1. But with its exceptional comfort, the Goldwing grew into an accomplished tourer and by 1980 was 'fully dressed', as Americans say, with an enormous fairing, panniers and more. At the other end of the spectrum was the 1985 Suzuki GSX-R750, an alloy-framed confection that was genuinely a road-going, mass-produced version of the firm's four-stroke endurance racers. There really looked to be nowhere an Italian manufacturer could compete, and both Ducati and Morini had to be rescued by the Castiglioni brothers' Cagiva concern in 1984 and 1987, respectively, while Laverda folded in 1987. MV Agusta had closed its doors in early 1980 and De Tomaso called an end to his Benelli project in 1988. While the Le Mans had sold well, and still looked a true sports bike in the early 1980s, it was looking irrelevant to a new breed of sports riders by the middle of the decade in the face of 150mph plus (240km/h plus) oriental competitors. Equally, while Moto Guzzi's California remained a charming and engaging tourer, the Japanese offered the luxury of a Goldwing or similar. A few riders still appreciated the character and personal relationship a Moto Guzzi V-twin might offer, but they were increasingly rare and unlikely to be Italian in the now open-to-all home market.

Yet there was one niche the Japanese repeatedly tried, and failed, to conquer – the so-called custom market. These were motorcycles unashamedly mimicking Harley-Davidson's styling cues, and in the early 1980s were proving surprisingly popular. Although the 1969 film *Easy Rider* led to a brief flirtation with so-called choppers, the unsuitability of this style of motorcycle for European riders meant that, within a few years, customizers had moved on to styling motorcycles that worked away from straight roads. Choppers were originally a US phenomena that sought to make Harley-Davidsons (often ex-war department) comfortable on long, straight roads by 'chopping' the frame so that longer forks with a shallow rake could be fitted. This, in theory, allowed the motorcycle to cruise in a straight line with little or no input from the rider, although custom-bike builders quickly moved from practical considerations to aesthetic. The engines of choppers were almost universally from Harley-Davidson, and Harley were soon adopting chopper styling cues in their production motorcycles, discovering a rich seam of buyers in an otherwise overcrowded market.

The Custom Cruisers

While a little of this style was arguably picked up by Moto Guzzi's own California, that bike, along with the original loop-frame V-twins, owed its looks to the older, touring Harleys, rather than the newly fashionable custom look. Yamaha, often the most innovative of the Japanese manufacturers, were the first of the Japanese to adopt the look, dressing their XS650 parallel twin up with high handlebars, longer front forks and a stepped seat to hint at the look adopted by Harley-Davidson's Sportster. Few in the motorcycle press were convinced, but

In 1989 a more Americanized California III was offered in a number of guises including this version with fuel injection and catalytic converter.
MOTO GUZZI

LEFT: **The touring version of the California III helped make the range Moto Guzzi's best sellers.**
MOTO GUZZI

BELOW: **California III was even offered with colour-matched touring equipment as the Carenatura Integrale, meaning full fairing.**
MOTO GUZZI

sales took off. Yamaha expanded the experiment to other models, including a 'Midnight Special' XS1100 four with linked brakes, similar to Moto Guzzi's. All the Japanese soon boasted similar models, including improbable versions of their small-capacity motorcycles, with surprising sales success. Magazine testers and many 'serious' motorcyclists treated these mass-produced custom bikes with distain, but a new breed of buyers – and many celebrities – liked the look. Even by the late 1970s there were a number of voices warning that the industry was painting itself into a corner by focusing on performance, concerned that this intimidated newcomers to the sport; also it encouraged governments to introduce legislation in the name of safety and created the expectation in existing buyers that performance could be increased indefinitely. These Harleyesque Japanese motorcycles addressed such concerns, and offered a lifeline to older models that weren't able to offer the performance and sophistication demanded by other market sectors.

Moto Guzzi's first toe into this custom market was a brace of mildly Americanized small-block twins, using the V35C and V50C monikers. Sixteen-inch back wheels with a lengthened swinging arm allowed the rear of the bike to be lowered, and a bigger 18in front wheel, along with the longer V65's forks and higher handlebars from the California II, created the required chopper-like stance. The styling was less gaudy than most competitors and, although the chassis changes exacerbated

the V50's sometimes flighty front-end handling, the bikes were an immediate hit when launched in 1982. Soon joined by a V65C, the trio proved an unlikely hit for a company with such a fine sporting heritage, and would prove a reliable template for Moto Guzzi to the present day: the relaxed nature of the Mandello V-twin, the promise of low running costs and the V-twins' happy marriage to the custom styling, all proving attractive to buyers. When Ducati tried the same trick with the Indiana, a Pantah-engined cruiser, it proved how difficult building a tourer that looks at home on US highways really is. To date, only Harley-Davidson and Moto Guzzi have ever really managed it, and only the Guzzis offer dynamics that are acceptable to a rider who occasionally likes to up the pace under testing conditions.

Over a five-year period, the V35C, V50C and V65C sold almost 16,000 units, the smallest bike accounting for almost two-thirds of that figure. To put that in perspective, Ducati sold just over 2,300 Indianas in various capacities. Given how difficult the 1980s were for Moto Guzzi, these were welcome numbers, and so when the Custom range was replaced in 1986, Moto Guzzi provided buyers with more of the same. The new Florida in 350 and 650 guises featured longer forks, styling ever closer to a Harley's and, eventually, a return to wire wheels. Not as successful as the Custom range, the Florida nonetheless generated important income, and would develop an even more West Coast style as they became the 350 and 750 Nevada in 1989. These would remain in production for almost a decade, proving to be almost the factory's best-sellers, despite launching a slew of new models in an attempt to regain a significant share of the sports and touring bike market. But by the mid-1980s, trying to convince prospective buyers that a shaft-drive, air-cooled, V-twin with just two valves per cylinder was anything but a cruiser, looked an impossible task. Moto Guzzi embraced the seemingly inevitable, and relaunched the California with squared-off barrels, as on the Le Mans III, but with the Spada's 949cc displacement and a beefier chassis to reflect the motorcycle's likely role as a heavyweight tourer. In the process it gained 55lb (25kg) over the earlier T3 California, although it was still lighter than the original loop-framed police model that had inspired the range. Guzzi even built a handful of California IIs with the Convert's Sachs torque converter, although this was to be the final experiment with automatic transmission. Instead, the big California grew to be the bedrock of Moto Guzzi sales, with nearly 10,000 produced between 1981 and 1987, and finding an enthusiast customer-base most valuably in America. Morphing into the California III, like the smaller Florida and Nevada, styling became ever more Americanized, but sales held up well, especially when compared to other non-Japanese marques. Tightening emission regulations across the globe meant various batches had different versions of Guzzi's big twin, some even gaining the Le Mans V engine, albeit with 30mm carburettors. These would give way to fuel-injection and, despite Guzzi marketing various updates of the Spada and the T3 becoming the T4, then oddly angular T5, it was the California that kept selling. Eventually, various versions would be offered to broaden its appeal, but in the meantime De Tomaso was happy to explore other avenues.

Adventure and Off-Road Bikes

The 1980s had seen a new type of motorcycle appear, one that would grow to eventually pushed the sports bike from the top of the best-sellers' list, and one that grew from improbable beginnings. In 1977, when French racer Thierry Sabine became lost in an African desert, he decided it would make an excellent backdrop for the ultimate motorsport event. The Paris–Dakar was born, a long-distance raid for cars, trucks and motorcycles. Originally running from Paris to Dakar in Senegal, it was an unparalleled test of endurance. The inaugural 1978/9 and 1979/80 races' (the event actually started just after Christmas and ran for 6,200 miles/10,000km, so ran well into the new year) motorcycle class was won by the new Yamaha XT500, the reinvention of the big four-stroke trail bike. Then BMW launched a trail version of their 800cc shaft-drive flat twin, the R80G/S (Gelände/Strasse, approximating to open country/road) and won the 1980/81 event with Hubert Auriol, who would also win the car class eleven years later. A 1000cc version of the BMW would later win the event three years on the trot, only being defeated when Honda decided to throw their considerable resources into beating them. Sales of the BMW took off, creating a new class of motorcycle and proving the commercial value of the widely televized Paris–Dakar event. Over 20,000 R80G/S were produced and the BMW GS series remains a cornerstone of the firm, with over half-a-million sold. Not surprisingly, Moto Guzzi decided that, given the similarity of the BMW's design to their own V-twins, a version of the small-block V65 should be developed for the event. A group of French riders had actually used modified V50s to enter the first Paris–Dakar and had exceeded most observers' expectations, especially on the first section across France. The bike's principal weakness had been the cast rear wheel – no wire-wheeled alternative being available – which snapped when subjected to serious off-road use.

Initially, Moto Guzzi launched a trail-style version of the V35C and V65C in 1984, introducing wire-spoked wheels and deleting the linked brakes for the first time on the small-block range. Dubbed the V35 and 65TT (Tutto Terenno – All Terrain) these were really little more than re-styled versions of the custom bikes with new suspension. Nonetheless, an architect from Bergamo, Claudio Torri, approached Tonti with the idea of competing in the Paris–Dakar on a factory-modified version of the V65TT. Agreeing to contribute to the cost, he was given access to the experimental department and an engineer. Within a short time, the pair had modified the just-released V65TT trail bike, fitting the basic necessities of a long-distance desert

RIDING THE BIKES | NTX650

Glen Parkinson almost bought his NTX, surely the butchest small-block Guzzi, on a whim, but after riding it for 20,000 miles (32,000km) it's almost his perfect all-round motorcycle.

The NTX range (New Type X: the 'X' symbolizing (moto)cross rather than the letter X) was Moto Guzzi's second stab at turning their small-block motorcycles into an off-roader. The Lino Tonti-designed engines grew from the original V35 and V50 to power a variety of models that enjoyed

varied success. The 'adventure' bikes were the least successful in terms of sales, not helped by the styling of the original TT on sale between 1984 and 1987. The TT's swoopy bodywork jarred with the lines of the angular Moto Guzzi V-twin and the lowered gearing damaged fuel consumption alongside Guzzi's reputation for economical motorcycles. Yet like everyone else in the industry, the success of BMW's GS adventure bikes convinced Moto Guzzi to try again. The result was the NTX.

Launched in 1986, the styling of the 350 and NTX650 was nicely aggressive, with brutal bull-bar looks hinting that the owner was circumnavigating the world rather than commuting to work. The 7-gallon (32 litre) fuel-tank certainly sent out the right message, and even with the low gearing, gives a 300-plus mile (480+km) range. It also makes the NTX quite a handful at walking pace with a full fuel load. The NTX was much improved over the TT as an off-roader, with features such as a high-level, tucked in, exhaust system and bigger 40mm forks. Yet the NTX still failed to sell well, not helped by lukewarm press reviews bemoaning that it wasn't as sophisticated as the competition. The later NTX750 revised the styling again, not entirely successfully, with a new fairing almost entirely enclosing the engine. The NTX was officially dropped in 1990, although production or unsold stock hung around for some years after that. The final NTX650PB soldiered on for some markets until 1995, when Moto Guzzi accepted a universal truth: people don't want 'adventure' bikes; they want something from the BMW GS range.

ABOVE: **Glen Parkinson's NTX is the production version the Baja was intended to promote.**

LEFT: **The hand guard and sat-nav are later additions, but otherwise original. Fit and finish are very good for a 44,000 mile, 20 year old, Italian motorcycle.**

Continued overleaf

Continued from previous page

RIDING THE BIKES | NTX650

Glen Parkinson is a long-time motorcyclist and has ridden across much of Europe and beyond. He has owned an impressive array of motorcycles, many of them Italian, and still has several bikes. Yet despite the fact that some are newer and more powerful than the NTX, the Guzzi is still his go-to bike. Whether just popping to the shops or going for an impromptu ride, Glen's late 1994 NTX650 has become his default ride, and despite denying it any major trips, has put 20,000 of the 44,000 miles onto the odometer. 'It's just such an easy, everyday bike,' Glen confirms. 'From the first time I rode it I liked the relaxed style and riding experience.'

Yet the NTX was almost an accidental purchase. Glen had gone to North Leicester Motorcycles (NLM) in Ellistown to look at a V65SP that shares much with the NTX, including the 643cc, 50bhp engine, but in a mini-Spada touring package. The SP unsurprisingly weighs the same 374lb (170kg) as the NTX, although that's with empty fuel-tanks – the SPs takes 3.3 gallons (15 litres) less than the NTX. Trying the SP, Glen found it cramped, despite the fact he's normally proportioned and not especially tall. Instead his eye was drawn towards a red and white NTX350 that NLM also had in stock. Although Glen felt a 350 would be too weedy for his needs, Stuart Mayhew, boss of NML, explained that he was sure he could find a 650 version and soon a deal was done. That was back in 2008, and with each passing year Glen finds his NTX becoming ever closer to the perfect motorcycle. Supremely comfortable, with a fuel range that makes the most of it, cost-effective to run and with a style that wears its twenty-five years well, it seems the ideal all-

rounder. Glen happily rode over on a crisp February morning for the photoshoot, and the NTX is about to undergo a minor refurbishment. 'I really must take it over to Europe and get some more miles on it,' he remarks while getting ready to leave. How many riders who have owned a bike for five years and have a choice of more glamorous steeds would say that? Maybe the NTX's sin was to be born too soon, because with long travel suspension and low running-costs aided by easy home-maintenance, it looks perfectly aligned to our current straightened times and potholed roads.

TOP: **The speed- and odometer in kilometres gives away the fact that this NTX650 was a later import from Italy.**

RIGHT: **The framework at the rear is not just for panniers, but to provide additional bracing to the frame if used off-road. Owner Glen is a little camera shy.**

SPECIFICATIONS MOTO GUZZI NTX650 (1986–93)

Layout and Chassis

90-degree V-twin four-stroke road-going production motorcycle

Engine

Type	90-degree V-twin
Block material	Aluminium alloy
Head material	Aluminium alloy
Cylinders	2
Cooling	Air
Bore and stroke	80 × 64mm
Capacity	643cc
Valves	4 valves ohv
Compression ratio	10.1:1
Carburettor	Twin 30mm Dell'Orto
Max. power	60bhp@7,800rpm
Fuel capacity	7 gallons/32 litres

Transmission

Gearbox	Five-speed foot-change
Clutch	Dry single plate
Final drive	Shaft

Chassis

Front	Telescopic fork
Rear	Swingarm

Steering

Tyres	3.00–21in front, 4.00–18in rear
Brakes	Triple discs

Dimensions

Wheelbase	58in (1,480mm)
Unladen weight	374lb (170kg)

Performance

Top speed	102mph (164km/h)

racer: long suspension, a huge fuel-tank and extended wheelbase for sand riding stability. Although Torri didn't finish the Paris–Dakar – partly because his back-up crew were in a small Fiat, where many entrants had a helicopter watching over them – his attempt gained valuable publicity for Moto Guzzi. The French Moto Guzzi importer was especially impressed and persuaded the factory to build him fifteen replicas, and so the Moto Guzzi Baja was born.

Today these are one of the rarest Guzzis, and in the end seventeen 650cc Bajas were built by the factory's experimental department during 1984–85. Also known as the TTC (Tutto Terenno Competizione – All Terrain Competition), they never quite made the grade in the Paris–Dakar but competed successfully in European rallies for many years. One neat touch was the fold-away gearbox kick-start lever, as used in the NATO V50 models. The Le Mans' rear hub, swingarm and final drive housing were adapted for use, with a Cagiva Elefant hub and floating Brembo disc fitted at the front end. Perhaps four or five 750cc racers were constructed after 1985. All the Bajas were

hand-built and many have different details. Spurred on by the publicity generated by the Baja, Guzzi showed various prototype off-roaders, although only the 125TT two-stroke and the TT/NTX (in 350, 650, and the latter the NTX 744cc version) would reach production.

The small-block off-roaders were joined by the enormous 1000cc Quota based on the California III, but none of these really sold as well as hoped. At least with the Baja, Moto Guzzi had rediscovered the value of racing as a means of generating not only publicity, but also loyalty and pride amongst owners. They might be using their V-twin Guzzis for touring or cruising, but the fact the engine below them had proved its mettle in racing makes it just that little bit more special. So when De Tomaso spotted that an American dentist had built a Le Mans III that could not just win the odd event, but an entire championship at his first attempt, he took decisive action. The clearly gifted Dr John Wittner was invited to fly to Italy from his home in Pennsylvania, USA, at De Tomaso's expense to start a new and remarkable chapter in Moto Guzzi's history.

The off-roaders in the museum include an enormous Quota in the background.

Dr John and a New Era of Racing Success

John Wittner was the son of aeronautical engineer, Howard, and much of John's youth was spent around motorcycles. He crashed his first big bike, a 650 Triumph, just days after passing his test, avoiding a dog that had run out in front of him. Studying engineering in the early 1960s, he worked part-time in a motorcycle dealership to pay his way through university. On qualifying he joined a Moto Guzzi dealership as service manger, and began dabbling with racing. But these were the years of The Draft, and after military service in Vietnam, Wittner qualified as a dentist, although the passion for motorcycles in general, and V-twin Guzzis in particular, remained. In 1984, now into his forties, Dr John ploughed most of his income into entering the new AMA (American Motorcyclist Association) endurance series that would allow an 850 Le Mans to compete with Japanese 4-cylinder motorcycles in the middleweight category. The rules called for entries to remain almost stock, and the series would involve a mix of four- and six-hour races held over eight rounds. Riding with Greg Smrz and Nick Phillips, Wittner thought the Guzzi's reliability and modest thirst for fuel would allow it to run with fewer pit stops than the competition, and he was right. The plan was tortoise versus hare, with Wittner getting his team to ride steadily, respecting red lines and keeping things smooth. At tracks like sweltering Ontario, the competition could pull a fifteen-lap lead in six hours – in theory. Dr John's team just plugged away, moving up the leader board as other teams ran into mechanical problems or the need to

refuel. At the first round, on 8 April 1984, held at the Rockingham circuit in Carolina, the Moto Guzzi team won their class comfortably, astonishing a motorcycle press that had written Moto Guzzi off as a sporting marque. 'I guess you could call us a factory effort', Wittner teased the press, simply because he had some sponsorship from the US Benelli and Moto Guzzi importer, as well as the owners' club. He would later admit that, in truth, his house had pretty much financed the team in 1984. Winning the middleweight championship convinced Wittner to sell his dental practice, as well as his house, take a part-time dentistry job and go racing with serious intent.

The AMA Endurance Championship in 1985 allowed bikes to be modified, and if you are going to find the expertise needed to tune simple pushrod engines, America is the place to do it. The hot-rod scene is huge, as is the community making simple, big-capacity V8 engines fly. It was this knowledge-base that Dr John tapped into, and he would need their expertise because for 1985 the Le Mans would be in the unlimited capacity class. The importers had ensured that the Wittner team had the first Le Mans V to land on American soil, with 949cc pistons and a raft of changes, although many of them were questionable. In particular, the chassis changes made the bike feel bigger but less stable than before, although power and top speed were up over the 850 – a glance down the entry list confirmed they needed to be, and the scale of the challenge ahead. Competitors included Kawasaki's liquid-cooled, 16-valve GPz900R, Yamaha and Suzuki's new FJ1100 and GSX1150, along with Honda's homologation busting VF1000R, a limited edition V4 built solely to win production racing events. According to road tests of the time, the Le Mans was as much as 20mph (32km/h) down on top speed, compared to the Japanese bikes, yet on the straights, Wittner's version could pass the Kawasaki. Wittner believed the exhaust system was the most important part to tune on an engine, and designed a bizarre serpentine system with ultra-wide pipes that curled up in front of the engine. A slew of other changes, largely aimed at making the engine happy to pick up revs, combined with Mikuni carburettors, would eventually provide an astounding 95bhp at the rear wheel, almost 50 per cent more than a standard Le Mans III. This, together with the Guzzi's comparatively slight frontal area, explained the speed and the stability of the racer, even

in an era of much-improved Japanese bikes' handling, and was a great aid to fast lap-times.

Riders for 1985 were again Smrz and Phillips, joined by Larry Shorts, as Wittner focused on developing and preparing the bike. The season was far more competitive, with teams running a much faster pace from the start, and combined with the Guzzi's higher state of tune, inevitably this led to reliability issues. The team suffered a broken driveshaft and bent pushrods but Dr John's calm demeanour and obsession with carrying a spare of everything, allowed them to arrive at the final round, alongside eighty-five other entries, with a chance of winning the championship outright. All they had to do was beat the previous year's winning team, running a Honda VF1000R, an all-new, clean-sheet design built to win races, and in theory a far superior motorcycle to the Le Mans. It was, therefore, an emotional triumph when, late on 18 October 1985, after six hours and over 500 miles (800km) of racing, a Moto Guzzi Le Mans had beaten everything the Japanese could throw at it. Yet despite the elation of winning the championship and the exhaustion of twenty-hour days, Dr John was already thinking of 1986, despite limited funding. Unfortunately, 1986 turned out to be a year to forget, with much-improved Japanese competition and some bizarre misfortunes: the bike was lost in transit to the Isle of Man TT, and when Mobil agreed to fund the team at Daytona, the event was rained off.

ABOVE: **Dr John's racing motorcycle was ingenious, original and very successful. De Tomaso saw this as the route to reinvigorating Moto Guzzi's sporting heritage.**

RIGHT: **The racer pioneered Guzzi's use of 4-valve cylinder heads and dealing with the effect of shaft drive on a motorcycle's handling.**

The Burden of History and Racing at Daytona

Wittner wasn't the only one finding that the motorcycle he loved was no longer competitive with the Japanese on a race-track. The British manufacturers had long realized that the Daytona Cycle Week meeting, and especially the 200 (mile) race, was the most important event on the calendar, given that America was the biggest marketplace. The meeting opened the AMA road-racing season, running at the banked race-track close to the Florida beaches that had hosted the racing from 1937 until the construction of the International Speedway circuit in 1961. Being Florida, even in March, the skies were usually cobalt blue and temperatures as high as the stakes. The races were just part of a whole range of events and meetings held under the banner of Cycle Week, with some 200,000 motorcycles turning up, often with rider and passenger, plus those who arrived on four wheels or more. The British had finally realized the Japanese were not happy just to build small-capacity motorcycles (which had grown the motorcycle market enormously, much to the advantage of British bike sales in the 500cc-plus sector) and had treated the 1970 Daytona 200 as a line in the sand. The legendary Mike Hailwood was paid an undisclosed, but clearly substantial, fee to race one of four specially commissioned BSA/Triumph triples, and three American Daytona regulars – David Aldana, Gary Nixon and Gene Romero – were secured to fill the remaining berths. Despite an early lead, Hailwood's engine failed, and American Dick Mann went on to win the race aboard a CB750 prepared in Honda's Grand Prix workshop. Although Romero's triple was closing on Mann's clearly ailing Honda when it limped over the finishing line, it was all too little, too late. History remembers only the winner; the production Honda CB750s started selling at above the $1,400 list price and would go on to sell more than 10 million units. Little wonder then that the 1970 Daytona 200 has been described as the most important victory in history for any motorcycle manufacturer. During the 1970s, the Japanese would build ever more exotic motorcycles to take to Daytona, culminating in the two-stroke 4-cylinder Yamaha TZ700 and 750, especially devastating in the hands of up and coming Californian Kenny Roberts.

To win the American championship, until comparatively recently, a racer needed to be multi-disciplined. Between 1954 and 1989 the title was decided by points accumulated across racing in five disciplines: four on dirt or shale, and only one – road-racing – on tarmac. This allowed Harley-Davidson's riders to secure the championship, even as their road-racing motor-cycles became uncompetitive. But when Kenny Roberts contracted to Yamaha, who had a competitive dirt-racer in their XS650 parallel twin, the status quo folded. Roberts won the 1973 and 1974 series, and went on to focus on road-racing, becoming three-time 500cc World Champion in 1979 through 1981.

Although Roberts' departure gave Harley-Davidson some breathing space, all concerned could see the writing on the wall. Cycle Week's races were being held in front of sparse audiences, despite record crowds coming to Daytona. The bare commercial reality was that perhaps 90 per cent of the riders at Cycle Week were aboard Harley-Davidsons, and did not want to pay to watch their beloved marque trounced by the Japanese. The AMA's solution was to introduce Battle of the Twins (BOTT), a road-racing class that allowed only twin-cylinder motorcycles. Initially run at Daytona during Cycle Week in 1981, the rules were geared towards favouring 1000cc overhead-valve engines in an anything-goes chassis format, intended to offer Harley-Davidson a showcase.

Odd, then, that it was fans of Italian motorcycles who embraced BOTT, with Harley-Davidson still preferring to focus on oval dirt-track racing. The 1000cc (and reputedly more) 'Lucifer's Hammer' factory road-racer from Harley had some success, but it was the Ducati Pantah-based racers that were the surprise stars of the series. On 11 March 1983, Jay Springsteen finally gave Harley-Davidson their first win in fourteen years at Daytona, when he took the chequered flag for the GP class victory in the 50 mile/13-lap BOTT race. Jimmy Adamo, who had been king of Battle of the Twins racing since its inception aboard a 748cc Pantah-based engine built by Leoni, had his winning streak at Daytona broken when he lost the horsepower duel to Springsteen, who steadily pulled away. Formula 2 World Champion Tony Rutter was third on another Ducati. Then in 1984, writer and racer Alan Cathcart entered the Daytona BOTT on a much modified Laverda 500, the bike running perfectly to lead from flag to flag, making Cathcart the first British rider to ever win a race at Cycle Week.

Even BMW was getting in on BOTT racing, with class wins. Clearly Moto Guzzi ought to be using the series to promote their V-twin, and De Tomaso must have seen that Wittner was his most likely chance of success. Dr John's thoughts were to design a chassis that would best suit the Le Mans' engine. His idea to use a deep, rectangular steel tube running straight from the headstock to aluminium plates supporting the rear of the gearbox, shared much with the thinking of British (but Australian educated) engineer Tony Foale, who had established a business building such frames in 1973. In fairness, the early

Aermacchi pressed-steel spine frames are also similar and, like Dr John's frame, took advantage of being deeper than they are wide to resist twisting. But on the Le Mans, the real advantage was that the spine would fit neatly between the cylinders, keeping the bike narrow and easy to work on. The other facet Wittner addressed was the torque reaction caused by the shaft drive to the rear wheel, which, although manageable in an endurance race, was magnified greatly in short, sprint races. At Daytona, Larry Shorts had been circulating ten seconds a lap slower than he would in an event like a Battle of the Twins race. Wittner's solution was to build a cantilever rear suspension – again like Foale's chassis and a widely used layout by the mid-1980s – and to have the driveshaft float independently of the swinging arm by introducing a secondary drive coupling. Contacting the factory with a plea for funding in 1986, a watching

RIGHT: **The Sport 1200 now features the 8-valve engine and so many styling cues from the Breva that Moto Guzzi initially considered calling it the Breva S.**
MOTO GUZZI

LEFT: **The upgraded Corsa 1200 Sport.**
MOTO GUZZI

and waiting De Tomaso was only too pleased to invite him to Italy. This might have been the point at which De Tomaso decided irrevocably that his future involvement with the motorcycle industry would be exclusively about Moto Guzzi and her V-twins, and that the experiment with Benelli and other engines formats would be forgotten forever.

Factory Support for Dr John

De Tomaso not only liked Wittner's chassis ideas, he could see that they had potential for mass production. De Tomaso and Umberto Todero, still with the factory after nearly fifty years, were also considering 4-valve cylinder heads for a new Le Mans, and Wittner's chassis would be a perfect home for the sporting V-twin. So De Tomaso was happy to send Wittner away with funding to build a race-bike for the 1987 season, and in just five weeks the new chassis was ready. The 2in by 3in (51mm by 76mm) spine of the frame was in 4130 Chromalloy, a material as loved in the USA as Reynolds 531 was in the UK. Although not as strong as a tubular section, the rectangular spine didn't need the gussets a round tube would, to connect to the headstock and engine. Aluminium plates connected the

spine to the engine, which became a stressed member. Combined with the swingarm in 2in by 1in (51mm by 25.5mm) mild steel, the frame weighed less than 30lb (14kg). Rear suspension was a Koni unit intended for a Formula 1 car, with a huge range of adjustment, which appealed to Dr John. The rest of the chassis was pretty standard for the era: a mix including components by Brembo, Marvic and Marzocchi.

De Tomaso had also agreed that the factory would supply Dr John with raw crankshaft forgings, allowing them to be machined in the USA. The race engine featured forged and machined pistons, with a 12.5:1 compression that demanded 100 octane fuel. Bore and stroke were juggled, stretching the Le Mans V's 949cc capacity to as much as 998cc, although a short-stroke version displacing 992cc was usually preferred as offering the most effective combustion chamber. Cylinder heads were based on the Le Mans' but so altered that the standard valve lifters were unusable. The camshaft was by Norris and carburettors were heavily modified 41.5mm Mikunis, developed for Harley-Davidson flat-track racers. The exhaust was much as before – with replicas now on sale to other Guzzi racers – and the transmission built by Swiss firm Transkontinental. The clutch was in forged aluminium that was less than half the weight of the Le Mans standard unit, which was prone to

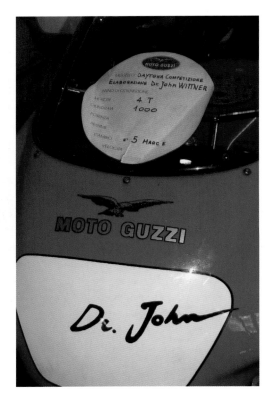

ABOVE: **The Daytona was the production version of Dr John's race bike.**

RIGHT: **The hope was that the Daytona would initially be a customer racer, building awareness of the road-going version.**

fracturing under racing conditions. Although only a handful of horsepower more powerful than the 114 dynometer-certified bhp of the 950 endurance racing engine, acceleration was much improved. The engine was also safe to 10,200rpm, although valve float from 9,700rpm meant there was little advantage in doing so – for now, at least. More impressive was that unfuelled and unfaired – but otherwise ready to race – the complete motorcycle weighed just 340lb (155kg) and generated enough newsprint and excitement to attract some high-profile advertising. This was not just from the motorcycling world – supporters included clothing brand Le Coq Sportif. The Battle of the Twins Championship was now called the Grand Prix Pro-Twins series, and expected to be a Ducati benefit. De Tomaso had accepted that Dr John's aim was to just finish each of the 1987's Pro-Twin's rounds and develop the bike for the reliability that had eluded him in 1986. Rider Doug Brauneck was a thirty-year-old from the city of Macon in Georgia just north of Florida, and an exceptionally versatile rider, as comfortable on a 250 two-stroke as Dr John's big V-twin. He debuted the new Moto Guzzi at Daytona with a safe sixth place, following up with second places at Atlanta and Brainerd to give him a one-point lead over Adamo on the Leoni Ducati. Finally scoring an outright win at Loudon after a race-long battle with Adamo, the pairing of Dr John's Guzzi and Brauneck looked increasingly unbeatable. They went on to a fairytale ending as Grand Prix Pro-Twins' 1987 Champions.

4-Valve Heads and Radical Competition

Winter 1987 saw Dr John back at Mandello and working with Todero to fit the new 4-valve engine into the racing chassis. Todero had originally built a dohc engine, but De Tomaso decided it looked too tall and lacked a strong enough visual link to the Le Mans' unit. Instead a 4-valve head, owing much to Cosworth thinking, was developed with a belt-driven single camshaft in front of each cylinder head, operating rockers and ultra-short pushrods. With 992cc, this gave 92bhp in road trim, far from competitive against the most powerful Japanese engines, but the design freed up space between the cylinder barrels. However, power was not significantly different in race-tune from the 1987 2-valve racer, although far fewer revs were required. Chassis modifications were minor, mainly aimed at making the most of the new 17in Metzler radial tyres, but appearance was much changed. Where the 1987 racer had at least hinted at its Le Mans V road-bike origins, the 1988 bike had

wind-tunnel developed bodywork and twin silencers, making it look like the full-blooded race-bike it had always been. Brauneck took a third place at Daytona's opening round, although it was clear that Pro-Twins was changing. Victory went to Englishman Roger Marshall on the prototype Quantel Cosworth, a liquid-cooled, all-new parallel twin intended to revive the Norton name. Second was Stefano Caracchi on the prototype Cagiva-Ducati liquid-cooled, 8-valve V-twin. Given the competition, and that Dr John had arrived at Daytona still awaiting his brace of 4-valve heads, third was a remarkable achievement. In fact, the Guzzi would have been fourth had the leading Honda, ridden by Paul Lewis, not snapped a conrod. His radical RS750 used a liquid-cooled V-twin that Honda were developing for dirt track, ostensibly developed from the engine in their road-going CX500, and proof that Honda were taking their advertising slogan 'Honda enters; Honda wins' seriously.

With the level of competition and questionable reliability, Brauneck and Wittner couldn't repeat the successes of 1987. Innovative design still pushed the Moto Guzzi racers' development, with ideas such as linked brakes controlled via the handlebar lever and gutted front forks controlled by a single Koni unit acting on the triple clamps. 1989 was more of the same, but the fuel-injected engine was now giving an astonishing 128bhp at a comparatively lowly 8,500rpm. It was time for Dr John to return to the factory full-time and develop a road-going version, and for Brauneck to hone his 250-riding skills sufficiently to become the 1990 AMA 250GP Champion. Dr John had built undoubtedly the most successful Moto Guzzi racer since the 1950s, and De Tomaso was keen to capitalize on the achievement. Sales at Moto Guzzi were collapsing and new models were urgently needed. With production down to fewer than 6,000 motorcycles a year and falling, De Tomaso sold his majority shareholding in Benelli and merged the company with Moto Guzzi to form GBM SpA in 1988. The Dr John racer-for-the-road was first shown late in 1989, in both carburetted and fuel-injected form, looking remarkably unadulterated. The press were invited to try the prototype, named the Daytona after the scene of many successes for Wittner's race-bike, and reaction was positive. Journalists were especially impressed when Dr John revealed that the only significant differences between the new road-bike and the racer was that the latter made widespread use of magnesium alloy especially on rocker boxes, yokes, sump and cycle parts, before delivering the killer blow: 'all you will have to do to release 128 bhp from the standard bike is to remove the airbox, change the exhaust, and fit a new chip'.

To bolster disappointing sales the Daytona was offered with a pillion seat, something Dr John disapproved of but dealers requested.
MOTO GUZZI

Getting the Daytona into Production and the End of an Era

But the reality of putting a racing engine, particularly an air-cooled racing engine, into production soon bit home and it would be 1992 before any Daytonas reached dealers' show-rooms. The most obvious change was a half, rather than full, fairing to help with engine cooling but nonetheless developed by Dr John in the factory wind-tunnel. There were also problems with the exposed drive train when the motorcycle was used on dirty roads, rather than a carefully maintained race-track. Yet the biggest problem was Ducati's 888, announced almost as the Daytona finally became available; the Ducati was cleaning up in superbike racing and reinventing Ducati as the ultimate sporting marque. Although the Daytona was as fast as the earlier Ducati 851, at around 145mph (235km/h), the new 851 simply moved the game on, although Japanese sports bikes were faster still. Some, like the Yamaha FZR1000 that was *Cycle World* magazine's bike of the (1980s) decade, even handled well. The Daytona had needed that 1990 launch date, because the glory years of the racer were now five years in the past, and Ducati had stolen the mantle of the most exotic Italian road-bike. Of course the Daytona, like the Ducati, was priced well above the Japanese competition, which by 1992 left the Daytona in something of a no-mans' land. Less than 500 were sold in the launch year, and that would prove

to be a high point, with only 1,433 Daytonas passing through the factory gates before production ended. In 1992 there was also a limited edition version of the California III to celebrate seventy years of Moto Guzzi, featuring a leather saddle and a certificate signed by De Tomaso, but with tragic predictability it was a year late – 1991 had been the anniversary. By 1993, the company was losing money and De Tomaso suffered a stroke. Control passed to his son, Santiago, although Alejandro would survive until 2003. There are those who still question whether he was a hero or villain, but with hindsight he was a man ahead of his time and understood the way the world was changing, whether we liked it or not. Without him there would have been no Le Mans and probably no Moto Guzzi by the time of his stroke. There would also have been no Benelli Sei, the world's first 6-cylinder production motorcycle, and fewer, if any, of Dr John's racing achievements. So for many, De Tomaso was clearly a hero, and would be sadly missed. With typical clear-sightedness and pragmatism, as his health faltered he invited bankers Finprogetti to establish a temporary integrated man-agement (TIM) company to nurse Moto Guzzi back to health, with new managing director Arnolfo Sacchi instigating a com-prehensive review of the business. De Tomaso would remain as notional president of Moto Guzzi until 1996, by which time the company would be back in profit and launching much need-ed new models. Given the devastation the Japanese motorcycle industry has wrought upon most of its European competitors, that surely amounted to De Tomaso leaving on a high.

CHAPTER SEVEN

REBIRTH AND REBRANDING

1993 saw a much improved and significantly changed California, the 1100, now unashamedly aimed at fans of American-style cruisers with a 17in back wheel lowering the seat and making for a chopper-like stance. The 1064cc engine used computer-aided design for the first time at Moto Guzzi, and would be offered with fuel-injection, as well as a 949cc engine for certain markets. While this version of the California continued to be Guzzi's best-seller, with some 7,660 being manufactured between 1993 and 1997, the factory was becoming highly reliant on the home and German markets, where this style of motorcycle remained popular. Elsewhere, however, there was a sports-bike boom that had grown out of the 1970s street-racing movement. Initially based around individual owners modifying their motorcycles to look and perform like racers – and especially endurance racers – models such as Moto Guzzi's own Le Mans had made sports bikes mainstream motorcycles, rather than an enthusiast's niche. With the launch of Honda's original Fireblade and Ducati's 916 around 1993, the interest in sports bikes became overwhelming and, in most countries, such models dominated the marketplace. Arnolfo Sacchi at the helm of Moto Guzzi not only recognized this sea change in buying habits, but also noted the rise of the 'born agains': buyers who had passed their motorcycle test many years previously but had abandoned the sport in favour of a quiet marriage, car and career. Typically in their thirties and forties, these newly affluent consumers had stable and comfortable existences, and were now looking to introduce a little excitement back into their lives. Motorcycle sales were also aided by the low interest rates intended to rebuild economies after the stock and property crashes of the late 1980s. Perhaps unwisely, if understandably, what this new breed of rider wanted was an affordable sports bike. The Daytona might have been a sports bike, and the Le Mans' heritage struck a chord with the born-agains, but it could not compete with the profile of the Ducati 916 or the price of the Fireblade.

Sacchi, therefore, had the 1100 Sport developed, a Daytona in all but price. The Daytona's chassis construction was simplified, less expensive components were used and a pillion seat – which dealers had wanted on the Daytona but Wittner had resisted – was standard. Although the transmission was from the Daytona, the engine was from the California, developed and upgraded by Wittner to give 90bhp. Road tests immediately recognized that the 1100 Sport offered pretty much everything that the Daytona had, and the reduced top speed of 135mph (217km/h) was really only of academic consideration. Like the California 1100, the original carburettors were soon superseded by fuel-injection, and the Sport outsold the Daytona by two-to-one. Unfortunately, the Sport killed off Daytona sales, and Sacchi responded with two limited edition, upgraded versions, the Racing and RS; the latter likely to become as collectable as the Telaio Rosso V7 Sport over time.

Monster Competition

Alongside the sports-bike craze was another phenomenon, driven by a single motorcycle that was to spawn a legion of impersonators. When the Castiglioni brothers took over Ducati, they had envisioned a range of unashamedly upmarket and high-tech motorcycles, but soon discovered they had misread demand. The sports-touring Paso 750 and 906 especially failed to sell (the 4,000-odd production run took almost five years to sell), so they quickly fell back on a 750 and a 900 version of the Pantah to sell on the reflected glory of the 8-valve Superbike range. After a shaky start and a re-style in 1991 by Miguel Galluzzi, these bikes revived the 750 and 900SS names and went on to become best-sellers. Galluzzi quickly became an essential part of the Cagiva/Ducati team, and was a man with an interesting past. A graduate of California's Pasadena Art

Center's College of Design, Galluzzi began his career with Honda following European styling trends, although one trend he picked up on seemed universal. Both in California and Europe he noticed that, if a sports bike was crashed, rather than return it to the factory specification owners typically took the fairing off completely, fitted flat handlebars and painted the bodywork that was left in a less garish manner than the original version; matt black was especially popular. When Galluzzi moved to Italy to join the Castiglioni's Cagiva Group, this was the idea foremost in his thoughts and led to the creation of the most successful Italian motorcycle for decades, and perhaps of all time: the Ducati Monster. The concept was explained by Galluzzi as providing everything a motorcyclist could want. 'All you need is a saddle, tank, engine, two wheels and handlebars,' he proclaimed.

Monsters eventually accounted for two-thirds or more of Ducati's output. The real beauty was that it involved little or no development, and saved the Castiglioni's at a time when Ducati was dangerously short of cash. The chassis was a mix of the 750SS and 851 Superbike, the engine from the 900SS and in truth only the bodywork, pared-down instruments, handlebars and footrests were new. The motorcycle offered all the

sporting credentials that buyers expected from Ducati in an all-round package that appealed to just about every type of motorcyclist. The new class was called 'nakeds', reflecting the lack of bodywork, just like the creations that Galluzzi had noted crashed sports-bikes owners were happy to ride. The Monster was the main reason Ducati were outselling Moto Guzzi threefold in their home market, and often by an even greater margin overseas.

Clearly Moto Guzzi needed a competitor to the Monster, since like Ducati they could promote a sporting heritage in a bike that could be enjoyed in every facet of motorcycling. Freelance designer Luigi Marabese was briefed to style the new motorcycle, intended to plug the gaping chasm between the California cruiser and the Daytona/1100 Sport models. The result was introduced in 1995 at the Milan Show, christened the Centauro after the half-man, half-horse creature of Greek mythology. Essentially, the engine and chassis were the Daytona RS, complete with forged pistons and Carrillo conrods. Unlike Ducati's Monster, there was no evidence of trying to keep production costs down and even the forks and wheels were Daytona specification by White Power and Marchesini, respectively. But like the Monster, here was a serious sports bike

The Centauro was next to the Daytona in terms of specification but did not sell well, and is rarely seen away from Moto Guzzi club meetings such as this one.

wrapped in unique bodywork. Early independent tests grumbled that the Daytona motor required more revs than the upright riding position led them to expect, but the handling was excellent and most observers concluded that everything that felt dated about the Daytona was perfectly at home on the brutally styled cruiser. Unfortunately, the styling was far from loved, and perhaps Marbese's previous work styling scooters was the blame for bodywork that one reviewer thought looked 'more like an upturned canoe' than a motorcycle.

The Centauro went into production the following year, with a launch making much of 1996 being Moto Guzzi's 75th anniversary. Sadly, sales of the Centauro not only failed to match expectations, it was almost completely ignored by buyers who were not already Moto Guzzi fans. The styling probably accounted for much of this, and the high price did the rest. The Centauro only survived for two years with just 207 built in the launch year and 1,265 in 1997. By comparison, Ducati sold well over 5,000 Monster 900s over the same period, plus another 13,000 of the 600 and 750 variants. Clearly there was demand for a cruiser-styled sports bike, even if Moto Guzzi hadn't yet found a way to satisfy it. For 1997, the Centauro was replaced by the GT and Sport updates, but production fell shy of 200 units while, despite a slew of competitors, the Monster continued as best-seller. The problem seemed to be that Guzzi fans preferred the torque, simplicity and reliability of the 2-valve heads over the Centauro's 4-valve items, and nobody else would even consider a Centauro. Although a poor seller, the Centauro gave an insight into the difficulties Moto Guzzi faced, unable to attract a new breed of buyers but with existing customers who were highly conservative and unwilling to embrace radical new models. It should come as no surprise that the Ippogriffo (half-eagle, half horse) 750 cruiser, shown in 1996, never made production, despite using a new V-twin engine. This was based around a Todero design for a twin-engined unmanned spy drone, initially built and operated by Israel and remaining in service with the American military as the RQ-5 Hunter.

New Management and New Ideas

Amidst this uncertainty, and despite rising profitability and production once again above 6,000 motorcycles a year, De Tomaso resigned (although retained a healthy share option) and in May 1997, Finprogetti sold its majority shareholding to US bank Tamarix. Oscar Cecchinato replaced Sacchi as chairman, and another thorough review of Moto Guzzi's operations and

opportunities was undertaken by American investment advisers. There was much made of the need to grow Moto Guzzi's market share, particularly among the European 'born-agains', and to attract younger customers across all markets. To achieve this, the new masters brought substantial new capital, aimed at not only model development, but also improving the factory and machinery. There was a new prototype engine, designed by an equally new team working with Danilo Mojoli and Ricardo Engineering in England: a super-compact, 70-degree, liquid-cooled V-twin, intended to be produced in various capacities of up to 1200cc and with racing potential, reflected in the intention to fit chain final drive rather than Moto Guzzi's traditional shaft drive. Advisers to Moto Guzzi's new owners expressed concern that up to 70 per cent of Moto Guzzi's production was bought by the Italian Government, mainly for the police. As Moto Guzzi had discovered before, Italy's membership of the European Union meant that such cosy relationships could not be taken for granted and that governments were required to give other member states the chance to bid for such contracts. So Cecchinato grasped the opportunity to build a Piaggio-designed, four-stroke, single-cylinder engine, alongside a scooter, to expand the Moto Guzzi brand and to appeal to new buyers, providing stability if the police contract was lost. Despite assessing Moto Guzzi's existing 54,500 square metre factory to be operating at just 55 per cent capacity, it was decided to buy a second factory in Monza (owned by Phillips Electronics) to take production away from Mandello. The Mandello premises would remain for 'spares and servicing requirements', as the new factory would be closer to transport links and new bedfellows Piaggio. However, this is the point at which Moto Guzzi's excellent relationship with its workforce faltered. Even through De Tomaso's changes and the industrial strife associated with the 1970s, Moto Guzzi employees had been loyal and willing. Tamarix's own report declared that:

> Relations with Moto Guzzi employees are considered by management to be good. Moto Guzzi was not subjected to any significant local work stoppages or strikes in 1997. In December 1997, however, Moto Guzzi experienced a work stoppage of one hour duration prompted by reports that management was considering alternative locations as part of its long-term expansion.

By now Moto Guzzi might only employ 360 people, but those people still view their – and Moto Guzzi's – home as Mandello del Lario. This fallout cost Cecchinato his post as managing director, as he was swiftly replaced by Dino Falciola, although

**The California continued to evolve
with the EV version.**
MOTO GUZZI

cancelling the move to the Monza factory also meant losing the opportunity to work with Piaggio. And then, in 1998, Moto Guzzi's worst fears were realized when BMW won the contract to supply motorcycles to the Italian police.

Moto Guzzi responded to a need for sales the same way they had for thirty years: upgrade the California. The 1997 California EV brought fuel-injection to the 1064cc engine, as well as detail improvements and a growing reputation for quality. More importantly, with decent suspension the California maintained Italy's reputation for making motorcycles that handled well, and this increasingly made it an exception in the custom or cruiser class, where the Japanese and American competition placed styling above all other considerations. When US magazine *Cycle World* declared the EV winner in a thirteen-motorcycle test, Moto Guzzi could legitimately claim to offer the best cruiser in the world; it also made a fine tourer and a useful all-round motorcycle – an increasingly rare commodity in a marketplace where models tended to specialize as touring or sports models. To expand the appeal of the California, and to ensure traditional buyers weren't alienated by the model's relentless shift upmarket, Moto Guzzi tried once again to take a leaf out of Ducati's book. In 1998, a 'Dark' version of the 600 Monster was launched under the banner 'Your first Ducati', with unlacquered matt black paintwork on the tank and components such as the side-panels and mudguards

left as unfinished plastic. A 900 version soon followed, and both models quickly became bestsellers. Alongside the new bikes, Ducati launched a range of customizing equipment, including custom-painted fuel-tanks, and supported this with competitions aimed at persuading owners to create unique motorcycles from a mass-produced model.

In fairness, the launch of Moto Guzzi's equivalent Jackal in 1999 followed the Monster Dark's so closely that there may just have been something in the waters of northern Italy. So while the 1999 California Special gained bigger mudguards, and an ever more laid-back riding position, the Jackal moved in the opposite direction, with sparse chromework, black paint and a sense of sparse purpose. In a way it was a T3 for the late twentieth century, an all-round, all-day, everyday motorcycle. There was the inevitable range of accessories and marketing, which sought to attract a new, younger buyer to Moto Guzzi. While it enjoyed some success, once again Moto Guzzi seemed unable to create a buzz around a product that might appeal to buyers other than the traditional Guzzi fanbase. At least that fanbase wasn't being ignored, and the Jackal was joined by the V11 Sport that had first been shown almost two years earlier, along with a 1064cc version of the resurrected Quota giant trail-bike. The V11 Sport was everything the Centauro should have been, in essence a Daytona with the 2-valve, 1064cc engine, finally fitted with a six-speed gearbox. Styling was nicely brutal and, like the

The Jackal was a stripped down California that created a new entry-level Moto Guzzi.

name, the green and red paintwork harked back to the Telaio Rosso. Options allowed for the by now *de rigueur* carbon-fibre replacement fittings, as well as a less aggressive riding position. There was also a fully faired touring version ready for production. Then in spring 2000, it was announced that Aprilia were about to buy Moto Guzzi, with the newest large-scale Italian motorcycle manufacturer buying the oldest.

Aprilia Take-Over

Aprilia was founded after World War II by Cavaliere Alberto Beggio, as a bicycle manufacturer in Noale, up in the northeast of Italy, close to Venice. Alberto's son, Ivano Beggio, took over in 1968 and set to expanding into mopeds and then small motocross bikes. In 1977, Ivan Alborghetti won the Italian 125 and 250cc motocross championships for Aprilia, moving on to the international stage in 1978 with two podium finishes and sixth place overall in the World Championship. This commitment to competition would, more than any other Italian manufacturer, define Aprilia. When Nicolas Terol took the 125 win in the Czech Grand Prix on 15 August 2010, Aprilia became the most successful motorcycle racers in history, surpassing fellow Italians MV Agusta with a record 276 victories. The commitment continues today with Max Biaggi's World

Superbike Championships in 2010 and 2012, even if Aprilia have had little success in Moto GP. But alongside the racing glory, Aprilia president Ivano Beggio craved a little of Moto Guzzi's heritage, and felt that the Mandello twins would complement Aprilia's usually avant-garde range perfectly, as well as ensuring the historic marque's future. He had tried to buy Moto Guzzi before, but the dawn of the new millennium was the first time Aprilia's cash reserves had coincided with Moto Guzzi being up for sale. In truth, the match between the two firms was perfect. Beggio also saw the value of keeping Guzzi at the Mandello plant, investing in new machinery to restore the marque's reputation for reliability and quality. Even better, the purchase would mean Beggio controlled Guzzi's model range for the firm's eightieth anniversary in 2001.

In the end, only one special edition would make the showrooms in time to see Moto Guzzi turn octogenarian – a titivated V11 Sport with a red, black and carbon-fibre makeover to justify the Rosso Mandello tag and 'limited edition' numbered plaques. It was joined the following year by the California EV80, with leather saddlebags to match the saddle, and another tweaked V11 Sport, the bright red, half-faired V11 Le Mans. Indeed, Aprilia mined Moto Guzzi's history ruthlessly with a series of V11s, most notably a green and silver Le Mans Tenni, painted to replicate Carcano's 1950 racers and honour Omobono Tenni. The Jackal became the even more stripped-

The Stone was another entry-level version of the California sold at a low price with the aim of persuading owners to personalize and upgrade the bike with Moto Guzzi's own range of accessories.
MOTO GUZZI

back Stone range, while Aprilia wisely focused on updating the factory and rebuilding Moto Guzzi as a global brand. There was also a new styling department at Mandello, an idea that had launched Aprilia onto the world stage. Beggio had always put design first, and the Aprilia design and development department employed more people than the manufacturing part of the business. Aprilia was a new breed of producer, one that designed a product and then outsourced manufacturing. Complete engines arrived from Rotax, to be bolted into a chassis that had also been built elsewhere. Design was considered to be the core business, and the first fruits of this concept were applied at Moto Guzzi late in 2002 and early in 2003, when two new concept models were shown. These were two of the most exciting Moto Guzzis seen for many years, and were quickly approved for production.

The Shock of the New: the Griso and MGS-01

First of these new models was the Griso, named after a character in *The Betrothed* by Alessandro Manzoni, one of the most famous works in Italian literature. Published in 1827, the darkly moralistic story is set close to what would become Moto Guzzi's home. Manzoni described the character of Griso

as having power 'greater in reality in the minds of others' and casts Griso as a tough and fearless leader 'who naturally undertook all the most daring enterprises... imposing upon himself the most unfair and dangerous jobs'. Given that Moto Guzzi's own Griso would have to take on much more powerful and successful motorcycles in the battle for sales, the name was well chosen. Initially shown with the 8-valve Daytona-type engine, it was the chassis and styling that marked it out as special. Thick, silver frame tubes snaked around the bike, mimicking the equally serpentine exhaust system. For the first time on a Moto Guzzi there was a single-sided swingarm with rising rate suspension and a new shaft-drive system to improve handling. This was labelled CARC, for Cardano Reattivo Compatto or Compact Reactive Carden, a carden being a transmission shaft with one or more universal joints in it. The idea behind this, like Dr John's efforts with the Daytona, was to separate power transmission from the swingarm. The swingarm was a large casting hiding the driveshaft and its two universal joints, which were free to float and could not apply the forces to the swingarm that traditionally spoilt a shaft-driven motorcycle's handling. In essence, it was the system Dr John had developed, but protected from the elements.

The Griso also brought something else new to Moto Guzzi, something arguably far more important. For the first in a long time, perhaps even since 1975 when the original Le Mans

This version of the Griso had the Tenni colour scheme that harked back to Carcano's green-painted racers. MOTO GUZZI

BELOW LEFT: **The Griso is what the Centauro tried to be, a sportsbike with an upright riding position.** MOTO GUZZI

BELOW RIGHT: **The 8-valve Griso is easily identified by the twin silencers designed to look like a figure 8 viewed from the rear.** MOTO GUZZI

débuted, people were talking about a Moto Guzzi that everyone loved the look of. Although it would be two years before the Griso made production, the 8-valve engine wisely replaced with the 2-valve 1064cc engine, the radical and aggressive styling would survive the transition from concept show bike to the showroom almost entirely unscathed.

But Moto Guzzi's new team had a second, and even more extreme, motorcycle to shock traditionalists with at the tail end of 2002: the MGS-01 Corsa (Moto Guzzi Sport 1 Racing), again using the old Daytona and Centauro 8-valve engine mated to the V11's six-speed gearbox. The MGS-01 was developed

by Ghezzi and Brian (the odd name refers to the founders Giuseppe Ghezzi and Bruno 'Brian' Saturno), who had been building limited-run Guzzi-based sports bikes for some time. The driving force behind the firm was Giuseppe Ghezzi, with business acumen from Brian and assistant Riccardo Teruzzi. Ghezzi was a long-time Guzzi fan, who had toured Europe on his Le Mans before donating its engine to a one-off chassis he had designed.

The founding partners joined forces in 1995 with the aim of developing a Moto Guzzi racer for the Italian Supertwins' series. The resulting motorcycle dominated the 1996 championship

– Ghezzi's Super Twin prototype winning nine of the thirty-two races it entered. The follow-up was the Ghezzi and Brian Super Twin 1100, designed to give road-riders a replica for the road. So it was understandable that in January 2002, Ghezzi and Brian were invited by Moto Guzzi to develop an official factory version, with all new styling. Basing their prototype on an engine developed for the American AMA Pro-Thunder series, and displacing 1225cc, the production version of the MGS-01 Corsa would claim 128bhp, while pushing along just 422lb (192kg). The plan was to build a limited run for racing, with a road-legal version following soon after.

ABOVE LEFT: **The MGS-01 was a radical departure for Moto Guzzi, and an instantly competitive racer.** MYKEL NICOLAOU

ABOVE RIGHT: **The 1225cc engine builds on Dr John's developments.** MYKEL NICOLAOU

LEFT: **Despite being built to order only, the MGS-01 is very competitively priced, especially given the quality of components.** MYKEL NICOLAOU

RIDING THE BIKES | MGS-01

The ultimate sporting Moto Guzzi, and one as different to every other sports bike as it is possible to imagine. Yet the MGS-01 is still a very special motorcycle and one that proud owner, Shaun Power, wanted before he'd even seen one in the 'flesh'.

Shaun Power came up through the ranks of motorcycling in a way typical of a certain generation of British riders: a sports moped at sixteen, followed by a climb up the Japanese capacity ladder. But fate intervened when, along with a couple of friends, he thought it would be fun to enter a six-hour endurance race on a 1990s Ducati 900SS. A class win sowed the seeds of an obsession, and even as his track-day habit grew, he became unwittingly bored with the benign excellence of Japanese sports bikes. During 2006, with magazines running images of Gianfranco Guareschi racing an MGS-01 on his way to becoming Italian Supertwins Champion, Shaun gradually became obsessed. In fact, the media had become obsessed with Guareschi themselves, since he started 2006 with a double win on the MGS-01 at Daytona just before Moto Guzzi's 85th anniversary.

The wins came in a Battle of the Twins event with no restrictions on engine displacement or modifications. Yet Guareschi's Moto Guzzi MGS-01 was apparently completely standard and available to anyone who would hand over the £16,000 asking price. Admittedly that's for a motorcycle that

Gianfranco Guareschi was almost unbeatable on the MGS-01.
MOTO GUZZI

cannot be legally ridden on the public highway (although some have succeeded in addressing that failing), but it still seems a bargain for such a highly specified motorcycle. Powered by an air-cooled, 8-valve, 1225cc, 90-degree V-twin, the MGS-01 features front and rear Öhlins suspension, Cosworth pistons and radial Brembo brakes; these were still rare in 2006. Each motorcycle is (they are still theoretically available to special order) delivered with a handbook recording the rider's details and the bike's frame number, along with a cover and paddock stand embossed with the MGS-01 Corsa logo. Even the packaging is personalized. Yet it still took Shaun a while to make up his mind.

Shaun Power was inspired by Guareschi to own a MGS-01 for track days. PETE WILEMAN

Continued overleaf

Continued from previous page

RIDING THE BIKES | **MGS-01**

I think images influence us so much, but then I'm a graphic designer so I would say that. The photo of Guareschi leaning this big Guzzi into turns kept coming back to me, and I really fancied an Italian track day bike. But the dealers said they were race-bikes and there was no warranty, so I tried to forget about it. But then Haywards (a Moto Guzzi dealer in Cambridge) said that if I let them do the servicing – which means new pistons every thousand miles – they would provide a two year guarantee. So that was it: I was the proud owner of a Moto Guzzi MGS-01 Corsa.

In fact, using it for track days helps to keep the mileage realistic, and even with new pistons, a service is a little over £400 all-in, a figure that will have Ducati 8-valve owners weeping into their cappuccinos when it's time to replace the cam belts. But in the end the real litmus test is – what's it like to ride?

It rides pretty well, and you do feel you're part of the equation, not just along for the ride; it makes you feel pretty special. The only real downside is the six-speed gearbox: you only ever can use top on the back straight at Silverstone, but by the afternoon of a trackday the gearbox has got so hot that you keep finding false neutrals. On a bike that lets you rely on so much engine braking it can make for some pretty hair raising moments. But in the pits it has a presence and uniqueness that has people coming over to look at it and chat. Most trackday bikes get ignored by other riders, but not this one. Everybody loves it.

The MGS-01 is also incredibly rare: there are probably fewer than 200 in existence and 18 at most in the UK.

You can see why everybody loves it. From every angle the MGS-01 looks brutally purposeful. If it was human, it would be a strong jawed, manfully biceped, action hero. This is not an anodyne sports bike trying to seduce you by being a tiny bit better and minutely different to the 4-cylinder competition; this is a bike that bellows, '*Viva la differenza*' to an awe-struck audience. The professional motorcycle photographer who came along to visit Shaun was as smitten as the rest of us, rating the bike 'The best looking production bike for years'. It really is that good in the flesh. Where Shaun's other

RIGHT: **Shaun has added a reference to another Italian beauty, Sophia Loren**

BELOW: **The MGS-01 features much carbon fibre and Öhlins suspension.**
MYKEL NICOLAOU

motorcycles have been impressively accessorized and uprated, the only changes he has made to the MGS-01 are the #85 decal on the tail piece, a nod towards this being the 85th MGS-01 built, along with the Sophia logo on the fairing. 'Sophia Loren will always mean something to a certain generation,' smiles Shaun. 'You can't beat *El Cid* on a Sunday afternoon.' Indeed. Or seeing an MGS-01 in action.

SPECIFICATIONS — MOTO GUZZI MGS-01 (2004–12)

Layout and Chassis

90-degree V-twin four-stroke racing motorcycle

Engine

Type	90-degree V-twin
Block material	Aluminium alloy
Head material	Aluminium alloy
Cylinders	2
Cooling	Air
Bore and stroke	100 × 78mm
Capacity	1225cc
Valves	8 valves ohc
Compression ratio	11:1
Carburettor	Marelli DFI 56mm chokes
Max. power	128bhp@8,000rpm
Fuel capacity	4 gallons/18.5 litres

Transmission

Gearbox	Six-speed foot-change
Clutch	Dry twin plate
Final drive	Shaft with double universal joints

Chassis

Front	Telescopic fork
Rear	Swingarm

Steering

Tyres	120/60 17in front – 180/55 17in rear
Brakes	Triple discs

Dimensions

Wheelbase	56in (1,423mm)
Unladen weight	422lb (192kg)

Performance

Top speed	Not quoted or tested

While the Griso and MGS-01 were intended to add glamour to the Guzzi range, the equally new Breva 750 was another fresh new design using a much improved 744cc version of Tonti's small-block engine. Breva is the southerly breeze that brings good weather to Lake Como, so seemed an apt name for a model intended to bring good fortune to Aprilia's vision of Moto Guzzi's future. Unfortunately, in reality storm clouds were gathering. Aprilia, like fellow Italian scooter manufacturers Piaggio, were trapped in a spiral of falling sales, dwindling cashflow and heavy debt. Aprilia relied on scooter sales, despite building motorcycles that could win races, because the big sports bikes were generating little in the way of cashflow. Aprilia had an offer from Ducati for Moto Guzzi, but it would have left the very real possibility that Aprilia, along with the Laverda name that Aprilia had also expensively acquired, would disappear altogether. As Beggio pointed out, 'the proposal presented by Ducati, while much appreciated… is less adequate to the immediate management demands and the expectations of important stakeholders'. So Aprilia threw their lot in with Piaggio, and Beggio salvaged the title of Honorary President of Aprilia after the takeover.

Piaggio's own problems had started when they had decided to invest time and money trying to market expensive Italian mopeds to the Chinese. Expanding scooter sales had allowed both firms to ignore their structural mistakes, but the market was about to shrink disastrously. In March 2000, the Italian Government had finally introduced legislation, commonplace elsewhere in Europe, requiring all riders of powered two-wheelers to wear a helmet, where previously scooter riders had been exempt. Historically, fewer than 20 per cent of scooter riders had chosen to wear protective headgear and with the new legislation rigorously enforced, scoter sales collapsed, leaving Aprilia's new range of large-capacity scooters especially affected. Then in January 2002, the Euro replaced the lira (as it had in some international trading from 1999) and Italian exporters found they could no longer rely upon the quiet but long-term devaluation of the lira to boost exports and deter importers. Worse still, both firms had expanded on borrowed

LEFT: **The Nevada 750 and California 1100 remain as entry-level Moto Guzzis in some markets.**
MOTO GUZZI

BELOW: **HM King Abdullah II and Piaggio CEO Roberto Colaninno admire a special California.**
MOTO GUZZI

money and reached the point where not only were they struggling to raise new capital, but also had nervous creditors asking about repayment schedules. In essence, they faced a perfect storm of falling demand, rising costs and an appreciating currency. Through no fault of anyone at Moto Guzzi, their fate was now tied to Aprilia, regardless of the devotion many felt towards Mandello's most famous child.

Another New Owner

Brand devotion was what Italian corporate raider Roberto Colaninno was relying on when he bought Piaggio for $133 million in October 2003. The bargain price-tag reflected the sagging fortunes of the iconic marque, immortalized by the Vespa scooter in the 1953 film *Roman Holiday*. In December 2003, Colaninno then used Piaggio to acquire Aprilia and Moto Guzzi in a $200 million deal, although it would not be finalized until the following August. Believing he could restore his collection of Italian two-wheelers with 'new, top-quality management, and growth allowing us to compete with the Japanese,' he sounded like De Tomaso thirty years earlier. But then, like De Tomaso, Colaninno had a chequered but generally brilliant money-making past. After working his way up to CEO at Olivetti and dazzling Italy with a $41 billion take-over of Telecom Italia in 1999, he was ousted three years later when shareholders backed a takeover by Pirelli. So in 2002, Colaninno was looking for a new challenge, and Italian motorcycling fitted the bill nicely. Starting

with a product offensive at Piaggio, he was an early adopter of the retro craze that is still with us, and launched a new range of scooters that wouldn't have looked out of place in *Roman Holiday*. In a remarkable reversal of fortunes, sales of these vintage-style bikes allowed Piaggio to post substantial profits in 2004 and claim a 24 per cent market share in Europe when sales of all marques – including Moto Guzzi – were taken into account. But Moto Guzzi's contribution to the whole was minimal, with production down to fewer than 4,000 motorcycles in 2004, almost as bad as 1993s post-war low and a far cry from the 46,000-plus units built in 1971.

Colaninno's real genius was then persuading creditor banks to swap debt for equity (shares), taking a huge amount of pressure off the group. He also introduced competition among suppliers, and began looking to China for cheaper parts. In April 2004, Piaggio signed a joint-venture agreement with Chinese group Zongshen for the production and marketing of Italian-designed engines, vehicles and parts for the Asian market. Not everyone approved, but it was exactly the sort of deal De Tomaso would have cut. Unlike De Tomaso, however, Colaninno didn't try and impose his ideas about what sort of motorcycles Moto Guzzi should build. Instead, in March 2005, he appointed the former president of Alfa Romeo, Daniele Bandiera, to reinvigorate Moto Guzzi. Fortunately, while the boardroom machinations had been grinding on, Moto Guzzi's engineers had kept their heads down and spirits up, and they

ABOVE: **The weather as you travel to the Arctic circle can be as grey as this Norge.**
MOTO GUZZI

LEFT: **Moto Guzzi CEO Danielle Bandiera poses on a red Norge. To promote the updated model in 2012 a group of journalists were invited to repeat Naco Guzzi's ride through Norway on his GT.**
MOTO GUZZI

had a new – or rather, much developed – 11 Evolution version of the 4-valve, 1064cc V-twin ready for production. Bandiera, therefore, had new models to hand, first with a Breva 1100, which mirrored the 750's styling but used the new Evolution engine. Then in September, the Griso was finally made available with a lightly tuned version of the 1100 Evolution engine, rather than the 8-valve Daytona motor it had originally been shown with. The MGS-01 project was quietly shelved, reflecting the decision to take Moto Guzzi in a new direction, abandoning the sports and custom models that had pretty much defined the V-twin era at Mandello. Giving up on sports bikes might have appeared logical, given that even the MGS-01's 128bhp was far from class-leading and Piaggio intended Aprilia to become their sports bike brand: there was certainly enough competition in the category without creating more in-house. So the Le Mans and the V11 range bowed out in 2005 with the high-specification, carbon-fibre and Öhlins-equipped, Scura R (Dark Racing).

The Griso Goes into Production and Sales Grow

Moving away from the custom look was more of a statement than a reality and, in practice, the revised Nevada, Breva and Californias looked much as before, although the latter gained the Breva 1100 engine and a 'Vintage' version in the black and white colour scheme of the original. So far, so business as usual at Moto Guzzi. There was also an 877cc, short-stroke version of the V1100 engine to expand the Griso and Breva's appeal. The big news was the Norge ('Norway', named after the pre-war Moto Guzzi that introduced the rear swinging arm), a fully faired, big tourer available in four versions to satisfy demands as varied as super-commuter to grand tourer. The Norge introduced an even bigger, 1151cc version of the V1100 engine, and proved to be a surprise hit to those outside Moto Guzzi. For the first time in over twenty years, production at Mandello in 2006 exceeded 10,000 motorcycles.

The touring Norge became Moto Guzzi's best seller when first launched.
MOTO GUZZI

Perhaps 150 of that 10,000-plus were of the racing-only versions MGS-01 Corse. When overseas importers discovered that development of the exclusive sports bike had actually got as far as building a production-line of sorts, the factory was persuaded to make the MGS-01 available to special order.

Although many disappeared into private collections, those that were raced met with some success. In 2006 and 2007, Italian Gianfranco Guareschi dominated the AHRMA Battle of the Twins F1 competition at Daytona, as well as winning the Italian Supertwins Championship. By the time Gianfranco's father

The Vintage version of the California harked back to the original model. MOTO GUZZI

For some the *Giornata Mondiale Guzzi* (World Guzzi Day) has been an opportunity to pose their bikes in front of Moto Guzzi's famous V8. This particular Le Mans has been much altered, something Moto Guzzi owners seem to relish.
MOTO GUZZI

Claudio had finished with his racer, it was making 136bhp, yet Moto Guzzi made little play of the MGS-01's achievements, and steadfastly stuck to their plan of producing nakeds and tourers. There was never a road-going version of the MGS-01, although there are at least two converted for road use in the UK, reflecting the comparative ease of registering racing motorcycles as road-legal vehicles in Britain.

The year 2006 was also Moto Guzzi's 85th birthday, so Piaggio made the most of *Giornata Mondiale Guzzi* (World Guzzi Day), an annual event held at the Mandello plant each September since 2001. Starting as little more than an invitation for owners to visit the factory, with the additional publicity and attractions on offer, a claimed 15,000 people attended in 2006. That figure has grown over the years, but even sixty years on, the numbers are still comparable to the hoards of Guzzino that joined in the street party Moto Guzzi had laid for owners in June 1949. In fairness, back then Moto Guzzi was a high-volume, low-value manufacturer protected by import quotas, where the Piaggio group's aim was to trade on Moto Guzzi's heritage and build quality to sell premium, large-capacity motorcycles to a world-wide audience. Given that a sizeable proportion of those who attend the Giornata Mondiale ride there on late-model Guzzi V-twins, there is clearly a lot of love for Mandello. It might well have been the turnout that caused management to backpedal on the no-more-sports bikes edict and introduce the 2007 1200 Sport, a pugnacious looking bike that successfully mixed elements of the Norge and Breva to create a traditional Moto Guzzi sports bike. Although by the standards of the time it was really a Moto Guzzi with a sporting edge, rather than the road-legal racing motorcycles that now defined sports bikes, the world's infatuation with sports bikes was coming to an end.

Adventure Bikes and a New Breed of Buyer

Early in 2005 a British television series came to an end, starting a craze for what would be come to be known as adventure bikes. Motorcycle programmes are rare on UK terrestrial television, but the programme did well enough to spawn further series largely due to featuring Ewan McGregor. At the time McGregor was starring in the *Star Wars* trilogy but was actually a truly versatile and loved actor ranked at thirty-six on *Empire* magazine's 'Top 100 Movie Stars of All Time' list in 1997; in short, he was a global celebrity who was able to bring motorcycling to a universal audience. The show followed McGregor and friend Charley Boorman travelling from London to New York, via Europe, Ukraine, Russia, Kazakhstan, Mongolia, Siberia and Canada. The total cumulative distance travelled was 18,887 miles (30,396km), using their motorcycles wherever possible.

Long Way Round started with Boorman advocating riding KTMs, a much admired Austrian off-road (and latterly sports)

Even a star like Ewan McGregor wants to try out the V8 while Charley Boorman looks on.
MOTO GUZZI

Ewan McGregor admires the factory 250 racers. McGregor had an old loop-frame V-twin with a sidecar for transporting his dog: apparently people stare at the dog and fail to notice the outfit's famous rider.
MOTO GUZZI

motorcycle manufacturer. Infamously, KTM turned them down, and the trip was ultimately undertaken using three R1150GS adventure bikes from BMW. Sales exploded, as the ageing motorcycling community suddenly woke up to the fact that sports bikes were uncomfortable and far too powerful for most riding conditions. Sports bikes might have offered the reflected glory of the race-track, but the big R1150GS suddenly offered the reflected glory of the *Long Way Round*, and BMW would sell nearly 78,000 by the time the six-year production ended. Sadly, Moto Guzzi had no even vaguely comparable model, since production of the unloved Quota had ended in 2001.

The follow-up series, 2007's *Long Way Down*, followed McGregor and Boorman from John O'Groats in Scotland to Cape Town in South Africa using BMW R1200GSs, the 1150's replacement. This time Moto Guzzi was ready. The programme showed McGregor preparing for the trip in London using a white Griso as his personal transport, and he was also guest of honour at *Giornata Mondiale Guzzi* in September 2007 shortly after completing the trip. At the end of the event, Daniele Torresan, the man responsible for Piaggio's external relations, handed McGregor the keys to a white California for him to ride back home. Once back in the UK, the bike was auctioned to raise funds for the United Nations Children's Fund (UNICEF), the charity supported and promoted by both *Long Way...* series. There might have been some Guzzi traditionalists horrified by this most traditional of firms embracing celebrity culture,

but it has become the modern way. And anyway, the traditionalists had the 1200 Sport.

By the time the *Long Way Down* aired at the end of 2007, Moto Guzzi had launched their own adventure bike, the Stelvio, named after the highest paved mountain pass in the eastern Alps. Fortunately, Moto Guzzi had addressed the issue of a replacement for the Quota very cleverly, and the new model had strong visual links to both the Norge and the Griso, without looking like a parts bin special. Indeed it looked a suitably rugged travelling companion and while suitably man-sized for this style of motorcycle, wasn't as ludicrously oversized as the original Quota. This new approach to styling was no accident, because Miguel Galluzzi was involved. He had left Cagiva to join Aprilia in 2006, twenty years on from designing the Ducati Monster and presumably wishing some of his other work would be recognized. Unfortunately, the Stelvio wasn't an immediate hit, largely due to a small (by class standards) 4-gallon (18 litre) fuel-tank and incongruously revvy 8-valve engine, a development of the Norge's 1151cc motor. While the new engine felt right at home in the newly launched 8v Griso, it didn't provide the low-end power that big off-road motorcycles need, even if very few are ever used in such conditions. A 2011 update addressed this, and increased fuel capacity to 7 gallons (32 litres). There was also traction control provided by Aprilia, who had updated the engine mapping, the overlapping skills within Piaggio now starting to pay off.

The latest Stelvio, a style of motorcycle made popular almost single-handedly by McGregor's 'Long Way...' TV franchise.
MOTO GUZZI

BELOW: **The NTX version of the Stelvio is aimed at occasional off-road use.**
MOTO GUZZI

Rationalization and a New Entry-Level Moto Guzzi

Having introduced an 1151cc version of the Guzzi V-twin, it would be 2011 by the time the Norge adopted the 8-valve version, partly because, in 2008, it was still Moto Guzzi's top-seller. Over that period there would be rationalization of the range to focus on the 1200 8-valve engine powering the rear wheel via a six-speed gearbox and the CARC shaft drive in a variety of formats: the Griso, Norge, Stelvio and (with 2-valve heads) 1200 Sport and Breva. Almost as left-overs, the California and Nevada 750 soldiered on and, in theory, the MGS-01 was still available to special order. The curious omission to the range was the lack of a retro-model; by 2008, Ducati had their SportClassic range, Triumph the Bonneville and there were various other manufacturers making forays into the market sector. The rather dated and less than beautiful Nevada was also the only 'entry level' Moto Guzzi and wasn't even available in some countries. The Bellagio, running a unique 936cc, short-stroke version of the 4-valve 1200 engine, was a nicely judged Ducati Monster competitor but in 2008 was priced at almost half as much again as the Ducati 695, Bonneville or even the Harley-Davidson 883. If Moto Guzzi was to grow, they needed an entry-level model that could compete with these icons of style, and quickly.

Taking the Breva 750 and the handy fortieth anniversary of the V7 Special, little more than new bodywork saw the launch of the V7 Classic. Wisely copying the styling of the V7 Sport, rather than the loop-frame Special, this was full circle for the innovations of Lino Tonti, who had passed away in 2002, still in service to Moto Guzzi. Here was a 744cc version of Tonti's small-block engine mimicking the first Guzzi he designed. The Heron heads made the new V7 rather breathless but the styling was perfectly judged and the price was a match for the bottom-rung products of competitors. Unsurprisingly, the V7 became Guzzi's best-seller by far, and Guzzi finally seemed to be on a path to follow Ducati on to the world stage. Grand plans were rolled out to undertake refurbishment and rebuilding at the factory, with cultural and exhibition spaces, a new museum and events that played to Guzzi's reputation as building excellent touring motorcycles. But there were problems ahead, and not just for Moto Guzzi.

In the six years running up to 2008, the world's borrowing – corporate, personal and government – had doubled, with most of the debt being accumulated in Europe and the USA, Moto Guzzi's prime markets. Inevitably a crisis hit and, in 2008, the West's financial system came crashing down, destroying many industries. The radical changes 2008 brought to many people's fortunes choked demand, not just for motorcycles, and the effects of the subsequent recession will doubtless be with us for many years. The hopes and plans laid out for Moto Guzzi to double the 2007 production run of 10,000 motorcycles were in tatters, and by 2010, production was in fact limping along at less than half that. It was time, once more, for Moto Guzzi to regroup and face an uncertain future.

ABOVE: **The Bellagio is named after the town at the northern end of the old Circuito del Lario, and used an unusual short-stroke version of the old 1100 motor that displaced 940cc.**
MOTO GUZZI

LEFT: **The Nevada is still built, but no longer listed as a UK model.**
MOTO GUZZI

LEFT: **The V7 Classic seems more at home in Italy than the more contemporary Breva 750.**
MOTO GUZZI

BELOW: **A lunch stop on the Circuito del Lario is a luxury the old racers didn't share.**

RIDING THE BIKES | RACING CLASSIC MOTO GUZZIS IN THE MODERN WORLD

Four-hour races for classic motorcycles have become big news in Europe, with Moto Guzzi often the main beneficiaries. Andrew Gray built a Le Mans-based racer and then flew it from Los Angeles to Spa Francorchamps to join in the fun.

Classic endurance racing is a phenomenon that has reinvented 1970s motorcycle racing. These days you

Manel Segarra senior racing a Le Mans to victory in the 2010 Spa classic four-hour race.
DG SPORT BIKERS' CLASSIC

Christopher Charles-Artigues on French Moto Guzzi importers' Moto Bel classic racer at Spa.
DG SPORT BIKERS' CLASSIC

can spend a happy July evening leaning on the fence below Eau Rouge at Spa Francorchamps, becoming increasingly nostalgic as the smell of sausages, campfires and oil carry in drifts of smoke or mist, just as they did when the Bol d'Or was still held at Le Mans. White headlights dazzle and then red tail lights smudge the night. There are the plaintive wails of Japanese fours, a solitary Yamaha TZ700 tearing linen in the dark and even the odd British triple. It's as if the last 35 years never happened. And then along come the Moto Guzzis, their exhaust note somewhere between the BMW's flat drone and the urgent buzzsaw of the Ducatis. But, unlike the 1970s, a Moto Guzzi isn't just leading: there are a brace of them fighting over the top steps of the podium. You would imagine that anyone who did think about racing here would look at the competition's 1123cc Hondas and 1135cc Kawasakis and realize that these are bigger and hungrier versions of the bikes that defeated Moto Guzzi first time around. By 1980, Mandello del Lario push-rod twin's thunder looked to be the death cry of old technology, beaten into history by 16-valve overhead-cam fours. Yet today the original Moto Guzzi Le Mans thrives in classic endurance racing, without any rule book favouritism, destroying the multis that were its Nemesis back in the 1970s. This could be the toughest racing in the world, with brutally simple rules: your bike must be at least thirty years old and needs to last four hours of racing. Most of the clever electronics and such from today's race shops is banned, although you can run any engine capacity you think will last the race. So it would be madness to simply pick a marque you want to promote. Prospective competitors need to think carefully, especially at Spa, perhaps the greatest closed-circuit still in use, because this is a crucible for testing engines, talent and resolve. Yet here the big Moto Guzzi V-twins look unbeatable.

Moto Bel is the French Moto Guzzi importers, and their Le Mans racer is usually a betting man's favourite in classic endurance racing. These events are run as either a single four-hour race, or split into a pair of two-hour races. The headline events are Spa and the Bol d'Or, now held at Magny Cours in central France. There is also a big event at Cartagena close to Spain's Mediterranean coast and a new

Continued overleaf

RIDING THE BIKES | RACING CLASSIC MOTO GUZZIS IN THE MODERN WORLD

race is being established at Imola. Briefly, the rules allow two-rider teams on a motorcycle that was in production during the 1970s, although flexibility allows for an incredibly varied spectacle that certainly captures the imagination of spectators and competitors alike. The one that holds enthusiasts particularly in thrall is the unbroken four-hour race at Spa, run on the longest (4.4 miles/7km) race-track left in the modern world. Appropriately, there's a Le Mans' style start, riders running across the grid at 8pm and racing – if they are lucky – until midnight. Moto Bel won here in 2009, and won both two-hour Bol d'Or races that year. They can trace their victories and lead rider Christopher Charles-Artigues back to 2003, but in 2010 newcomers from 2009 tasted victory. Team Guzzimotobox drove a thousand miles from their home in Tortosa, south of Barcelona. They arrived at Spa with tools and two motorbikes packed in a van, towing a caravan called home. Their number one bike brought the father and son riders, Manel and Manel Junior Segarra, home as victors. Although subsequent events have brought mixed fortunes, Moto Bel and Motobox have proved that the Moto Guzzi Le Mans makes a formidable endurance racer, leaving far more powerful motorcycles floundering in the wake of the Le Mans' remarkable stability.

Moto Bel's 1150cc 1980 Le Mans is rumoured to make almost 100bhp at the back wheel, which is more than Mike Baldwin's Leoni tuned, US Superbike racer could manage. That might have been back in 1977 and running under the 1000cc class limit (the Le Mans' standard 850 capacity boosted using barrels from the automatic Convert), but Baldwin's bike was a short-circuit racer that only needed to last a sprint race. Moto Bel boss and engine builder Jacques Ifrah manages to make his simple 4-valve twins last four hours and well over 300 miles (480km) by using specially commissioned steel conrods, crankshaft and pistons. That tells how far metallurgy has come in the 35 years that have passed since the original races that the classic series mimics.

To classify for the finish, a team doesn't just need to be running at the chequered flag, they need to have completed three-quarters of the winner's laps – for 2010, that was fifty-eight laps, and just thirty-seven of sixty-seven starters made the cut, even though forty-five bikes crossed the line. Spa kills

engines, the climbs wrecking bottom-ends, while the descents tempt over-revving. Yet still people come, talking of the event as the greatest on the current motorcycle calendar. One such rider is Andrew Gray, who débuted his Guzzi racer here in 2011. Andrew Gray is a long-time Guzzi fan living in Los Angeles, but his native British humour shines through in the name of his race troupe: he calls them Team Guzzi Nerd. He started racing in 2007 and decided to build a Moto Guzzi V-twin for the Vintage Superbike class of the US national AHRMA series. He's raced at Mid Ohio, Utah, New Mexico, as well as Portland and Seattle in local club Vintage races. Andrew tells what made him decide to pack his Moto Guzzi racer and much of his workshop into a huge crate, air-freighted to Brussels, ready to race in the 2011 Spa four-hour race.

I read an article by [American motorcycle writer and TT racer] Mark Gardner about the Classic Bol d'Or about five years ago. A Guzzi [Team Moto Bel] won, which piqued my interest. I think something formulated subconsciously and it became something that if I lived in Europe I would do. Then two years ago I was sitting in a bar in Portland with

Andrew Gray (*right*) and Chris Page raced in the Spa Classic in 2011. Beth Reddick (*centre*) was one of their team.
ANDREW GRAY

my riding partner Chris Page and we were discussing how
badly our US national series is run, and I just blurted out,
'Let's do the Classic Bol d'Or'. I started researching and
came upon Team Glam, a UK endurance team. I contacted
James Clark of the team and he convinced me that Spa is
The One. Basically the idea was to take a year's racing
budget and blow it on one event. We succeeded.

Being the eternal optimist I was hoping for a top ten at
Spa. I think more than anything I hoped to finish, build a
great-looking bike and have a life-changing experience. It's
amazing what can happen when you just decide to go do
something. And I had Chris as my co-rider, a very
experienced club racer and instructor who's someone that
wouldn't do anything silly. Like crash.

Team Guzzi Nerd came eighteenth in the 2011 race, despite
this being their first visit to the circuit. They were also the
first Moto Guzzi home. Yet they weren't even certain they
had an entry until they signed on, as Andrew recalls:

My brother Mark was our fixer. He worked for the
European Union President and gets things done for a living,
so if we needed a translator or enforcer he was our man.
Mark is someone you definitely want on your side. I arrived
in Belgium not knowing if I was actually entered in the
race, even though I had sent my application and money
months before. Mark called the head of Spa and had a
'chat'. I was officially entered an hour later.

Team Guzzi Nerd's race machine started out as a cobbled-
together melting-pot of various bikes, but has evolved over
time. As Andrew says:

The beauty of Guzzis is they are so modular. Our frame
and tank is Le Mans III. Bodywork is Magni Sfida. The forks
are 38mm SPIII, the engine is Sport 1100 retrofitted with
41mm Dell'Ortos carburettors and a distributor. When I
built the engine I knew I'd be the limiting factor, so there
was no point building for outright power. The engine is
fairly mild but bulletproof. The perfect endurance motor,
really. It still runs the stock pistons. Guzzi build things so

Chris chases down a Laverda.
ANDREW GRAY

well, durability is not a worry. Tuning comprises porting,
Megacycle midrange cam, titanium pushrods and skimmed
heads to up the compression to around 11:1. The bottom
end is balanced and blueprinted. It makes 80 rear wheel
horsepower. The chassis has Maxton suspension and we've
good lights.

Andrew found Spa in the flesh daunting enough, but in his
own words, his first thought was 'to get my finger out'.

Andrew's turn on track.
ANDREW GRAY

Continued overleaf

Continued from previous page

RIDING THE BIKES

We had never seen the track before and had limited practice so things were a bit overwhelming. I had taken it a bit easy in the first session and afterwards we were qualified 60th or something out of 80 teams. Only the top 70 teams qualify so there were some nerves. That's when I realized that Spa is for grown-ups. Surprisingly I found night riding fairly easy. Of course that could've been because I was going so slowly… but there are plenty of markers so you can soon remember braking and turn in points. The 100 watt headlight bulb helped. At one point in night-qualifying it started to rain and I remember thinking, 'bloody hell, I don't even ride in the rain let alone race in it. I live in California'. But at least the race went smoothly and to plan.

Nothing broke, we were steady, didn't push. Refuelling went smoothly. Probably after the second hour I thought 'we're going to do this'. Most bikes break in the first hour or two. I started to get a bit jumpy waiting for Chris to finish

Andrew's home-brewed Moto Guzzi racer.
ANDREW GRAY

about 30 minutes before the end. I had spent a lot of time prepping the bike so I was fairly certain it would hold up.

As soon as we finished I started thinking how we could've finished higher. I'm very proud. Of course it's very different to compete for the win, which is what many of the other Guzzi teams do. The bar has been raised by Moto Bel and Moto Box and to be top ten you have to risk blowing up. We competed to finish so the bar is much lower for us and we could potter around. We were consistent and fairly quick at night, so that helped. That's the wonderful thing about endurance racing. It's not all about absolute power. First Guzzi home is wonderful but that was on a technicality as Moto Box were disqualified. I'd much rather be second Guzzi home and see them win. They deserve it. They are blindingly fast.

Hopefully we'll see Team Guzzi Nerd back in Europe. Andrew certainly has plans.

I'd like to improve the bike: lose 30lb (14kg) off it, build a second 95bhp engine and join the ragged edge guys. I'm hoping to be working in Europe. If that's the case, Spa and the Bol for sure. If not I'll find a way to be there. I'm hooked.

There are always others running Moto Guzzi's in the Spa 4-hour race, of which this was just one.

CHAPTER EIGHT

THE FUTURE

The current V7 range outside the famous factory gates. MOTO GUZZI

Visiting the Moto Guzzi factory is easy. You get off the train at Mandello del Lario and there it is, pretty much right in front of you. Getting in is trickier: the museum is open most Monday to Fridays at 3pm, but being Italy it might not be, especially during the summer break. And when they say 3pm, they mean it. Ten-past and you'll find the gates shut, and even if you do get in, all visitors are expected to have left by 4pm. On the other hand, admission is free and, although the 'museum' could also be described as a load of old bikes lining a few first-floor corridors, if you know what you're looking at, then prepare to be astounded: the very first Moto Guzzis ever built, the outrageous V8 racer, a full-size statue of Omobono Tenni and a scale model of the wind-tunnel. You might think the exhibits deserve a better setting, with more perspective and, happily, Piaggio agree. In fact they've been promising a truly imaginative redevelopment of the factory for years. Certainly, Italian timetables

are notoriously flexible, as any number of disappointed would-be museum visitors will attest, but there are those sceptics who feel Piaggio are not serious about revitalizing the factory. Indeed, there are plenty who think that Piaggio are just wriggling until people stop twisting their arm and they can dispose of the factory. Following a 1998 sale-and-leaseback arrangement, the Mandello del Lario facilities are owned by Unicredit and rented by Piaggio, making them one of the few facilities that the parent company doesn't own. So when Piaggio announced they would close it for refurbishment in 2008, locals were certain this was just a ruse, especially when up to five years to complete the work was being talked about. Despite the fact that a new version of the Stelvio, the TT with chunky tyres and panniers, was shown in November, the newspapers and unions viewed the darkened windows of the factory with grim suspicion. There was talk of a judicial review, Unicredit

ABOVE: **With what amount to road tyres the Stelvio is a fine handling motorcycle on tarmac.**

BELOW: **The NTX specification includes panniers.** MOTO GUZZI

wanting to redevelop the site and pretty much any version of events you cared to imagine. Even when the factory did reopen in February 2009, there were mutterings that the 190 employees wouldn't be there for long, and that production would be shifted to the modern Aprilia facilities in Noale.

Even a cursory look at the crumbling edifice of Moto Guzzi's factory will make it clear that there are issues. If you are lucky enough to visit in brilliant sunshine that bleaches the water-stains and paintwork into romantic soft focus, they might seem manageable. See it in the rain and the scale of the neglect and, more importantly, the obsolescence, become more obvious. How can you need all these buildings, pay for and maintain all these buildings, even if you reach Piaggio's target of 20,000 bikes a year? Yet if you arrive just before the museum opens, there's a fair chance that a Guzzi fan from some far-flung corner of the globe is standing by those faded red gates having his photograph taken in front of the Moto Guzzi logo. It may not be at the level of American tourists blocking the Ponte Vecchio, but it is a more frequent occurrence than you'll find at any other Italian motorcycle factory, Ducati included. But while the current Ducati premises might adjoin the older factory, the Guzzi premises are the real deal, a factory that's produced pretty much every Moto Guzzis built since 1921.

If you can get into the factory, perhaps on a Giornata Mondiale Guzzi, it is genuinely awe-inspiring and far bigger than Ducati's current home, although Guzzi never had redevelopment forced upon them by war-time bombing. Pre-war Guzzi were Italy's biggest manufacturer, building 30,000 bikes a year. Production peaked in the early 1970s at over 46,000 bikes, with the new V-twins reflecting glory onto the best-selling singles. These days turning out 10,000 bikes in a year with a workforce of 150 would be considered a cause for celebration, although Piaggio still talk about doubling those figures. More than 1,500 people once worked here, and there was far more than mere manufacturing facilities. There was a medical centre, libraries, shops and a canteen, accommodation for employees, and the racing department's workshop, which is now almost empty, apart from the ghosts. The sad truth is that a factory big enough to do all that forty years ago needs a fraction of that space today. So all those metal window frames and north-light roofs stare blindly at the sky, seeming to ask, 'what next?'. The fears of the people of Mandello looked more than justified.

At least they had new – or rather, updated – motorcycles to build. The first was a new version of the V7 Classic, the V7 Café, with clip-on handlebars, a humped seat and the usual café racer accoutrements. Available with a matt green tank that was a fair facsimile of the original Sport, it harked back

Prototype V7 racer caught outside the factory gates.

to Carcano's magnesium alloy fairings. The other new model was the Griso SE (special equipment) with darker matt green bodywork described as the (Omobono) Tenni colour scheme. Both were well-received by the press, and solid sale success followed. It would be naive to believe this didn't influence what happened next, and on 17 September 2009 Roberto Colaninno, still CEO of the Piaggio group, issued a press release.

A Commitment to Moto Guzzi's Future

'The historical Moto Guzzi factory in Mandello del Lario, in the province of Lecco, will not close. This has been proven by announcing that a meeting with the unions will be held on September 22nd. Our intention is to avoid the cassa integrazione.' *Cassa integrazione* is literally 'cash integration' but colloquially means layoffs under an Italian system that, in brief, means the government pays workers a reduced salary while a business restructures or during economic emergencies.

Colaninno concluded, 'It will remain Guzzi's factory and we will provide strong investment to achieve industrial and technological restructuring; for new models and for a new line of

Moto Guzzi products which we are working on.' Alluding to the talk of court and boardroom battles, the statement simply stated 'We rationalized the group' he concluded. But when the factory closed again in spring 2010, the rumour-mill went into overdrive, with speculation that the museum was being emptied and Moto Guzzi was dead and buried. Despite journalists being reassured, at an Aprilia launch, that it was for more 'investment', it seemed time to fly to Italy to get to the truth.

While I sit outside the factory, well before the mythical 3pm museum opening, a factory test-rider arrives on a test mule of the Café Racer, and waits for the gate to roll aside. Briefly lost in conversation with the man who opens the faded steel barrier, he doesn't notice my camera until it's too late. The bike looks nicely judged retro with more than a touch of Italian bling. This touchstone to the past with Art Deco highlights is what Piaggio believes will save Guzzi. Trying to escape the camera the rider stalls the Guzzi. Hopefully it's not an omen for Piaggio's plans.

Above the gates is an architect's hoarding proclaiming that phase one of planned improvements is completed. But then phase two should have been completed in 2009, providing newly glazed facades, a tidied-up site and some quid pro quo demolition and rebuilding: the new 'factory' would run to 90,000 square metres. But rather than emphasize manufacturing, phase

LEFT: **Mandello del Lario's Moto Guzzi dealer, established by factory racer Duilio Agostini.**

BELOW: **Duilio Agostini on his way to victory in the 1953 Milano–Taranto aboard a Guzzi 500.** MOTO GUZZI

two emphasizes 'cultural and exhibition spaces'. Spaces people will visit to spend money, and the artist's impressions seem to feature more happy children, shopkeepers' mannequins and artfully placed motorcycles than a typical factory. But there's no sign of building work and newspapers talk of mayorial concerns and local beliefs that the factory is dead and buried in Piaggio's eyes. It's hard to get a consensus on whether Piaggio's plans were misunderstood or rethought under pressure.

'I don't know where these stories came from,' says Nico, a long-time staffer at the local Guzzi dealer. 'For sure we hear them, voices from all around the world saying that Piaggio will sell the factory, but they will never sell the factory because this is where Moto Guzzi comes from. We have customers who come from every part of the earth to rent a Guzzi because if you have ever owned or wanted a Guzzi it is a dream to ride one out from Mandello.'

Nico Arnaudo works at perhaps the most famous Guzzi dealer on earth, Agostini's, based just around the corner from the factory on the outskirts of Mandello del Lario. It's named after Duilio Agostini, who was Italian motorcycle champion and won the Milano–Taranto on a Guzzi Dondolino in 1953. He went on to be a works Guzzi rider and then set up the eponymous dealership in 1956 to fund his retirement. There are old Guzzis scattered around the showroom with handwritten *Non in Vendita* (Not for Sale) notices on their saddles.

DUILIO AGOSTINI . VINCITORE DELLA MILANO–TARANTO 1953.

Motorcycles that are evidence of the long history of a family business still run by Duilio's daughter Alis. So Nico should know the truth of what Piaggio and Moto Guzzi plan for the future. He continues: 'Now Moto Guzzi sell all the bikes they can make, they have all the people back, they have new models. The factory is full. Parts of it were not safe for the workers, now they are.'

Nico's excellent English and fervent belief in his beloved Moto Guzzi make it clear that he at least has no doubts about the truth, and living and working in the shadow of the factory means he should know. Yet looking around there's little or no evidence of any improvements, just an unloved old factory that could have been making anything: apart from a few old pictures and the rather tired museum, it just looks like another white elephant clinging on to Europe's manufacturing heyday. Even if the factory can be saved as a modern manufacturing facility, who is going to buy the motorcycles? Being a publicly listed company, Piaggio have to issue regular audited trading statements, and these make fascinating, if brutally honest, reading. The sub-750cc motorcycle market is in decline in Europe, as computer-gaming children grow up and become mainstream consumers. Motorcycles will not be for them, certainly not in enough numbers to make being a mass producer viable. Bigger bikes do a bit better, especially in the USA and Canada, but it is South America and Asia where the growth is. Piaggio have just opened a research centre in Foshan, China, and are pushing ambitiously into new markets. They understand that Guzzi is no longer a cutting-edge brand, and write about 'the pleasure of travel, elegance, passion and tradition'. So Piaggio certainly seem to understand what they've got in Guzzi, and how they might match products to demand, but to many fans the bigger question is whether or not they will keep Moto Guzzi at Mandello del Lario.

Plans for Mandello del Lario

'I don't care where they're built,' was the reaction of one hugely respected, and Guzzi-owning, journalist when asked what he knew of the rumours the factory might be sold off. Why try to build consumer durables for the modern age in a leaky old building squeezed into a hard-to-reach corner of Italy? Especially when that same leaky old building would be snapped up by property developers, keen to make the most of a site nestled below the mountains that overlook Lake Como. In the end, Piaggio's business is building two-wheelers that the customer really wants at a price he's willing to pay. If you can email component designs to a place where wage rates are a

quarter of what you'd have to pay at home, the essence of what you're doing might stay intact. Even so, some components add cachet, including Brembo brakes and Borrani wheels, for example. But if the complete motorcycle is made outside Italy and still badged as a Moto Guzzi, the question is would buyers be attracted by the lower price, or shun what they see as a fake? Especially given that Moto Guzzi has given up on racing as a means to build on past glories.

There are some examples to consider. Ducati and Triumph have manufacturing facilities in the Far East, although they do keep quiet about them, perhaps deliberately; perhaps wisely. Benelli have pretty much moved production to China, having struggled to rebuild the brand in Europe from the original founder's Pesaro base. But then the Chinese presumably would rather sell to their home market using a ready-made historic brand with a simple token presence in Benelli's home town. Fiat have proved they can sell every one of the 500s they make, despite the fact it's built in Poland, but then it is not targeted at the car enthusiast, let alone the notoriously obsessive motorcycle buyer. Along with the increasing age of Western motorcyclists has come relative affluence and often loyalty to a

The new V7 racer is a premium product within the range, where the matt black Stone model is the cheapest. MOTO GUZZI

Attention to detail justifies the V7's higher price.

**The Breva 1200 retains the 1151cc
2-valve per cylinder engine.** MOTO GUZZI

marque. They may have several motorcycles, all from the same manufacturer and will typically have a sound grasp of the history of that manufacturer. Yet this does not make motorcycle manufacturers immune to the rules of economics, and the cheaper you can sell a product, the more likely it is to sell well. And you can make things a lot cheaper in the Far East, where the cost of living and people's expectations are much lower than those in the West.

But that assumes someone else can't make the identical product at less money, and the growing Asian markets aren't going to pay a premium for a product built in their own country by their poorer cousins. They'll want, as we all do, association with a brand that shows off their discernment and appreciation of human endeavour. Apple does this in electronics by being associated with Silicon Valley, some incredible Apple stores

and the fact that those who work in creative industries tend to favour Macs. Motorcycle manufacturers have traditionally tried to do this by going racing, but this is a route largely closed to Moto Guzzi, and in any event would see them spending money to compete with Piaggio bedfellow's Aprilia. For Guzzisti the legends are in the past, but their blood, sweat and tears seep from every pore of those old buildings in Mandello: here's where Carlo designed the singles; here's where Carcano fettled the V8; here's where Dr John met De Tomaso. Moto Guzzi is unique in that production is still based on the same spot it started at. There have been attempts to move it, but all fell by the wayside. It now looks like the factory may become Moto Guzzi's unique selling point. The old Fiat factory in Turin (the one with the test track on the roof) has made a start as a motoring-themed shopping centre and hotel, and there's the Bikers' Loft in Belgium – an old factory that's now part motel, part museum, part event venue. Guzzi clearly have a chance to do something at least as special. It's not just the factory you could visit either, because if you ride out past Lecco there's the old Circuito del Lario, the 'circuit' Guzzi testers used to develop every road-bike up until the Le Mans III. After all, once you've sold a bike you need the owner to use it, wear it out, service and ultimately replace it.

Europe is still good at cutting-edge manufacturing – fashion, cars, aerospace – but success in these areas benefits from a focal point, a Mecca for pilgrims to dream about. Milan fashion week, a Formula 1 race, Farnborough air-show. Given that moving around the world is now cheap and easy, compared with motor-cycling's golden age, manufacturers could nurture this, encour-aging customers to get involved and build on their loyalty, rather than focusing solely on making a cheaper product. If you need less space to build motorcycles, then use the old space to sell more bikes – or tee-shirts, a meal or a room for the night.

On my way home there are a couple of UK-registered Guzzis at the ferry terminal, so I go over to say hello. The riders turn out to be South Africans, keen to hear about the factory's state. Relieved at the happy ending, they decide to ride straight down to Mandello, even though it will soon be dark: 'We can camp in Nico's garden,' they decide. 'He'll get us into the factory tomorrow.' Pilgrims to a personal Mecca: Piaggio have got a huge following they could build on. Sadly, if understandably,

the plans for new buildings aren't a priority for Piaggio, but there should be a new museum by 2016. Other work has been required, as it is across Europe, to clean up past industrial

LEFT: **The 90th anniversary of Moto Guzzi in 2011 was celebrated with another limited edition California.** MOTO GUZZI

ABOVE: **This version of the California had colour-coded pannier and legshields as well as distinctive paintwork.** MOTO GUZZI

THIS PAGE:
**Riding to the factory
from the UK.**

OPPOSITE PAGE:
TOP LEFT: **Scott Pommier,
a prize winning Canadian
photographer, was
commissioned to photograph
the 2012 V7 range. Pommier
photographed them around
Lake Como.** MOTO GUZZI

TOP RIGHT: **The 2012 V7 is much
improved and keenly priced so
represents 40 per cent of Moto
Guzzi's production.** MOTO GUZZI

BOTTOM: **The Moto Guzzi V12 Le
Mans concept was shown to test
buyer's reaction to a new breed
of Moto Guzzi.** MOTO GUZZI

contamination or waste. During 2012, working with the regional agency for environmental protection in Liguria, Piaggio are cleaning up the site, having already removed underground tanks. This is all necessary if the proposed phase two of the building work – including the new museum – is to happen.

The New V7 Range

Sales have steadily revived, especially of the V7 range and boosted by the 2011 launches of updated versions of the Norge and Stelvio, featuring the 8-valve engine first seen in the Griso. Moto Guzzi also launched a refreshed V7 range with a new engine delivering more torque and power, especially at lower speeds; in truth the original engine was barely powerful enough, its deficiencies masked by the bike's low weight. Inevitably the new engine offered lower fuel consumption and reduced emissions. As with the entire range, Moto Guzzi are also recognizing that the little details – often called 'jewellery' in the industry – have a marked effect on buying intentions and the ownership experience. But there was something else that gave the impression Piaggio was serious about Moto Guzzi. For the launch of the updated V7, they not only invited the world's press to ride the new model around Lake Como, they

also hired Scott Pommier, a Canadian Piaggio claim is the world's best motorcycle photographer. Pommier won a PDN Photo Award and places in both the Communication Arts Photo and Luerzer's Archive. Famous for 'on the road' shots and only working with natural light, his work captured the spirit of the original V7 Sport's era brilliantly. 'I'm happy to be shooting Moto Guzzi's campaign' Scott told admirers from the seat of a V7 on set at Mandello. 'It's a real brand, with a real history.'

Alongside the revitalized V7, the Nevada range made a comeback with the new 750 engine. With improving sales and demand, fixed-term contracts and newly flexible working hours were agreed with the trade unions with a view to increasing production. From the 2008 crash, sales were up to 5,800 in 2011 and 7,000 in 2011; 40 per cent of those were the new V7, with the Norge and Stelvio more than pulling their weight. What Moto Guzzi really needed next was a range leader, a prestige model that would sell at a premium and make Moto Guzzi special again. So, of course, they wanted a new California, and for the first time in Guzzi's history, it would be an all-new California that owned nothing to other models.

Styled by Miguel Galluzzi, now Piaggio's vice-president of design, it owes little to the V12 concept series shown in 2009. Describing the challenge he and consultant Pierre Terblanche faced reviving Moto Guzzi's image, Galluzzi says, 'The Guzzi

Later concepts showed the California, which is now in production. The V7 Scrambler cannot be far behind. MOTO GUZZI

The Scrambler is such an obvious expansion of the V7 range that UK dealer Corsa Italiana is already building their own version. MOTO GUZZI

crowd is extremely conservative, but if we only concentrate on those, we are going to lose eventually. So these bikes are looking into the future.' This is similar to the challenge Terblanche had faced when he was at Ducati and styled the controversial 999 to replace the 916.

The advantage Guzzi has versus Ducati is that Ducati makes sports bikes, Guzzi can do anything it wants because they've been doing it a long time and on all sorts

of bikes. We are not in a box; we can do anything we want as long as we are able to make it. New ideas once again mark a turning point in our history, an impalpable, yet very real force in the history of Moto Guzzi. It lies in the ideas and in the unrelenting research work that led Moto Guzzi to build its tradition on innovation. The prototypes showcased today are only the beginning: such unparalleled care for detail and neat design would be unthinkable without our twin-cylinder engine.

The California 1400

The California was first shown at a US dealer conference in Miami by Galluzzi, alongside Marco Lambri, director of Piaggio Group style. As well as showing the California, they also announced that a planned Piaggio advanced design centre was being established in Pasadena, California; the very place Galluzzi studied design. The aim was, 'as Piaggio goes global... to look forward ten to fifteen years to see what buyers will need... (Pasadena is) a melting pot of cultures and it's a melting pot of engineering and new thinking.'

The new production line for the California went into Mandello during 2012, and the Touring and Custom versions were presented at the media launch on the Côte d'Azur in southern France during November 2012. Dealers were almost immediately able to stock the new model. The level of organization reflected Piaggio's new-found commitment to Moto Guzzi. The reports that came out of the road tests gave the distinct impression that this was the bike to fully revive Moto Guzzi, as long as the price and thirst for fuel didn't put buyers off, although in fairness these are competitive with the obvious competitors from Harley-Davidson and Ducati's Diavel.

This ultimate Moto Guzzi V-twin was developed by Piaggio's research and development department based alongside Aprilia in Noale. Apart from crankcases carried over from the 1200, everything is claimed as new. Wider bore and the 1200 engine's stroke give 1380cc and the inevitable vibration that results is dealt with by rubber mounting in an all-new, but very traditional, steel frame. Wheels are the now traditional 18in front and 16in rear, and the radial-mount four-piston Brembos feature anti-lock braking. Indeed, as seems essential in new motorcycles in the last few years, there is a raft of electronic rider aids. Further cleverness is in the fuelling, with an idea pioneered on the V7; a single 52mm throttle body sits under the seat, feeding the 4-valve heads via a siamesed manifold that clears up the space where riders wants to rest their knees and creates a lazy, torquey character. It might be heavy – 743lb (337kg) for the Tourer – with a long 66in (1665mm) wheelbase, but it is all hidden well.

As they say in France, 'The first taste is with the eyes' and it is the styling that has to attract people. The clever thing is that in Tourer guise it's instantly recognizable as a Moto Guzzi California, but very different in the lowered, grey Custom version. One idea from the concept bikes that is developed in the new California is the V-twin cylinders 'exploding through the fueltank' as Galluzzi puts it. Overall, the look is almost Art Deco, with lines running from one component to the next and remarkable attention to detail. There will be four versions launched over a period of around a year, starting with the California Touring, with an Ambassador tag for the metallic black option and Eldorado for the white, reviving other great names. Next will be a lower, single-seater drag-racer inspired version, aimed squarely at the Ducati Diavel and Harley-Davidson V-Rod. 96bhp may not sound much from 1380cc but it is delivered at 6,500rpm and the 88ft/lb (12.3kgm/120Nm) is delivered by 2,750rpm. Moto Guzzi plan to build 2,000 in 2013 and

The metallic black touring version is the Ambassador.
MOTO GUZZI

RIDING THE BIKES | **CALIFORNIA 1400**

Paul Harris runs Corsa Italiana near Walton-on-Thames, the UK's largest solus (single marque) Moto Guzzi dealer. Not only has he ridden the new California, he also has an earlier T3 California – and some forthright views on what Moto Guzzi needs.

'You've read the road tests,' is how Paul answers the obvious question: what's the new California like to ride? 'It's fantastic: quick, smooth, beautiful.' But what about the weight?' '337kg' Paul laughs, before adding 'but you don't notice the weight, you really don't, it's all so low down. And anyway it's the same as the competition, the Victory or Triumph Rocket Three. And the Cali's a much better bike than any Harley-Davidson.' Another laugh; Paul clearly

ABOVE: **Detailing reflects the California's price and range-topping status.** MOTO GUZZI

The white touring California is called the Eldorado, another famous name from the V-twin's past. MOTO GUZZI loves a bit of controversy. So, is the California the right bike to build on Moto Guzzi's recent success, even at £16,000? Paul certainly thinks so:

Motorcycling's now either Poundland or money doesn't matter. Old T3 owners grumble that a clutch cable is £9.99, but the people who buy Grisos, Norges, Stelvios and the new Cali just walk in, pay and say, 'I'll collect it next week'. Don't even bother with a test ride most of the time. Whatever you think of it, that's motorcycling these days. I've told anyone who would listen that Piaggio should have given us a badge-engineered Galletto scooter or the Derbi Mulhacen (a 696cc single-cylinder roadster) badged as a Falcone, but I'm beginning to wonder if it's too late to bring people into motorcycling, never mind Guzzi. The new V7 Stone is a cracking bike, much better than its predecessor (the Classic), and has sold well, but we could sell something between that and the Griso and Stelvio; a meatier version of the V7 – a V9, if you like. I'm a big fan of the old Bellagio (with the short stroke 940cc engine and 'power cruiser' looks): that was a cracking engine and it was just that the styling wasn't for everyone. Make it look more like the V7 and we could sell that. We sold over forty V7s last year, so it would go well.

A few years ago, the bigger 8-valve engines were collecting a reputation for camshaft wear, and owners were increasingly frustrated that Piaggio seemed unable to get to the root of the problem. Today's motorcyclist expects reliability to be a given, along with high customer satisfaction. Any new model cannot afford to be tainted with a less than outstanding reputation for trouble free ownership.

ABOVE: **Brakes have ABS: indeed, there are many other electronic rider aids.** MOTO GUZZI

RIGHT: **A restyled Bellagio 940 might usefully expand Moto Guzzi's range.** MOTO GUZZI

Continued overleaf

Continued from previous page

RIDING THE BIKES | **CALIFORNIA 1400**

'The issue with the eight valve head is absolutely sorted,' affirms Paul, 'everything was recalled and some bikes even got a new oil pump and bigger oil cooler. It might have been component suppliers dropping standards: all I know is that we were told to do the work and we did it. I'm not aware of anyone having any problems anymore.' And indeed that seems to be the case, and certainly Moto Guzzi has a fine reputation for reliability and build quality, which is exactly the back story the California 1400 needs. Paul is certainly confident:

> *I think we'll sell ten to fifteen Californias this year. Guzzi were very clever launching it so late in the year, got the bike to the shows over the winter and*

the tests in the magazines. Guzzi planted the seed early and got people thinking about it. As soon as the sun starts shining we'll start selling them. They are sunny weather bikes really, whereas people use V7s and Grisos all year round.

> *Comparing the new Cali to the old T3 California – well, there's no comparison. Maybe the riding position; after all the T3's over thirty years old, but the new California definitely has the spirit of the original.*

Certainly the wide and proud rising position of the new California Touring has the road presence of the original, and clever electronics make it very easy to ride. The handling is

The California tourer certainly is a case of handsome is as handsome does. MOTO GUZZI

head and shoulders above the obvious competitors, as is low speed running. Just watch the width of the panniers: beautifully integrated, it would be a shame to scratch them in a gap that isn't quite wide enough. In fact looking over the California, the word 'bespoke' keeps popping into your head. Where other bikes in the range share parts – and the V7's instrument binnacle is remarkably similar to the item on Ducati's Monster – the California impresses with unique features and attention to detail. Sitting on it for the first time, the weight is obvious, but Paul's right: it's very low down, even compared to the Ducati Diavel. The Diavel might have far more top-end power than the California, but low down the California feels so much nicer and the detailing puts Ducati to shame. The California also feels longer, lower and slower steering than the Ducati but on the road it's hard to think of a reason for that to matter. The California just cossets its rider and offers a relaxing, joyous riding experience. In short, it makes you feel good about being out on a motorcycle and happy to be riding. Over the years people have forgotten that away from a race-track it's the experience that matters, and the feeling you get out riding is why motorcycling holds us in its thrall. If people remember that, and are happy to be seduced by the heritage of the name, Moto Guzzi should sell all the Californias they can build.

The Custom version of the California 1400 will be released during 2013. MOTO GUZZI

SPECIFICATIONS

MOTO GUZZI CALIFORNIA TOURING 1400 (2013–)

Layout and Chassis

90-degree V-twin four-stroke touring motorcycle

Engine

Type	90-degree V-twin
Block material	Aluminium alloy
Head material	Aluminium alloy
Cylinders	2
Cooling	Air
Bore and stroke	104 × 81.2mm
Capacity	1380cc
Valves	8 valves ohc
Compression ratio	10.5:1
Carburettor	Marelli multipoint DFI, single 52mm choke
Max. power	95bhp@6,500rpm
Fuel capacity	4.5 gallons/20.5 litres

Transmission

Gearbox	Six-speed foot-change
Clutch	Dry single plate
Final drive	Shaft with double universal joints

Chassis

Front	Telescopic fork
Rear	Swingarm

Steering

Tyres	130/70 18in front – 200/60 16in rear
Brakes	Triple discs

Dimensions

Wheelbase	66in (1,685mm)
Unladen weight	741lb (337kg)

Performance

Top speed	Not quoted or tested

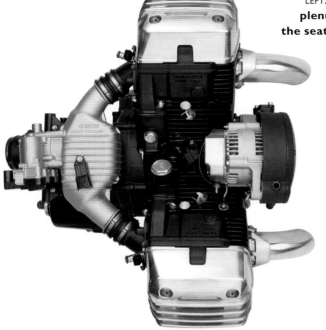

LEFT: **The California 1400 engine is pretty much all new. The long plenum chamber allows the fuel injection to be positioned under the seat, improving toque and space for the rider's knees.** MOTO GUZZI

Details of the shaft bevel drive. MOTO GUZZI

RIGHT: **The California's chassis is also new, with rubber mounting to deal with the vibration inherent in a 1400cc twin.** MOTO GUZZI

BELOW: **This version of the 1400 is intended to lure buyers from other marques including Ducati.** MOTO GUZZI

pre-orders indicate they will sell those. If they do, and the continued efforts to market the brand bear fruit, sales should once again pass the psychologically important 10,000 mark. The main target markets are Germany, France and Italy, Guzzi's traditional hunting grounds. They have the dealer network and customer-base in those countries, and it makes sense to focus on customer service and quality control rather than volume, for now at least. Despite being named after an American state, the only US dealers you can buy a California from are based around Los Angeles or New York.

Of course, there is the question of what will happen if the California doesn't sell as well as hoped, but Piaggio's Daniele Torresan, while not complacent, is realistic and believes Guzzi's future is secure. 'For sure the new California is a strategic model. After her we've planned other new models and engines (which will appear) by 2016.' Indeed, there is clearly a carefully planned route map within Piaggio to get Moto Guzzi to 2016. With the new 1400 engine, a revamped Norge and Stelvio are not hard to speculate about, but there is a far more intriguing possibility. In the past Moto Guzzi dealers have looked jealously at Piaggio's other brands, and thought the range could be easily expanded with a little badge engineering. By 2012, the scope of Piaggio's interests was truly impressive, including scooters, mopeds and motorcycles from 50 to 1200cc, marketed under the Piaggio, Vespa, Gilera, Aprilia, Moto Guzzi, Derbi and Scarabeo brands, plus three- and four-wheel light transport. The main headquarters in Pontedera, near Pisa, also has production plants for Piaggio, Vespa and Gilera two-wheelers, those light transport vehicles, along with engines for scooters and motorcycles. At Noale there is the motorcycle development centre and Aprilia Racing's base. Scorzè, like Noale close to Venice, produces Aprilia and Scarabeo branded two-wheelers. And, of course, Moto Guzzi's home at Mandello del Lario. And then there are the overseas' interests including the Derbi factory close to Barcelona, as well as facilities in India and China. Piaggio really are ready to go global, and although Moto Guzzi is far and away the smallest of their interests, like many before them, Piaggio have fallen in love with the marque.

Moto Guzzi's imagery for the Custom is predominately urban. MOTO GUZZI

The Tourer's photoshoot reflects the wider ambition and greater comfort on offer, especially for a pillion.
MOTO GUZZI

A New Falcone Single? To 2016 and Beyond

So when dealers were asking for smaller Moto Guzzis to expand the range, suggesting rebranded scooters or single-cylinder 500s from other Piaggio brands, they were disappointed at the response. No, came the reply, this is not the future. Yet it is difficult for a dealer, especially a solus (single marque)

dealer to make a living from such a narrow range. With the California they have the glamorous range-topper, and with the V7 they have the class-leading daily ride. But dealers would really love a cheap yet stylishly cheerful commuter that brings new fans to Moto Guzzi, and a 500 single would do just that. Having once been seen as an archaic layout, rising fuel prices, changing expectations and the rise of period style has changed the fortunes of one motorcycle in particular. Royal Enfield

ABOVE: **Attention to detail on the Custom Nero Basalto apparently extends to Moto Guzzi branded tyres.** MOTO GUZZI

RIGHT: **As Moto Guzzi contemplate a new single, they could do worse than look to Copenhagen bike builders Wrenchmonkees' Falcone Nuovo for inspiration.**
WRENCHMONKEES

350 and 500 singles have been produced in India since the mid-1950s, gradually improving the mechanical aspects, while retaining the classic looks. In 2012, production exceeded 70,000 motorcycles, and with a new factory the intention is to double this. Far from being knocked by the global recession, Royal Enfield and their dealerships have found that a classically good-looking 80mph (130km/h), 85mpg (3.33ltr/100km) motorcycle is perfectly attuned to the new world order – especially one that is simple to care for and comes with an instantly recognizable and historic name on the fuel-tank. Moto Guzzi dealers must

eye this success with frustration, and will be pleased that Daniele Torresan is now more forthcoming, and in an extraordinarily positive way.

> If Moto Guzzi builds a single it must be a horizontal cylinder, like the old Falcone. We agree that it's the right moment for a new single-cylinder motorcycle, but we need time and we cannot to put another log on the fire now (having just launched the new V7 and California).

More good news came at the beginning of 2013, when Britain's biggest selling motorcycle magazine, *Bike*, included the base V7, the matt black Stone, in a group test. Almost remarkable in itself, Moto Guzzi's having been largely ignored until comparatively recently. The V7 was up against the usual suspects, all priced within a few hundred pounds of the V7 and appealing to the retro-all-rounder market. Even so the names are impressive: the Harley-Davidson 883, Triumph Bonneville and the Kawasaki W800. Yet the Moto Guzzi won the riders over and the test concludes with 'our money would go on the Italian'. Certainly, for the first time in forty years, and perhaps forever, a Moto Guzzi won a group test. The Moto Guzzi V7 is not part of a reinvented brand; it is the evolution of the Dondolino, the V8 and the Le Mans.

Time to ride my borrowed Classic back along Lake Como to possibly the most magical motorcycle factory on earth. To be part of Moto Guzzi is to be part of something that started in Mandello del Lario in 1921 and is still there, stretching into the future. To ride any Moto Guzzi from a Guzzino or Zigolo, a Falcone or V-twin, even a Benelli Sei or the magnificent new California, is to be part of something very special.

ABOVE: **Moto Guzzi owners are always happy to help others.** MOTO CLUB VETERAN SAN MARTINO

LEFT: **And Moto Guzzis certainly like to cover distances, ideally in Italy.**

RIGHT: **Helping out and endurance racing at Spa Francorchamps.**
ANDREW GRAY

BELOW: **Riding back to the factory from Lake Como.**

INDEX

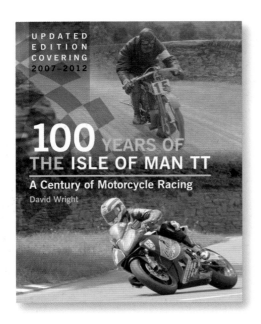
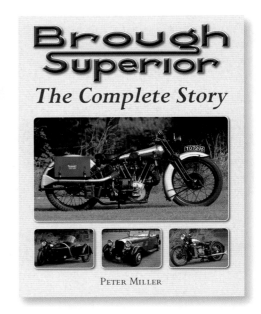
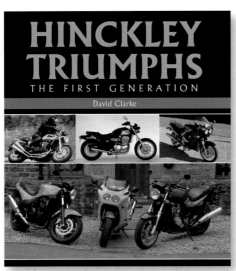
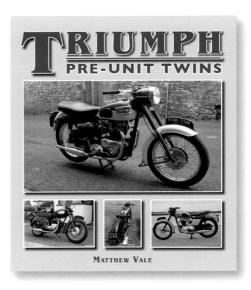